JUANITA!

The Madcap Adventures of a Legendary Restaurateur

BY SALLY HAYTON-KEEVA

Published by

Sagn Books

P. O. Box 216

Vineburg, CA 95487

ISBN: 0-9626295-9-6

Printed in the United States of America

September 1990

For my husband, Joseph. Whooeee!

Acknowledgements

I would first like to thank my deft and perceptive editor, Susan Hayton Magorien, who also happens to be my sister. No one has ever had a stauncher ally or a more generous friend. Surely no writer could wish for more.

Nan Perrott handled the typesetting and manuscript preparation with sensitivity, speed and skill, all the while cheering me on into the stretch with her unfailing enthusiasm for the book.

Thanks to Ken Winston and Don Ponte for the cover design and photo layout.

Although many of the photographs in this book were not only bent, folded and mutilated, but charred as well, Richard Ingalls brought them back to life. Gary Campbell retouched the well-travelled cover photo.

Bouquets are due to the wonderful staff at the Sonoma Public Library for their patience and expertise, as well as for their remarkable ability to keep a straight face when asked strange questions.

I want to thank all of the wonderful people who gave me their time in interviews. I have never laughed so hard or so often in my life.

Finally, how could I not thank Juanita, who has brought both joy and exasperation to so many? It was my great good luck to be in the right place at the right time and not do too many stupid things – except for driving too fast in her driveway and having an answering machine. After two years of togetherness, we are the best of friends.

Other books by the author:

Valiant Women in War and Exile
America in Rebellion
The Mission

and the upcoming:

Juanita Cooks!

Table of Contents

San Francisco was pretty square in the mid-Fifties. We were just starting to head into unknown waters, and Juanita was really at the forefront of this. Juanita's Galley was a whole new atmosphere, a whole new setting, a whole new character. It was Bohemianism at its best, and it was fun to be in at the beginning of it all. Unlike anything we'd ever seen before, it was folksy and friendly, with Juanita exuding an atmosphere of good feelings and generosity. And the food! We didn't know about cholesterol in those days, but the cholesterol count of everything must have been in the millions! I remember how wonderful all those english muffins were with gobs of butter, and the buckets of eggs and huge portions of everything – and with Juanita standing there like a gentile mother saying, "Eat, eat, eat!" So we did. We loved her because she really *was* like a mother and gave to everyone in the place a real warm feeling.

There was a genteel bawdiness about her that was very appealing. You could tell her a dirty joke and she'd laugh, and then she'd tell you a dirty joke and you'd laugh, but she'd still be a lady through it all. She was great copy and I wrote a lot about her through the years. She got pretty wild at times and threw things around, but that was because she was so exuberant. Just wacky and wonderful.

Her places were always untidy, which was nice. They weren't *dirty*, understand, just nicely untidy so that you really felt at home. The atmosphere was like a big boardinghouse, only much crazier. There hasn't been another place like it since.

One time I remember very fondly was when a friend took the Director of the Morgan Library to Juanita's. He was a very distinguished fellow and was introduced to Juanita as "the Director of the most famous library in New York City." At that, Juanita turned to him and said, "Then you would probably like to have an autographed picture of me, wouldn't you?" He said he would, so she wrote on this photo of herself lying nude in a bathtub, "Don't judge a book by its covers."

Nobody could ever forget Juanita, even after meeting her just once. She's a lot more than a mere footnote to local history – she's a whole chapter by *herself*!

– *Herb Caen, Columnist*

Introduction

"What Ever Happened to the Legend of Marin?" – *San Francisco Chronicle*
"Buxom Juanita Still Tells it Like It Is" – *Associated Press*
"Her Bark is Worse Than her Bite" – *San Francisco Examiner*
"Muumuus, Jackasses, Junk and a Place" – *Sacramento Bee*
"The Salty Life of a Legend" – *Independent Journal*

Three hundred pounds of dynamite, and almost anything could set her off. People gossiped about her long before her second restaurant burned to the ground—actually, the dirt was dished years before the *first* one went up in a squall of smoke and scorched chickens. From her earliest days, Juanita Musson seemed marked for notoriety, her character being an inflammable mix of meddlesome feistiness and a devil-take-the-hindmost honesty. People have loved her. People have thought her pure poison. Few people, once meeting her, have ever forgotten her. Probably the world's most unusual restaurateur, whose ample proportions have graced the pages of *Playboy, Australian Vogue* and the *New York Times,* Juanita has fed the famous, the infamous – and the simply cowering – with equal parts bluster and butter. With "Eat it or Wear it" as her motto, Juanita has sent hapless diners forth decorated with syrup, splattered with pancake batter and, on more than one occasion, with hamburgers stuffed into their pants. Anything was possible once the doors of Juanita's Galley swung shut behind you. Suddenly in a three ring circus, *you* were part of the show.

Though her succession of restaurants first began in Sausalito, north of San Francisco, and marched with a conquistadore's determination and ferocity into the heartland of the Wine Country, Juanita has always been treasured as a San Francisco character. Not since the days of the divinely disordered Joshua Norton, who with Napoleonic self-confidence declared himself in 1859 "Norton I, Emperor of the United States and Protector of Mexico," has there been an eccentric more cherished in the city in which eccentrics have not only been tolerated but practically required to flourish. Herb Caen, long-time columnist for the *San Francisco Chronicle,* was at least partly responsible for Juanita's initial success. He, along with other local notables, such as the impresario Enrico Banducci, discovered in the large, bawdy, generous woman an authentic and celebrated character, who bellied up to the Bay Area's gentrified image and punched it right in the nose. From "a lovable tomato" she became—in Caen's forthright words—"a Mau Mau in a muu muu."

One incident neatly illustrates the Jekyll and Hyde nature of Juanita's personality. Two young men once parked their car in front of Juanita's and she asked them to move it. She didn't like where it sat hulking in front of her front door because ...well, just because she didn't. They refused, being young and feckless. She asked them again, her voice ascending in volume and scale in such a way that more knowledgeable customers sank in their seats and prepared to duck. "Screw you!" one of the young men offered in reply. At this, Juanita armed herself with a cast iron frying pan, marched outside and smashed out all of the car windows, one by one. Then she turned on her heel and marched back in to flip the burgers left sizzling on the grill. "And what will *you* have, boys?" she asked them sweetly.

"A lot usually happened to me in a year," Juanita once said with the innocent air of someone taken wholly by surprise by the capricious nature of Fate. "I always seem to be in the wrong place at the right time."

Being in "the wrong place at the right time" often landed her in jail, where the matrons were so fond of her they "always put clean sheets on my mattress." Judges who passed sentence on her frequent peccadilloes have had to suppress smiles at her colorful and obscene recounting of events leading up to the latest unfortunate incarceration. Hauled in on a citizen's arrest by a man she had called a "son of a bitch," the judge on the case turned to the injured party and assured him that "from Juanita, that's a term of endearment." He advised the defendant, however, that in the future it would be prudent for her to refrain from insulting her adversaries' families when aroused. "Just call them an asshole," he allegedly advised her from the bench, "and then they have to prove that they aren't one." Juanita has often remembered his advice—and sometimes even followed it—if not too riled to rein in her tongue.

Survivors of her slash-and-burn form of verbal fisticuffs have included such celebrities as Mort Sahl, Tommy Smothers, Joseph Cotten, Joan Sutherland and Noel Coward. Shelley Berman once came dangerously close to being ushered outside by the seat of his pants. Unimpressed by name, beauty or wealth, Juanita has always been most impressed by people who ate her food, lots of her food, without being picky or harassing the help.

"I love serving men," Juanita has always said, "and the only way I could do it legally was feed 'em."

Well, yes, *mostly.*

I joined Juanita's circus in 1988. Having lived in Northern California, I had read Herb Caen's column about the volcanic Juanita Musson who served up her biscuits with plenty of backtalk. Because she had a tendency to holler at her help and to harass her customers, I had resisted tasting her wares, either edible or temperamental, until it was too late and she had unplugged her grill forever. Juanita herself would never have stooped to such pigeonhearted behavior, but I feared she would sense my timidity and lash out with her spatula.

It was too late for regret; I would never make the acquaintance of Chickenshit Smith or Beauregard the drunken monkey or see the fabled prime rib that draped a dinner platter like a beerbelly over a pair of too-tight shorts. The best I could do was to see if I could find out where she had gone to ground like a fox from the baying hounds of fame. I had an ulterior motive. I was writing a weekly column for my town's venerable newspaper, the *Sonoma Index-Tribune.* I mostly wrote profiles of amusing and/or interesting local characters and I had the happy idea of using the column as an excuse to meet Juanita, who might lay down her spatula in the interests of Journalism.

As it turned out, she was easy to find and easy to talk with. Hers was the last in a row of modest cabins, once part of a resort in this area of hot springs north of historical Sonoma. It was festooned with Christmas garlands and faded mementoes of other holidays, giving it a festive and rakish air. The covered "patio" in front of the door sheltered a deaf white cat, a dog so old it appeared to be petrified, large leaking bags of kibble, plates of half-eaten table scraps, dead plants in plastic containers, a plaster Indian, a mangle, a lawnmower, an unoccupied birdcage, an assortment of peculiar but possibly useful implements, a tottering pile of terracotta tiles and a golf cart.

I knocked at the door. Receiving a muffled but robust "Come in!" I stepped inside a room that resembled nothing so much as a thrift shop after a hurricane. In addition to the usual complement of chairs and tables, most of which were adorned with plates of half-eaten table scraps, there were even more decorative items; shadeless lamps and lampless shades, trunks and trays and large ceramic roosters, lace doilies and doll dresses, a mask made of cowrie and coconut shells, and an impressive array of knickknacks. The walls were hidden behind posters, paintings and pictures of Jesus, framed entirely in seashells.

"Well, for godsake, come on in!" The voice was not without a certain sweetness in its soft southern cadences, and also not unlike a cackle. Through a beaded curtain I stepped into a smaller room filled corner to corner with an antique wooden bed which was, in its turn, filled by a woman who was leaning back against its headboard in welcoming charm. On the coverlet lay a mother cat suckling newborn kittens. I wondered, in the space between her smile and my stammered introduction, if the kittens had entered the world right there on Juanita's bed. It seemed likely. Although she had never met me and had no reason to expect my visit, Juanita was as welcoming as long-lost kinfolk. "Sit down, honey," she urged, patting the bed. I did so tentatively, dislodging one of the kittens so that it rolled, blind and mewling, into a crevasse where it poked around for a friendly teat until I helped it scale the chenille landscape back to home.

We had an animated discussion. Could a conversation with Juanita be anything else? We parted with my happily accepting an invitation to "Come again, honey." I wrote about her in my column and we spoke three or four more times on the telephone. Then I was thrown from a horse two months later, right before Thanksgiving. When I mentioned that a broken pelvis would prevent any intimate encounters with a turkey, Juanita touched and delighted me by offering to cook dinner for any number of my friends and relations. Wild horses wouldn't have kept me from accepting such an offer. Thanksgiving Day, twelve people gathered — more friends than I had thought I possessed, but the lure of the fabled Juanita had made me a very popular girl. She poured forth from my kitchen a cataract of food. A forest of stuffed celery gave way to a raft of nut-stuffed dates, followed by the bird itself and two kinds of stuffing (loaded with butter, hold the sage) accompanied by a mountain of mashed potatoes and a sea of gravy. Creamed onions filled in the cracks and there were mincemeat cakes as a sort of suicidal final flourish. Between twelve reasonably gluttonous people we consumed six pounds of real butter, a box of Vege-Sal, and enough of everything else to eliminate famine in one of the smaller Third World countries. Everyone waddled home in happy agony, armed with leftovers.

The next Thanksgiving my husband and I went to Juanita's house. Since she didn't own an oven at that time, everything had been cooked in neighbors' ovens and was being kept warm in a primitive microwave and two electric woks. As we arrived we heard her shouting, "Just go get the fuckin' table, John! I asked ya twice already!" Several harried women were hurrying in and out of a nearby cabin. Juanita sat just outside her doorway with a huge bowl of potatoes on her lap, stirring them furiously and cursing them, too, from time to time. It was like a Tobacco Road version of the lunatic cook in *Alice in Wonderland;* I found myself wondering how soon she would start throwing utensils at her guests.

Quietly, smiling nervously, we tiptoed safely past her reach and on into her house which had been spruced up some and filled, north to south, with tables. In her tiny kitchen, in which the bubbling woks sat precariously on narrow ledges, there was another table upon which rested the turkey, a huge ham, half a dozen salads and enough chili rellenos for the whole of Chichicastenango. There were rolls. There were pies. There were about a thousand nut-stuffed dates. I put my small offering of cranberry sauce in among the rest where it looked like something Scrooge might bring to the feast.

You never saw so much food for so few people in all your born days. Nor such an odd collection of guests— unless, of course, you happen to have been luckier and smarter than I and to have seized the opportunity to dine at one of Juanita's restaurants where, as impresario Enrico Banducci told me, the "flannels" rubbed shoulders with the "furs." One guest was stoned and one was drunk. One was a born-again Christian who was so nervous that she remained huddled mouselike in a corner, her frightened eyes darting about as if she expected at any moment to be set upon by atheists brandishing drumsticks. A woman came in with her husband and an autoharp and proceeded to sing a medley of obscene songs, all in a sweet, clear voice.

Since it was a buffet, all of us were expected to wedge ourselves into the kitchen simultaneously. We did, with hearty encouragement from Juanita, who at last came inside with the bowl of potatoes she had beaten into submission. It was nearly impossible to slide in between the table and the tipsy woks, let alone do it in the company of ten dinner guests, some of whom were the worse for wear and ladling gravy all over themselves. While the rest of us staggered around with plates full of food, trying not to trip over cats or footstools, Juanita sat watching, a beatific smile on her face, completely in her element. Not having so much as a single taste herself, she urged everyone to go for seconds, for thirds, to eat more! More! More! All the while most of us had shoveled our way through barely half of what we had first heaped on our plates and were still miles away from the mincemeat. It was, at the very least, a memorable holiday.

Inspired, I broached the idea to Juanita of writing her biography. "Well, why not?" she said, "I guess it's time." Thus began two wonderful and maddening years; fitting my perfectionistic work habits into her mañana-is-soon-enough-for-me way of life. I arrived for interviews only to find her needing me to drive her thirty miles to pay her utility bill before they cut her off. Or she had decided that, after all, it was a good day to rearrange her furniture, drive around in her golf cart, check out the action at the nearby Agua Caliente pool, or go yell at some shiftless neighbor. Once she sent me for water — hers being sulphurous with minerals — and her voice rose gently in my wake, "Poor thing, she's being treated no better'n a stepchild."

Whatever she is and whatever she is not, Juanita is most certainly her own person with her own way of doing things. Heaven help you if you are so disengaged from reality that you think you can change her, persuade her, or get your own way once she has set her mind on something else. As she has said countless times to so many people, often in the red face of tearful protest, "There is a right way, a wrong way, and Juanita's way." I did it Juanita's way, just like everybody else who wanted to stick around.

Writing the biography of someone still counted among the living can be a perilous enterprise, something like shooting the rapids with rocks on one side and alligators on the other. On the one hand there is Truth, and on the other there is discretion, outright falsehood and the natural inclination in all of us to appear in public attractively dressed. There are few of us who would ever agree to appear as God made us, warts and flabby thighs and all, preferring the safety of anonymity to the dubious delight of standing in the limelight stark naked, stripped of everything but ego — and *that* sadly wilting in the heat. Therefore it has been both a relief and a pleasure to work with the live Juanita, who assured me from the very beginning that "My life's been an open book, honey. You're just puttin' it between covers."

In a regional sense at the very least, Juanita is a living legend. What is it that most becomes a legend? Well, in Juanita's case, the answer is "fame and infamy." Did she really burn down those restaurants? Was she really one of Sally Stanford's stable of light ladies? Is it true that she has "saved" men, women and children by her fierce – if quirky – sense of justice and overwhelming generosity? Ask a few people and you'll receive a bewildering variety of answers, all sworn to just as passionately whether the teller was eyewitness or merely the recipient of yesterday's news.

Larger than life in every sense, she has had an entire mythology wrapped around her once-mammoth frame, veiling the figure beneath like one of her trademark muumuus. During the fifty-five interviews conducted with people who have known her, I heard several stories several times, each slightly different from the last, reminding me of the game called "Telephone" in which children sit in a circle and one whispers a sentence to the child sitting alongside, who then passes it on to the next, and so on until it returns to its place of origin, invariably transformed. Attesting to the power of individual imagination and perhaps to what a psychologist might call "creative listening," the sentence "He wore red suspenders to the ball" becomes "She runs her head into all fenders." Oh, most of the stories in this book are true although some names have been changed to protect both the innocent *and* the guilty. Some stories have been altered slightly in one direction or another to suit the inclinations of the teller. The thing is, Juanita seems to fit our need for modern myth. Just as we have a need to tell each other about the poodle in the microwave and the rat in the Whopper, we need people with enough personality, enough chutzpah, to bear up under the weight of so many expectations, projections, anticipations. I am sure that once a living legend steps into Never-Never-Land, the stories become even more outrageous and apocryphal, what with the subject unable to correct or deny them.

In Juanita's case we may still rest assured that most of the stories are true, with a few creatively embroidered but losing none of their appeal for those of us who prefer our news delivered colorfully, by bush telegraph. I say this with assurance since I know that if Juanita ever heard someone telling a big lie, they'd better be wearing a rubber apron and a hard hat. There aren't too many of us that brave!

Overanalysis is no fun, though. No one really wants to chart the exact distance down the rabbit hole to Wonderland. It's enough just to get there, look around, meet the Mad Hatter, grab a teacup and … listen.

1

"The Inimitable Juanita"

– Press Democrat

Juanita Lois Hudspeth came out fighting on October 16, 1923, halfway between Collinsville and White Springs, Texas. Oscar Hudspeth was a cowboy who travelled in the center of a pack of twenty hound dogs. Louise Mitchell Hudspeth was a resourceful, pretty woman with poor eyesight, gentle ways and a backbone of granite. The summer Juanita was not yet one year old, Louise got work in the cotton fields in order to pick enough cotton to fill a mattress with enough left over to buy ticking. She took her daughter along with her, armed with a small bag into which Juanita put the cotton bolls her mother dropped along the furrows. At noon Louise would cover her child with a piece of burlap to shield her from the hot Texas sun. In a few weeks Louise had picked enough for the mattress and Juanita's bag was full enough to pay for her very first doll. Louise brought it home one day, a beautiful baby doll with a china head and arms and a flowered dress. Juanita clasped it tightly with delight. Running to show her father, she perched it on Oscar's crossed legs and awaited Daddy's admiration. Without taking his eyes from the newspaper he was reading, he gave it a swipe with one heavy hand, sending it crashing to the floor. Juanita gathered up its broken body.

"Fix it, Mommy," she cried.

"I can't, Juanita," her mother replied, eyes fixed on her husband's face. "It's ruined."

As soon as Oscar was out of the house for a whole day and the coast was clear, Louise packed a suitcase, dressed Juanita, slapped on a hat and left Texas and her husband forever. A Greyhound bus dumped them off in Hominy, Oklahoma, homeplace of Louise's maternal kinfolk. Louise filed for divorce and went straight to work and, as soon as she was able to, bought her daughter another china doll. "It was real pretty," Juanita remembered, "but it wasn't the same."

One morning when Juanita was three years old, she and her aunt were on their way to Sunday school when Oscar Hudspeth showed up. Forgetting about the broken doll in her excitement, Juanita flung her arms around his neck. "Do you think it'll be all right if I take Juanita for an ice cream?" he asked her aunt, who readily succumbed to his cowboy charm and agreed that she would pick Juanita up at the drugstore after church.

An hour later she arrived to find the fountain empty of men with little girls in tow and hurried home with the woeful responsibility of telling Louise she had handed over her child to a kidnapper. For two dreadful weeks the police and several irate male relatives beat the bushes for a cowboy and his short sidekick. They started off in Texas and then, gaining some information along the way, circled back into Oklahoma where he was finally collared.

Juanita remembered this as a happy holiday, full of kittens. Although she was still wearing her Sunday-go-to-meeting pongee dress, and was lavishly tattooed with scratches, she was none the worse for wear and was carted on back home, eager to see her mother but mourning the loss of the kittens. Louise chose not to file charges because, she said, she didn't want him in jail, just out of Oklahoma. He was sent packing back to Texas with a warning that if he ever returned, he would be thrown in the slammer so fast his dogs wouldn't know who to bite.

From that time on Oscar was out of Juanita's life, although she wrote to him when she was eleven years old and he wrote back, telling her how much he loved and missed her. Louise found the letter and cried. Not wanting to hurt her mother again, Juanita put an end to the brief correspondence and saw him but once more in her life, many years later. The little pongee dress was folded up and stuck inside Louise's big Bible, perhaps as a reminder about cowboys.

Maybe the truth was that Louise didn't quite trust Oscar to keep his word about staying out of Oklahoma, because she packed up her suitcase once more and headed for Tulsa, where she got a job in a bakery and rented an apartment upstairs. Juanita took to city life as if to the high-rise born. The only child on Main Street, she found an abundance of maple doughnuts downstairs and the grocer on the corner gave her an apple every day. Soon she was a familiar sight, wandering the streets and making friends with all the shopkeepers, her blond hair curly and uncombed, her knees skinned, her eyes alight with mischief.

After awhile Louise went to work at a department store in the children's clothing section. Sometimes she would lose her temper with her daughter and threaten to give her away and get another, nicer little girl, maybe from among her customers. Juanita would state, with a steely glint in her eye and her chin unquivering, that she knew her mother was a lot kinder to the children who came into the department store and so they had less reason to sass her in the first place, "Well, I'm paid to have patience with them," Louise would reply, "Nobody pays me to be patient with *you*." Nevertheless, on the chance that her mother might make good her threat and trade her in on a sweeter model, Juanita tried hard to behave for as long as she could—or at least until the threat had been forgotten.

Although Louise was determined not to remarry until her daughter was grown, fearing that a stepfather might mistreat her, she did occasionally accept dates. Juanita didn't cotton to the idea of sharing her mother even for an evening, but was open to being bribed not to throw tantrums upon the arrival of a young man carrying flowers and with a speculative gleam in his eye. The usual bribe was the right to sew on Louise's sewing machine. By the time her feet could touch the pedal, she was able to sew simple outfits for herself.

She also learned to cook when very young, standing on a chair in order to reach the soup pot. One memorable day she was supposed to be cooking beans for supper but a game of kickball proved too tempting and she forgot to check on them. Two batches had to be flushed down the toilet. For a third time, now dangerously close to the zero hour of Louise's return, Juanita ran back to the grocery store for another bag of beans. In her hurry, she stumbled and spilled them all over the sidewalk. Scooping them back into the bag, gravel and all, she raced home and threw them into the pot. They had just reached the al dente stage when Louise walked wearily in the front door.

"She couldn't understand why the beans had so many rocks in them," Juanita recalled. "She cracked a tooth on one of them, so I didn't tip her off as to what really happened."

These were still Depression days, when men with families stood in line for the chance to pick up the city's weekly garbage so they could be first to hunt among the leavings for an apple or a soup bone or a serviceable piece of scrap iron. Louise, who wanted her daughter to have the luxury of a carefree childhood and who was often at the end of her rope where parental responsibility was concerned, found foster homes where Juanita could stay in the summertime. One summer she was sent to a farm in Kansas owned by folks down on their uppers due to the catastrophic loss of their horses and barn in a fire. They had started taking in city kids, three of whom accompanied Juanita on the trip.

The first morning there the children awoke to the sound of the farmer's voice, shouting, "Hey, you kids, get up! We need your bedspread for a tablecloth!" The children crawled out of bed wondering what mess their parents had sent them into. Silent with misgivings, carrying the bedspread, they trooped downstairs into the kitchen only to find the farmer and his wife sitting with welcoming smiles at a long table piled high with all kinds of food, including pie. To these children, who had been living on what amounted to beans and table scraps, it was a feast that made them forget on the instant everything but their empty bellies.

Juanita grew to love the farm, although the children were expected to work for their keep, drawing water from the well and tying up shocks of freshly-cut wheat. Years later she was to find a table (with five legs and five leaves) just like the one belonging to the farmer and his wife. Every time she sat at it she remembered their many kindnesses to her.

"I really think the Galley was born there, at that farmer's table," she said. "All that food and all of us so happy!"

Another summer she was sent to Arkansas for two weeks of camp with children of other poor families. She learned to swim in the camp's lake and spent her days happily making bookmarks and potholders. One day the children all decided to explore a nearby cave. Deeper and deeper they wandered until the tunnel they were in grew so narrow that they could only continue on their hands and knees. Apparently the thought of turning back did not occur to them, or the prospect of crawling through the darkness was too tempting to resist. Gratifyingly lacerated, they eventually wormed their way into a dimly lit chamber and saw, to their relief, a hole full of daylight overhead. Evidently Juanita's merry band was not the first to find itself in so uncompromising a situation since there also was a pole that extended upward from the floor of the cave to the surface. It became a point of general discussion that somebody would have to climb the pole and go for help. Since no one else seemed to be so inclined, Juanita tied her shoelaces together, slung her shoes around her neck, shimmied up the pole and ran off to recruit a rescue party.

Not all of the foster homes and summer camps were as pleasantly full of food and adventure, however. Once Juanita found herself alone with a curmudgeonly couple in a house in the middle of an oilfield. There was little to do but scrabble around in the dust and watch the oil rigs, like the heads of grazing horses, moving slowly up and down. The worse part, however, was the carrots. The lady of the house—who hennaed her hair with a heavy hand—insisted upon feeding Juanita grated carrots, which reminded her unpleasantly of shredded coconut, which she also detested. The bowl of grated carrots returned with the bleak inevitability of death and taxes until, her spirit broken by the thought of how disgusting they were sure to be in another week, Juanita choked them down. Never would she be able to eat a grated carrot again — or like a woman with hennaed hair.

When Juanita was five years old, she moved with her mother into a house belonging to people who supplemented the family income by taking in paying boarders. The patriarch of the family, affectionately known as "Grampa," spent most of his time in a rocking chair on the front porch. When Louise was away at work, the family kept an eye on Juanita. "Go out and sit on Grampa's lap for a spell," she was told. Heart sinking, she would shuffle off to the porch to find Grampa waiting in his rocking chair like a vulture. Though she would try to occupy herself at a safe distance, Grampa would threaten her with a spanking, or worse, if she didn't come sit on his lap. Then he would put sly hands where grandfatherly hands were never meant to be.

"Now, don't you tell nobody," he would warn her, "or I'll tell your mother you're a bad girl."

Every time Juanita managed to escape back into the house, his daughter would say, exasperated, "Now, you git on out of here, Juanita, and sit for a spell on Grampa's lap." Out again she would go, head hung with shame and feet dragging, to suffer more invasions of the prune-like but purposeful hands.

Louise decided to move closer to town, much to Juanita's

unspoken relief. Two of Louise's younger sisters were eager to try their wings outside the confines of rural Hominy, so together they rented an apartment. Juanita's youngest aunt loved to show her off and would put Vaseline on her eyebrows and eyelashes to darken them. Once by mistake, however, she put on Vick's Vaporub, and instead of being winsome and charming at the movies, Juanita cried until her eyes were red and swollen and she didn't look cute at all. This was the same aunt who was taking a bath when the "revenuers" came into the apartment building in search of hidden hooch. After they broke up the casks in the basement, they were emboldened to storm the building room by room without benefit of formal announcement. One agent opened the bathroom door to find Miss Mitchell wearing fingernail polish and nothing else. Leaving a trail of apologies, he backed out, too mortified to return. "This was lucky," Juanita remembered, "since my uncle had hidden a bottle of moonshine in the toilet tank."

It was shortly after this that Juanita got restless. The aunts had gone their separate ways and though there was now considerably less giggling, there was also no more Vaseline on the eyelashes. Wandering aimlessly down the street one day, Juanita saw a "Room to Let" sign in the window of an apartment house and marched upstairs in search of the landlady. Overcoming her initial disbelief that a seven-year-old child would have been given the responsibility of househunting, the woman showed Juanita the light airy rooms and received her promise that by evening they would be occupied and the first week paid in full.

Juanita went home, packed her belongings in a cardboard box, gathered up her mother's possessions, and ferried everything armload by armload to the new Hudspeth residence.

Louise was taken somewhat aback when her daughter came into the department store to tell her they had a new address, but she accepted change as she would continue to accept it in the disordered lifestyle Juanita was always to create and enjoy. After these new rooms seemed less light and disturbingly less airy, Juanita moved again, this time carting their worldly goods in a taxi paid for with money she had earned doing odd jobs for neighbors. "Just tell me what the address is," Louise modestly requested, "so I'll know where to go after work." She did put her foot down on the accumulation of personal possessions and told Juanita that she could move them as many times as she liked as long as she could fit everything she owned into two shoeboxes. While this certainly curtailed ownership, it also expedited delivery. One of Juanita's cherished finds was a small house with a piano. Though she couldn't play a note and had no desire to learn to play, she was drawn to the special look of a house containing a piano and moved her shoeboxes with a comfortable sense of having gotten quite a bargain. There was something about old furniture that she found comforting. A piano, a chipped chest of drawers, a tarnished brass birdcage—these were signs of stability, of permanence, of family. When a piano was by her side, all was right with the world. She belonged.

The next house proved to be a less pleasant package deal, as far as Juanita was concerned, since down the block was a school housed in an old Victorian. Louise was pleased, but Juanita was not. She wanted to go to a school that looked like a school, not a school that looked like a house. Soon after she was enrolled, she came to class with her arm bound up wrist to elbow with cereal box tops for splints and a rag to keep them in place. She presented herself at her teacher's desk with a pitiful moan and the explanation that her arm was really *quite* badly broken and she couldn't do anything at school that day and, likely as not, couldn't ever do anything again—at least not at that school and not until her arm was much *much* better.

"Oh, I'm so sorry you hurt your arm, Juanita," her teacher said with the cunning of her kind, "Because I was going to let you do the penmanship exercises on the chalkboard today." Ah, the lure of glory! Juanita prided herself on her superior writing ability and found herself seized with an urgent longing to be up in front of all the other children, making swoops and pothooks. In a remarkable display of the power of mind over matter, Juanita rose to the occasion and did not even seem to feel the pain. Her teacher was, of course, no booby. She called Louise at work to inform her of Juanita's unfortunate accident and when Juanita awoke from her afternoon nap, her mother was sitting on the side of the bed, removing the "splints."

To make up for the unseemly appearance of the school, there was their next door neighbor, Rose. Here, all was fitting and proper. From first story to second, the house was furnished entirely with family heirlooms. For Juanita, who sat only on rented chairs at rented tables and slept in rented beds, this was a most genteel setting. It was, as a matter of fact, the most perfect place Juanita had ever seen in which to give herself a birthday party. It wasn't her birthday, but details seldom deterred her. Fired with inspiration, Juanita "borrowed" all of Rose's empty Coca-cola bottles and all of her own and took them to the grocery store to get the deposit money. When this sum was augmented by a week's worth of lunch money, she had just enough to buy cake and ice cream for a gaggle of friends who gathered in Rose's parlor while Rose was having her hair done. The children all had a fine time and managed not to break a thing. Though Louise was furious when she found out about it, Rose simply said, "Now, Louise, don't you go spank that child! She was only havin' herself a good ole time." Juanita couldn't have agreed more, always believing that a party, no matter how frivolous or ill-conceived, needs no apologies.

One house became a Hudspeth residence because it not only had a skateable sidewalk in front, but also a large and well-laden cherry tree. All of the kids in the neighborhood would gather on that stretch of concrete to race each other up and down the block. When the cherries ripened, the children would snatch a cherry as they clattered by. This was more than Juanita's flesh could stand. The next day she ditched school, climbed the tree and proceeded, with admirable thoroughness, to eat the tree bare. Red cherries, green cherries, cherries the birds had pecked and cherries that came complete with bugs, disappeared one by one until Juanita, too full to walk, curled up under the tree to die. When Louise got home from work the empty branches and the green child told the sorry tale and off she rushed the little glutton to the hospital where her stomach was pumped out. "I never ate a cherry after that," Juanita said sadly, "I was forever cherried-out."

Juanita loved all animals, especially goats, but her gypsy-like ways precluded having pets. Not even for the easygoing Louise was it thinkable to travel from house to house with a Barnum and Bailey caravan of rescued strays such as Juanita would have enjoyed. One Easter, however, Louise decided to surprise her daughter with two baby chicks. Juanita was thrilled to have pets at last—even ones with such limited means of being amusing—and cared for them devotedly until they began to lay eggs. One day when she got home from school, Juanita explained, she went to the nest she'd made in an old refrigerator carton and they were gone. That evening her mother confessed that she had run out of money and had sold them. "I was so mad at her that I was going to run away," Juanita said, "only I never did."

The next year two new chicks arrived on Easter morning and, once again, Juanita was delighted and gave them the run of the living room where they ran in circles, peeping and pooping with clockwork regularity. That night Louise's brother came to dinner. Being a man who kept frequent company with John Barleycorn, he was pretty soaked by midnight and passed out on the living room floor. Next morning Juanita bounded happily downstairs to play with her new pets, only one of which was jumping on and off Louise's unconscious brother like a fluffy Lilliputian. Search as she might, Juanita could not find the other chick. Late that morning, when her uncle was finally roused from his stupor, the other chick was found flat on the rug, another innocent victim of demon rum.

The next Easter Louise decided to let Juanita have a real pet at last and surprised her in the morning with a rabbit. Juanita turned it loose and it took up residence behind the piano where it ate all the nap off the rug. Louise, unaware that the rug was disappearing, decided that the kitchen linoleum needed a little more glamour. With Juanita's help, she spent one long day painting it a cheerful apple green, with the intention of stencilling red dots on it the next day. They left the bucket of red paint with its cover loose conveniently near the newly painted floor. Having apparently eaten its fill of carpet nap for the day, the rabbit hopped into the kitchen in the night, knocked the red paint over and hopped with mindless determination around and around the room, leaving hundreds of red pawprints behind him. Next morning Juanita and her mother stood in the door, surveying the damage. "Well," Louise sighed, "there certainly doesn't seem to be any point in putting on the dots now." Juanita solemnly agreed and they went downtown to get breakfast.

One boardinghouse they lived in for awhile was particularly attractive to Juanita because of all the tapestries the landlady had strung out along clotheslines so as to separate large rooms into smaller ones. Juanita has credited this creative living arrangement as the inspiration for her lifelong love of hanging carpets and tapestries on any wall as yet unhung with one. Louise found this almost-Oriental approach to public housing rather less than charming and considerably too public and as soon as Juanita could find another residence, they decamped.

Along with the succession of foster homes and summer camps, Juanita also spent time with her Oklahoma relatives—the Mitchells in Hominy, the Luickharts in Enid—during Christmas and Thanksgiving and for a month in the summer. One aunt had a daughter named Margaret Crabtree who was less than welcoming to her bumptious younger cousin. "She'd make a cake and not even let me lick the bowl!" Juanita recalled, aggrieved. "I'd cry and my Aunt Mag would make up another batch and let me eat the whole bowlful." She taught her niece how to do needlepoint and together they stitched a comforter Juanita would use for many years. She also showed her how to cook more than bean soup. "It was good Okie-style cooking," Juanita explained, "with everything floating on a sea of fat."

Juanita travelled back and forth between Tulsa and Hominy by bus for awhile. This came to an abrupt end on the day she missed her connection and was taken home by a couple who found her sitting on a bench outside the deserted bus stop. "Their name was Tanner," Juanita recollected. "It was a name I never could forget because they were so nice to me." The Tanners called Louise and explained things and Louise allowed that, yes, her daughter could stay for supper and sleep the night. She thanked them and then asked to speak to Juanita, reminding her to say "please" and "thank you" and not to take more than two helpings, even if they had cake.

One of the guests at supper was the famous humorist, Will Rogers. But Juanita had eaten too many meals of plain boiled spaghetti and the occasional breakfast egg, with a spoonful of grease mixed with Karo syrup as a special treat. The Tanner's dinner of roast beef and ice cream was far more absorbing than the happy raconteur across the way. Besides, the whole house was furnished with antiques. Will Rogers just couldn't hold a candle either to the roast or to the table it sat upon.

Being by nature color-blind, Juanita liked playing with the black children who often lived in the even seedier neighborhoods than those where the Hudspeths hung their hats. One day Louise came home early to find her little girl pulling a whole wagonload of kinky-haired kids up the street. Louise had learned that "niggras" were positively beyond the pale at her mother's religious but racist knee, and through tight lips ordered her daughter home. A whipping ensued, with the neighbor children gathered outside the window to watch, much to Juanita's humiliation.More painful than that, however, was the realization that her mother and grandmother, good church-going Christians, were such frightful bigots. (A few years later, after a white dentist had pulled the wrong tooth, Juanita went to a black dentist who did the job right. She couldn't wait for the next time she visited her grandmother so she could tell her all about it. Predictably, Grandmother Mitchell was scandalized that any kin of hers would so lower themselves as to seek the professional ministrations of "one of *them*.")

Rebellious to the core, Juanita entered puberty with a vengeance. She already knew what men liked to do with little girls and was soon to take advanced courses on the subject. Once in a movie theatre a man had taken her hand and placed it in his lap where, in a manner of speaking, the barn door was open and the horse ready to bolt. Without a word, she got up and cooly moved elsewhere. Another afternoon a man came to the door and asked her to unlock the screen so he could see "how nice and fat" she was. "I thought this was a little strange, so I didn't do it," she explained. "I just told him I was too busy and closed the door."

Louise was worried. She had married young and had borne Juanita several months less than nine after the ceremony, and she desperately wanted her daughter to do things differently. Knowing she was out on the streets of Tulsa worried her. Now that puberty was casting a long dark shadow over the sunny meadows of childhood, she decided to send Juanita back to Hominy to live with her mother, to whom she agreed to send money for room and board. The fat, so to speak, was in the fire.

The Hominy Public Library was housed in rooms over a mercantile store. Juanita loved to wander among the bookshelves and visit with the librarian and take home books to read out on the porch swing at her grandmother's house. Several times a week she would make the journey upstairs, noticing that an attorney had his office directly across the landing and that his door was frequently and hospitably open. Out of curiosity, one day Juanita tapped at the door and a man with friendly eyes and nice hair looked up, smiled, and invited her to step right on in. It wasn't long before the law office door was closed more often than it was open. "I used to love to go to the library," she explained, "but after awhile, going to the library was just what I told everybody as an excuse. I went to his library, really, and we'd lay on this wonderful Freudian leather couch and fiddle around. It didn't strike me until years later why I was always collecting couches like that." They carried on all summer, doing everything but "it," and when she got a part time job helping out in a dentist's office, she started fiddling around with him, too. Either Louise sensed what was going on, or had somehow gotten wind of what her precocious daughter was up to, because she decided to send her away to a convent for a year of testosterone-free education. "There weren't any attorneys or dentists there," Juanita confessed, "so I got in a different kind of trouble."

Grandmother Mitchell was furious. They were Methodists and good Methodists didn't have any truck with such papist hocus-pocus as convents. But Louise prevailed, and her decision was made easier by an event which came close to shattering the family. According to Juanita, one day while she was still living with her grandmother she got into some kind of mischief and her uncle beat her so severely that she had not only multiple bruises but a very black eye. Mrs.Mitchell, who treasured her only son, sauced or not, stood by and did nothing. The next day one of Louise's sisters came by for a visit, caught sight of the black eye and demanded an explanation. Juanita needed little urging. "She called my mother, who came right down to get me and took me home and never let me stay at my grandmother's house again if my uncle was going to be there." When the beginning of the school year rolled around, Louise packed up Juanita's school uniform of skirt, middy blouse and black lisle stockings, hustled her daughter aboard a Greyhound bus, and waved her off to spiritual reclamation in Missouri.

That first day inside the big red buildings full of small solemn nuns, Juanita's first thought was to cut and run. But she knew how much her mother wanted her to be there and how much money it was taking from her limited means, and so she put up her chin and tried to make the best of it. "I didn't like it one bit when I first got there," she remembered, "but I didn't want to leave when the year was over."

Louise returned to Tulsa and promptly fell to pieces. Now that she no longer had to worry about Juanita, the years of deprivation and overwork swamped her like a leaky dinghy in an incoming tide. As Juanita explained it:

"Those had been real hard days before 1934. I guess the minute my mother got me off her hands she just sorta broke down. She'd always been real thin, but what I didn't know was that while she'd been sending money to grandmother for my room and board, she hadn't been eating much herself. So about the time she got me situated and didn't have to worry about me runnin' around wild, she just let go somehow and had to be taken to the hospital where they immediately operated by cutting her stomach away from her backbone to save her from starvin' to death."

As long as the tuition was paid, Juanita ate with the wealthier girls in a private dining room with tablecloths and linen napkins. With Louise unable to work, the money she managed to send—often fifty cents was as much as she could scrape together—was not enough for such luxuries as linen napkins and Juanita was directed henceforth to eat in the large public dining room with the poorer girls. "I didn't care at all," she said, a defiant glitter in her eye, "because we all ate just the same, even if it was off tin plates instead of china." Though it sounds a little like Jane Eyre in these more egalitarian times, Juanita remembers it as a pleasant sort of sisterhood; all of them sitting in their dark uniforms at the long, wooden tables, their hair tightly braided, and with the nuns constantly on guard to nip girlish silliness in the bud. Though the food varied only slightly for lunch and supper, breakfast was always the same—mush. "Oh, I just loved that mush!" she exclaimed. "It was the same stuff people fed to their calves and I guess since it made the calves grow so well the nuns figured it would do the same for us."

Instruction covered the usual academic subjects, but the girls also learned such womanly skills as crocheting, embroidery, hand sewing, both plain and fancy, and the proper methods for preserving fruits and vegetables. Sister John drove the school tractor and slopped the hogs and though Juanita always begged to be allowed to accompany her, she was kept—perhaps prudently—inside the convent walls. She made friends with Sister Josephine who was elderly and sweet-tempered, loved by all the girls. One day Juanita said to her, "Why didn't you get married and have a bunch of kids of your own?"

and was told in reply, "But I have more children this way." Once when the Mother Superior was out of town, Juanita talked Sister Josephine into sewing the hems on the "dinner set" she had crocheted and embroidered. When the Mother Superior returned, she called Juanita into her inner sanctum for questioning.

"I thought you were going to roll the hems before you stitched them," she said, her eyes like lasers behind her steel-rimmed spectacles. "Well, I was going to," Juanita stammered, "but then...I asked Sister Josephine to sew them up for me so I could have them all done as a surprise for you when you got back!" Some nuns were quite clearly less prone to being outwitted by artful little girls with blond curls and wide blue eyes. "It looks very nice, dear," this shrewd judge of girlish venality continued, "but it will look much nicer with rolled hems. So you will take out all the hems and roll up the thread you have wasted so you can use it again when you do your work the right way."

Juanita recalled, "I picked out all of the machine stitches and rolled up the thread and it seemed like I worked on those damn doilies for years until I finally got 'em done. But when the Mother Superior told you to do something, you did it right. That's how I came up with my slogan, 'The right way, the wrong way, and Juanita's way.'"

This same rock-ribbed example of Christian rectitude again caught Juanita skidding from the straight and narrow and gave her the backside of her hand. "But sister!" Juanita cried out in shock, "You slapped me with your holy ring!" To which the dry-eyed nun replied, "Yes, and if you sass me once more, I'll slap you with it even harder!" In the convent, wooden floors were scrubbed with bricks wrapped in rags until they shone, and beds were made with hospital corners, tight as drums. The convent kitchen was where Juanita found herself most often, canning garden produce and peeling potatoes. One day she was assigned the duty of dipping peaches into boiling water in order to peel them for canning. One peach suddenly looked so beautiful to her, so tantalizingly perfect, that she was unable to stop herself from taking a big bite out of it. That was when she got another taste of sister's holy ring, and while the peach sailed uneaten in one direction, Juanita sailed in the other.

Sauerkraut was her punishment. Standing at a machine that shredded cabbage, Juanita turned the crank while other girls brought in basket after basket until a two-ton truck was empty. She'd switch to her left arm but then her elbow would smack the crank as it rounded the bend, forcing her to switch back to her right arm again. "It took me three days to get all that fuckin' cabbage done," she said, "with only time off to eat and sleep. I decided then that I'd be a lot of things in this world, but I'd never be either a sauerkraut maker or a nun."

Mother Superior did not see Juanita as nun material anyway. "You're going to put on make-up," she told Juanita dourly more than once, "and probably flirt. As a matter of fact, and though I hate to say this to you, I think you are going to be quite wild." In one year Juanita learned a lot of things. But the most important might have been the lesson Sister Theresa taught her one day in a single sentence. "It is as much a sin to think a thing as to say it." From then onwards, Juanita said whatever she thought on every possible occasion.

The return to civilian life required an immediate search for a place to live. Rooms were found in the large home of a couple by the name of Redliffe. Mr. Redliffe worked nights on the railroad and so Juanita had to keep her rowdiness to a minimum during the day. Since the Redliffe backyard abutted an icehouse, Juanita was often to be found hanging around on the other side of the fence, watching the men make ice. Mrs. Redliffe, who was unhappily childless, decided to adopt a baby. One weekend she took off for Oklahoma City and returned with "the sorriest-lookin' baby I ever saw," Juanita remembered. "Just awful. It was blue as a robin's egg. Once she got up to the orphanage, she decided to choose that one because it looked like it might die and she didn't want it to end up in a pauper's grave." The baby girl lived, though, and grew up to be a beautiful young woman. "After it looked like she wasn't going to die after all, I used to babysit her and wish she was my own. I really think that was one of the happiest times of my life."

When the summer of 1935 settled stickily down upon the Oklahoma cornfields, Louise decided to send Juanita to stay at her Grandmother Mitchell's house in Hominy. A boy named Freddie Filbert caught her eye almost the first day. Soon they were fast friends. One morning Freddie invited his new friend to come with him on a house tour sponsored by the Methodist Church, in which his mother was, ecclesiastically speaking, a head honcho. Juanita happily accepted. They settled themselves in the front seat of the Filbert Buick, awaiting the upcoming refreshments with the eager anticipation of twelve-year-olds. Suddenly Mrs. Filbert opened the car door and after one horrified look at her son's companion, told her, "You are not riding in the front seat with my son!" and though Freddie tried to make his mother see reason, Juanita burst into tears and ran home crying. Grandmother Mitchell did the best she could to console the heartbroken little girl, but next day, when the formidable Mrs. Filbert showed up on the Mitchell's front stoop, she was welcomed into the parlor with Midwestern graciousness.

"I'm sure you understand that I simply cannot allow Juanita around my son, and I think you know why," Mrs. Filbert announced. "We don't want to have any accidents happen, now, do we?"

"But..."Mrs. Mitchell began. Mrs. Filbert held up one hand, fixing on the old lady a sharp and disapproving eye. "I regret the necessity of saying this," she interrupted without seeming in the least regretful. "However, we know what happened to Juanita's mother, don't we?"

Mrs. Mitchell was forced to own up to the unpleasant truth. Juanita, who had watched the entire interview through a keyhole, was shamed and hurt. When her grandmother gave Freddie's mother a big bag of beefsteak tomatoes from her garden as if it were a kind of party favor, her bitterness knew no bounds. This was to be the last time Juanita stayed at her grandmother's house, although this wasn't entirely due to her sense of having been betrayed with a bag of tomatoes. Louise and her sister had agreed that it was time to move their widowed mother into an apartment in Tulsa, and they soon carried her off, protesting, after they had lodged her worldly goods in a barn.

It would be reasonable to assume that Juanita's affection for her grandmother might have undergone a sea change, what with the cold shower it had taken in the Filbert affair, but it did not. When, in later years, her grandmother's possessions were stolen from the barn—and there may be a genetic factor in those unlucky souls prone to having their things stolen, as Juanita's own history would later suggest—she just felt terrible for the woman. "Through the years I ended up collecting everything I could remember that she once had. I had Hoosier cabinets up the ying yang, and lace doilies and pincushion dolls and hair receivers, the whole bit. Maybe I was trying in a way to bring her back, or put her life back together again. I don't know. But everything that woman treasured, I treasured. Everything she lost, I found."

As things turned out, Freddie Filbert became an alcoholic and never amounted to much. Though Mrs. Filbert had thoughtfully informed Mrs. Mitchell that her grandchild "will never amount to a hill of beans," destiny proved otherwise. As for the drunken uncle who had not only squashed her Easter chick but had given her a shiner, he ended up falling down an elevator shaft. "Slowed him down some," Juanita observed. However, this did not happen until after one incident in which his drinking was to have a more significant impact on her life...but the cart is ahead of the horse and consequences had yet to be meted out.

Back in Tulsa, Juanita entered high school and, with a sixteen-year-old friend, bought a 1928 Chevrolet for fifty dollars. "To get it to run," she explained, "you'd have to adjust the carburetor. So I had to ride out on the fender, turning it one way and then the other and most often not get it right so the car would stall. We'd pick mother up to take her to work and if it was raining, she'd have to carry an umbrella because the roof leaked." Juanita had earned her share of the money by cleaning houses and sewing clothes for her mother's friends. Louise's on-again-off-again beau, Joe Chancellor, who would marry her many years later, often gave Juanita money when he saw her in town. "Sometimes I gave it to my mother and sometimes I kept it, depending."

Unreliable and damp as it was, the car still provided for the under-age Juanita, as cars always have for American teenagers, a pair of steel wings on which to explore the world beyond childhood. That adult world was opening up and possibilities for adventure and mischief were limitless. Juanita figured that she'd finish high school, fool around a little, get married, have a bunch of kids, and with a picket fence out front and ruffled curtains at the window, settle down forever in a world of meatloaves, mumps and mortgages. This idyll was not to be.

Louise's youngest sister had married a man and set up her household in Tulsa. Visiting at their house one afternoon, Juanita thought nothing of it when her aunt decided to run an errand downtown. No sooner had she gone, however, than her uncle grabbed her and carried her to the bedroom. At first she thought he was playing. As his intentions grew clear, her nervous protests became terrified pleas for him to let her go. Speed and self-satisfaction were the order of the day, and he tore one of his niece's legs out of her pants and raped her.

After it was over, Juanita stumbled bleeding to the bathroom, overwhelmed by shame and the unbearable notion that she might get pregnant and, in Mrs. Filbert's prophetic words, "never amount to a hill of beans." She found a douche bag hanging on the back of the bathroom door and a bottle of Lysol under the sink. Unaware that she was supposed to dilute the powerful anti-bacterial, she poured it full strength into the bag and used it. Her first thought after the initial burning agony had passed was to wonder how women could bear to voluntarily inflict such pain on themselves. Curled on the bathroom floor, sobbing, she heard her aunt come home. After dressing and splashing cold water on her face, Juanita cleaned the blood off her aunt's linoleum and walked into the living room as if nothing had happened. Without another word to her uncle, she left. Although she was thrown into his company from time to time, Juanita refused to speak to him again, nor did she ever mention the rape to anyone. It would not be for several years that she would finally learn the full impact of what he had done. For her uncle, it was over when the act was completed. For Juanita, life was changed forever.

"I was so afraid of having a child by him that I just burned everything inside," she said. "As it turned out, because of what I did, I couldn't ever have a child by anybody." Alone in her shame, Juanita dealt with her feelings the only way she knew how, by pretending they weren't there. At that time, society inclined toward the belief that girls who were raped often "asked for it." Juanita sure didn't expect society to be lenient with her, especially since she knew full well that while technically she had been a virgin before the rape, she had still been no Shirley Temple. She buried the pain and the terror and the humiliation, tried to convince herself that what Mrs. Filbert had said wasn't true, and went on with her life.

Juanita at 15.

Mr. and Mrs. Richard Musson on their wedding day, 1944.

Suffering "secretary's syndrome" at Douglas Aircraft, 1943.

Woodcliffe Lake, New Jersey, 1944

Top: *Putting it all on the line. Woodcliffe Lake, New Jersey*

Bottom: *Grandmother Mitchell, Louise Hudspeth and Juanita
in a tulip field, 1944.*

Demonstrating the Chambers Stove. Dayton, Ohio, 1945.

2

"What Happened to Juanita?"

– California Living Magazine

Now that Juanita was growing up, a larger segment of her family began thinking about her future. Every time she went to Enid, it was mentioned in the society pages because she had so many relatives there, quite a few of whom had done well for themselves. Her Aunt Lizzie, for one, had buried one husband and then married a millionaire. "Even though he had all the money," Juanita explained, "he still had to do what Aunt Lizzie said and live up to her ways. Nobody ever put anything past old Lizzie!"

Lizzie and the rest, who were really quite fond of the harum-scarum young Hudspeth, wanted her to go to college, attend church, and marry well. Their preference was for a young man named Edward Cort III, who was considered quite a catch. But Juanita had other ideas "I didn't want to go to college because I wasn't all that interested in learnin' what they were interested in teachin'. I thought high society was just about ankle-deep and that most people who went to church did it to show off their new clothes and pretend to be goody-goods. I just wanted to have fun."

So she drove around in the leaking old Chevy, played touch football in empty lots, and went to school because her mother made her go. "Don't you dare get married, Juanita!" Louise warned her over and over again. "You finish up your schooling and *then* think about getting yourself a husband."

One day, Juanita decided to drive over to Pryor to visit some kinfolk she hadn't seen recently. In the distance ahead of her, a funnel-shaped cloud was also making its way toward Pryor, and Juanita followed in its wake, ignorant of the havoc it would create in the minutes before her arrival.

"When I got to town," she remembered, "the fronts were gone from all of the buildings downtown. The hotel looked like a dollhouse with all the furniture still in it. The funny thing was, the only front left

24

on a building was on my aunt's coffee shop, the only place left intact on the whole street. When I got to the neighborhood where my aunt and uncle lived, my uncle was still sitting on the porch swing where he'd watched the tornado blow away all three houses on the other corners. I guess he didn't know what in the hell was goin' on, what with everything happening so fast. On the other side of town another uncle of mine got hit on the head with a brick. I guess you could've thought it was all some kind of judgement from God, and my uncle and aunt had been spared because they were so God-fearing. But, to tell you the truth, my uncle was one of the sweetest men alive and my aunt was a bitch – so that's justice for you!"

Soon after that cosmic comment on the folks of Pryor, Juanita was playing touch football with a bunch of her friends when she noticed a good-looking young man hanging around and watching. When he saw that she had noticed him, he asked if he could play and Juanita answered, "Sure, come on!" and proceeded without further delay to tackle him. "Hey! I thought this was *touch* football!" he protested, laughing, to which Juanita replied,"But you're so much fun to tackle!"

Jimmy, a handsome Greek-American, was twenty-seven years old to Juanita's fifteen. They started stepping out together, and though Louise thought him far too old for Juanita, she was already resigned to the superior force of her daughter's will.

"Just don't get married before you finish school," she reminded her.

Jimmy took Juanita to the Greek Orthodox Church his parents attended, and introduced his family to the girl he was determined to marry. Juanita helped Jimmy's stepmother with her naturalization papers and she in turn taught her future daughter-in-law a few Greek words and the basics of Greek cuisine. Though Jimmy had been, and continued to be, quite the lady's man, Juanita took to heart something her mother had told her about jealousy: "Anything you're not sure of, you're jealous of," and tolerated his flirting as long as she was always the girl he took home.

In 1940, Juanita's uncle—the one who had yet to fall down an elevator shaft—embroiled himself with both John Barleycorn and a car he was driving, and ended up broadsiding a truck full of kids on their way to a picnic. A child was killed in the accident, according to

Juanita, and Louise's brother thrown in jail. He spent the one dime he was allowed on a phone call to his sister to ask her to bail him out. Blood being what it is, Louise borrowed money and over her daughter's angry protests, hopped a bus to Illinois. They couldn't make the charges stick, for some reason, and Louise hired a lawyer who managed to spring him.

"I thought she had no business getting that lousy bastard out of jail," Juanita explained, "and so as soon as she left I said to Jimmy, 'Wanna get married?' He thought that it sounded like a good idea and so we decided to flip a coin, heads we would go to a movie, tails we'd get married." Tails it was.

The Justice of the Peace in Claremore, where the bride and groom went to get hitched, got to the point in a hurry. "You two have it in mind to get married," he said gruffly, "and so be it. I pronounce you man and wife." Their brief honeymoon consisted of several days of going to the movies and spending quantities of time in Jimmy's bedroom. "I knew what my wedding night would be like, since by that time we'd had quite a few of them," Juanita explained. "We'd gone to bed together whenever and wherever we could beforehand. Marriage didn't change that part of it at all."

While Juanita finished high school and Jimmy worked, they also found plenty of time to dance and go on picnics with her husband's older crowd. For awhile they lived in Bakersfield, California, where Jimmy worked for a relative and Juanita adopted pet rabbits that hopped around their house, leaving a trail of "marbles" wherever they went. Then came Pearl Harbor. Returning to Tulsa, Jimmy joined the Air Force while Juanita went to work for Douglas Aircraft, then the Spartan School of Aeronautics, as a sort of Rosie without a riveter—although she would have certainly loved one, they were so satisfyingly noisy.

Jimmy was sent to England where he made quite an impression on the local girls. A Red Cross worker paid a call on Juanita one day with the news that since Jimmy would be leaving more than his heart in England, she might consider divorcing him so that he could marry the English girl he had inadvertently knocked up. "Fly boy," Juanita thought at the time, "you should have kept your fly closed." When Jimmy came back on R and R—one would think he'd had enough of that already, but war is hell—he discovered that Juanita had filed for divorce and had no intention of sharing baklava with him again. Beyond the disappointment that he had not been true to her—and after all, she had also been whiling away the lonely hours not entirely alone—was the deep hurt that while she had not managed to become pregnant with Jimmy's child, another woman had done so with military dispatch.

"His place was with her, not with me," Juanita said. "I felt she had a stronger claim to him than I did."

Leaving her secretarial work at Douglas, she moved on to Spartan Aircraft to be a mail clerk. This was when it first became apparent to her that she had not been created for sedentary labor. It made her sleepy. It made her grumpy. It made her feel faint and see double. It was lousy. Opportunity knocked in the gilded personage of J. Paul Getty, who needed a chauffeur. Dressed in slacks and cowboy boots, she went to work, driving and taking dictation while on the road. At Getty's house she would answer the phones while he was busy and play with his dogs. Though she wasn't a guest at any of his swanky parties, she did once encounter Charlie Chaplin in the living room. This was during the Hollywood hoo-rah about his paternity suit. Juanita was fiercely partisan."Of course I was all one-sided, all for Charlie. He was every bit the gentleman. Cute, too."

But Getty went on to greener pastures and, on foot again, Juanita ran through a series of brief jobs, including a stint where she kept the books for a hostelry called, appropriately enough, the Pascock Inn. When a job in airplane overhaul opened up at the Tulsa Airport, she jumped at it and immediately fell in love with her patients. "Boy, did I love to fly!" she admitted. "I became just a crazy kid for airplanes. Got so that for years after I'd go with anybody anywhere in an airplane. All I needed was an invitation and enough time to get to the airport. Sometimes I didn't even ask where we were going – it was enough just to go!"

"One More Time for An Indefatigable Lady" – *Reporter*

One winter day toward the end of the war, Juanita decided to make some warm flannel gowns for a friend's new baby. She didn't know how to get them to where the baby's parents were stationed in Muskogee, near Camp Gruber. Figuring that she might find a soldier in the city who was also stationed in Muskogee, she took the package of baby gowns downtown and soon spotted a car in which was sitting a soldier with a most promising appearance of idleness and good looks. She tapped at the car window and when he obligingly rolled it down, asked if he would run an errand for her. When he said no, he had other plans, she put a fist on one hip in a gesture that would in later days mean Trouble. "Well, what the hell's the matter with *you*? All I want is a simple favor." They went back and forth and finally the soldier admitted that he didn't much like Tulsa, to which she responded that he might like it just fine if he saw it with the right person. He allowed that maybe that might be so, and wondered who that right person might be.

Feeling the tug at the end of her line, Juanita told the soldier she'd be only too pleased to show him the town if he would, in return, deliver the baby clothes. Pressing his advantage, he upped the ante and agreed to everything, provided she come to Muskogee the next weekend and have dinner with him. They shook hands on the deal. Final details were finessed, such as her favorite liquor, and when she arrived in Muskogee according to their agreement, it was to find a nice dimpled bottle of Scotch sitting on the dresser of the hotel room, keeping company with the soldier who most likely was feeling he'd gotten much the better end of the bargain. Not one to stand on formal rules of etiquette when temptation beckoned, Juanita joined Dick Musson in Scotch, joined him in bed and then, two months later, joined him in matrimony.

"First time I saw him, all I thought was that he was a ride for my baby clothes," she admitted, "but after that first time, I could see he had lots more potential than that. He'd just been on a roundabout trip to see which one of his girlfriends he wanted most to marry when he ran into me like a buzzsaw—me being the saw. His mother, Toots, had already picked out the girl she wanted him to marry and for years she'd say, 'Well, my boy shoulda married Mary Lou!' and I'd always answer right back, 'But he didn't. He married *me*.' Her nose was outta joint and never got back in. I guess Mary Lou was more daughter-in-law material, but I think what Toots really wanted was a doormat. A doormat and a dishrag, both."

Juanita Hudspeth and Dick Musson were married on September 22, 1944 in Wichita Falls, Texas. The photograph taken soon after the wedding shows a man past his boyish years, with dark curly hair and a generous mouth. Juanita, fifteen years his junior, sports a crop of curly blond hair above a remarkably pretty face. It would be easy to be taken in by the sweet expression , the dimples, the flawless skin, if one did not take notice of the dangerous sparkle in the soft blue eyes. Although his mother thought he'd "reaped the whirlwind, that's for *sure*," Dick and Juanita were crazy about each other and vowed to remain forever together, come what may. Dick shared Juanita's dream of the picket fence and the little house, its walls bulging with children, and though the war had not yet ended, they took no measures to ensure that the children did not start arriving before the little house did.

Two of Dick's spinster aunts were about as delighted as Dick's mother by the nuptials and wrote a note of "welcome" to the new bride in which they invited her to come for lunch so that they could instruct her on the "standards and traditions of the Musson family." Though they refrained from calling her white trash, they made it otherwise clear that they believed the Okie their nephew had married was in desperate need of a little cultural education. Toots seemed totally in agreement with the letter, but Dick tore it up in anger. Juanita cried, fearing in her heart that what the snippy aunts had said was possibly true.

"I asked my own aunts what my grandparents had been like,"she said, "and whether there was any reason for me to feel embarrassed about being who I was. They told me that our family had fine people with fine houses full of antiques, which was good to hear since I'd grown up mostly in apartments and hotel rooms with a lot of junk. I did know that my Grandmother Mitchell had nice things, but it was still real comforting to know I had every bit as much reason to be proud of my family as Dick was of his."

Much to Juanita's delight, in later years a cousin showed the two spinster aunts a copy of an article about their Okie in-law in the *New York Times*. "So they cashed in their chips knowing I'd made good," Juanita said with satisfaction. "Or that I'd made bad, maybe— but they sure did know I had made it."

The newlyweds lived for awhile in Lawton, where they were swiftly joined by Toots, who was determined to allow them no more than one week of married bliss. Knowing it was only a matter of time before Dick would be shipped overseas, they returned to the Musson stamping grounds in New Jersey, travelling by way of North Carolina and Washington, D.C. In North Carolina it was snowing. Icy roads were not something Juanita had had to contend with before and when she hit a slippery spot she skidded into a car that had stopped in front of them. "Well, I only hit his bumper," Juanita recalled, somewhat defensively, "but he called the police and everybody got all upset at me, making fun that I'd been J.Paul Getty's chauffeur and all. I was so flusterated by this time that I picked up a lemon from a bag on the seat and started suckin' on it. The police arrived and this little man was raising all kinds of hell, and Dick was out there arguing with him and then this insurance guy shows up and Toots is just raggin' and raggin' at me, whinin' that she'd hurt her head, that I'd given her whiplash, and I was just so upset by all this that I ate that lemon whole. Rind, seeds and all, and never even knew it.

"The cops finally laughed and said to the man that was so irate, 'Nothin' wrong with your bumper. This young lady didn't hurt you none!' They checked my driver's license and when they asked me why I had a chauffeur's license I told them about J. Paul and they kinda winked and said, 'Well, better luck next time, honey!' and away we drove, with Toots in the back still whinin' about whiplash. Dick was at the wheel in Washington, D.C. and because they didn't want to, he refused to stop to let me see the Lincoln Memorial. He just drove around it once and said that would have to satisfy me because Toots was anxious to get on home."

Dick received his orders and settled his wife and mother together in an apartment in New Jersey so neither of them would be lonely and he wouldn't worry about either of them so much. This, of course, provided both women with their own battlefield where, unlike the practice followed overseas, no prisoners were taken. Right away, it was war.

Capable and thrifty, Juanita had made for herself as part of her trousseau a beautiful and perfectly modest taffeta robe. One night after her bath, she put on a nightie and the robe and went into the living room where Dick was reading and Toots was smoking and doing a crossword puzzle. Looking up, she remarked sourly, "What are you trying to do, Juanita? Seduce him right in front of me?" In tears of rage and embarrassment, Juanita fled to the bedroom and never again wore anything other than street clothes in front of her mother-in-law, nor did she ever again join their intimate circle of two in the living room after dishes. Juanita would read in the bedroom until Dick came to bed and if any noises ensued from the connubial chamber, Toots would be sure to call out, "What are you two doing? Can't you be quiet?"

Every morning Dick would tell the women goodbye. The newlyweds would kiss and sniffle, and he would march off to where his ship was to sail. Every night he'd march back home again because the ship had not yet arrived, and the next morning the goodbyes would start all over again. After a few days of this, Toots had had enough of the sniffles and far too much of the kisses and told her son, "Oh, don't come on back home again if your boat isn't there today. I just can't stand this coming and going!" As destiny would have it, the next day he left for the ship and when night fell and he did not return, they knew that he had gone to war.

The domestic battle began in earnest the moment Dick and his duffel-bag were gone. A brief period of detente preceded strategy, the sneak attack and the midnight foray, escalating within a period of days into the siege by silence, intermittent crossfire, and then the all-out blitz. This was how it began:

"We were havin' dinner with some friends one night, and Toots pulled out these disgusting yellow napkins and proceeded to put them on the table. So I started washin' everything I could lay my hands on, starting with those napkins. Then I washed the tablecloths and all the china and the plates up on the plate rail, and then I oiled all the furniture and scrubbed all the floors on my hands and knees like I learned at the convent. After this, Toots just assumed it was my job. While I worked, she would sit there smokin' and doin' crossword puzzles and thinking up letters to write Dick about what a lousy housekeeper I was and how I was runnin' around with other men. She kept her two sons on their toes and upset most of the damned time."

Dick's brother got married and Toots kept an eye on them, too, though never what one might call a satisfied eye.

Juanita got a job at Teterboro Airport working for Robinson Aviation, which operated a shuttle between Ithaca and Buffalo. Her boss was sympathetic to Juanita's desire to learn to fly and would let her take off when the occasion presented itself. One day Arthur

Godfrey flew in and, seeing the voluptuous young blond, invited her for a spin. She accepted. That was the first of many such aerial adventures. The hopeful aviatrix managed to get only four hours under her belt, but the company she kept was good. Besides, up in the air she was not afflicted with the secretary syndrome which caused her to see double.

She was thrilled when a truck spotter didn't show up for work one day, and her employer decided that she had enough horse sense to take over the spotter's job. In her element, she shouted at the drivers bringing in loads of gravel for a new runway. She stood in the rain, sopping wet, mud-splattered and happy. It was too good to last, however, and she went back to her desk as into exile.

Louise Hudspeth, naturally curious to see how her daughter was faring as a married woman, came East. Proudly Juanita showed her mother the sights of New York City. They were enroute to the Empire State Building when they stopped to have a cup of tea. Over their cups and buns they heard a thunderous explosion and ran outside to discover that a B-25 had crashed right into the side of the tallest building in the world with catastrophic results. Thirteen people died and an elevator full of passengers slipped its moorings and plummeted 18 floors. "That coulda been *us* in that elevator," Juanita said, "makin' history like that. Instead we just ate doughnuts."

Toward the end of the war, Juanita moved so that Dick wouldn't need to find himself out of the army and into an armed camp. She didn't have much to furnish the rooms with, so she made a dressing table out of orange crates and tables out of boxes. (Juanita and Dick had already decided that someday, when they had money, they would buy only hand-rubbed maple furniture because, in Juanita's words, "If our kids peed on it they wouldn't ruin the finish.") Dick returned unscathed and the newlyweds took up where they'd left off. He went back to work as an insurance auditor for Travelers, and commuted every day to New York City.

Toots still kept a watchful eye on things, just in case whoopie got out of hand. Every day Dick would stop off at her house on his way home from work to see how she was doing and Toots, a resourceful woman, generally managed to find something for her son to do; a leaky faucet to fix or an errand to run. All the while she knew Juanita was waiting down the road, standing by her stewpot and getting more steamed by the minute. This perhaps afforded her mother-in-law some quiet pleasure, but it made Dick's homecoming less than festive what with his bride at the door armed with a spatula and a mouthful of pithy observations.

Now that Dick was home, Juanita began to take cooking seriously. This was fortunate since Dick enjoyed good cooking and was a competent chef. The first meal Juanita cooked for him must have come as an unhappy surprise since she was so capable in every other room but the kitchen. As she recalls, he taught her to cook in self-defense: "The first night I made chicken fried steak swimmin' in about two inches of Crisco. My mashed potatoes Dick called 'potato poultice,' and he had to cut the gravy with a fork. He figured I needed a few lessons before he got a heart attack, so I paid attention and learned."

Months passed without a sign that the pitterpatter of little feet would be heard any time soon. Juanita couldn't understand it and grew increasingly anxious that Dick was disappointed in her. "I didn't marry you for children, Juanita," he told her, "I married you for yourself." But his reassurances didn't convince her. Finally she went back to Tulsa to consult with the doctor who had operated on her for a kidney infection. While conducting exploratory surgery to see if the diseased kidney would have to be removed, he had found evidence of the deep scarring that was the result of the rape-induced lysol douche. "I knew then that you'd never be able to have children," he told her, according to Juanita, "but I didn't tell you that then because you might never have gotten married."

"And he was right," Juanita admitted, "If I'd known I couldn't ever have children, I'd have become the biggest whore in Oklahoma." She went home desolate with the news and asked Dick for a divorce. Again he repeated what he had said to her before, adding, "I don't think I would've made that great a father, anyway, so stop worrying about it."

Soon after Dick had returned from the war, he told Juanita she was too skinny and that they ought to have wine with supper to fatten her up. Pretty soon, Juanita says, they were having wine before dinner, too, and then wine afterwards. She blossomed every which way, first pleasing Dick and later alarming him some when she didn't stop. Johnny Walker supplanted rosé and eventually, in later years, she blossomed all the way up to 300 pounds and beyond. "Much later," Juanita said, "Toots complained that I'd given her ulcers, and I told her, 'Well, you made an alcoholic out of *me*!'" – although in all fairness it would seem that three pair of hands helped hoist those first glasses.

In 1947, Dick was transferred to Dayton, Ohio. Feeling that at last they might be free of Toots, Juanita went house-hunting with a light heart. She found a house and bought it. Unfortunately, the people they bought it from refused to move. Perhaps this was an experiment in the "having your cake and eating it too" philosophy of material accumulation. Juanita, temporarily stymied, found a construction shack on an empty lot down the street and covered it with tarpaper so it wouldn't leak, nailing on the outside wall a sign that read, "We apologize for this eyesore. It will be torn down as soon as we are able to move into our new home." The sign captured the attention of the local press which ran articles about the "Okies" who had come to live in a tarpaper shack in residential Dayton. To hear them run on, it was like *The Grapes of Wrath* all over again.

Juanita furnished the shack with crates and boxes and other recyclables, made friends with the neighbors, cooked on the shack's potbelly stove and took out the slop jars every morning to empty them in the geraniums. She worked for awhile in an appliance store and sold roofing and learned to bake bread. Perhaps it was the absence of Toots that made their primitive lifestyle so unexpectedly pleasant. But, eventually the procrastinating folk moved out of the Musson domicile and Juanita and Dick moved in. They painted and poured concrete and once, while Dick was away with the Army Reserves, Juanita ripped out a wall of the closet so that they could walk from bedroom to bathroom without a detour into the hall. When Dick called her from camp that night and asked what she had done with herself all day, Juanita told him about ripping out the wall and throwing it, piece by piece, out the window into the hydrangea bushes.

"Why in the hell did you do that?" he demanded testily. "That might have been a bearing wall!"

"Well, I don't guess it is."

"How would you know?" he pressed on with increasing irritation.

"Because the house hasn't fallen in, silly."

Soon after, Dick drove up to where his mother was doing crossword puzzles in Maine, where her other long-suffering daughter-in-law lived, and brought her back to live with them in Dayton. Juanita remembers the Toots of those halcyon days coming downstairs, cigarette in hand, and to the cheerful greeting,"Good morning!" answering sourly, "What's good about it?"

One night while the newlyweds were doing what newlyweds do, their bed collapsed. Toots called out her usual refrain, "What's happening in there?" To which Juanita, losing patience, yelled in reply, "We're fucking, what do you think?" Maybe that was a mistake, she admitted, "because Dick had trouble getting it up for months after that."

Dick took up gardening and learned to "put up" the fruits and vegetables of his labors. The day came, however, when Juanita found Dick, the perfectionist, sorting peas according to size. "I just took one look at that jar labeled 'petite peas' and took off my apron. I mean, who in the hell *cares*? I left the canning up to him after that." One day Dick took the lid off a pressure cooker full of corn without releasing the steam first, and was peppered from the waist up with kernels like boiling buckshot. When she heard about it, Toots gave Juanita hell for going off to work and leaving her husband alone at the mercy of a pressure cooker which, as anyone knew, was something a woman had to keep an eye on.

"We had fun in Dayton, though," Juanita remembered. Everybody in the neighborhood would jump in their cars at sunset and drive on up to the city dump with our .22's to shoot rats." Forty years later, her voice soft with remembered happiness, Juanita added wistfully, "Boy, I bet nobody has fun like that in Dayton, anymore. The town has grown up so that rats probably have a hard time finding a place to live."

It was in Dayton that Dick was overcome with the urge to make soap. "It's my philosophy," Juanita declared, "that men want to make soap sometime in their lives. This was Dick's time." They ate a lot of bacon and sausage and saved up several large cans of grease for the day when Dick, like a pioneer of yore,would stir it all up with wood ash in a cauldron—preferably in the front yard, to the amusement of the local children—and end up by nightfall with a gratifying row of square white bars. As are so many of the dearest dreams of man, this was doomed from the start. Juanita explained, "I put a can of grease on the stove so I could melt it down enough to get it out of the can and I dropped it. It hit the floor and grease splashed all over everything. I had to wash the floors and repaper the walls. Dick gave up the idea right then of ever making soap again."

This did not prove to be the young couple's greatest disappointment. Toots took it into her head to sublet her apartment since it was such a waste to pay out good money like that when she had two children with homes in which she had not the slightest doubt she was welcome whenever and for however long she wished. Her visits had been frequent and extended before; now began the infernal cycle of spending three months with her other son and nine months with Dick and Juanita every year. "I'm staying with you longer," Toots told Juanita graciously in explanation, "because you don't have any children." Her other daughter-in-law was less considerate.

Glad for any reason to get out of the house, Juanita took odd jobs, went flying with whomever, whenever, and drank prodigious amounts of wine until she decided it made her too fuzzy-headed and started drinking Scotch. She also began, defiantly, to see other men, Arthur Godfrey among them, and if they had an airplane or knew how to fly one, so much the better. One night at a dinner party at which some friends of Toots were guests, Juanita got a call that a friend of hers was heading skyward. Without more ado, she put down her fork, put on her coat, and scrammed. She was always raring to go. Anywhere. Everywhere. And as far from Toots as possible.

Juanita had harbored a longing to see the Lincoln Memorial ever since Toots and Dick wouldn't let her out of the car in Washington, D.C. When the opportunity to do so presented itself, she was gone. Without a word she took off, but once she reached Washington she called Dick to tell him she wouldn't be home for supper. "The cherry trees are in bloom too!" she told him happily. Though it would be reasonable to assume he did not share her enthusiasm, he merely told her, with considerable restraint on his part, that he hoped she would have a good time. "You bet!" she assured him. Then she returned to the bar and a group of friendly strangers she had joined in the pursuit of spirituous frivolity after the party she had flown to D.C. with had passed out. While she stood there, shooting the breeze, a young man came up to her with an intent look in his eye and when he managed to get her somewhat to himself, asked her why she was with "all those hoods." "Hoods?" Juanita asked innocently. "What's a hood?" When he went on to explain that she was amusing herself with an assortment of notorious gangsters— a term she did understand—Juanita thought for a moment and then said, "Well, they haven't propositioned me yet, so I wouldn't worry if I was you," and returned to the merry group.

One of Juanita's casual friends was a call girl. Her car having broken down, she found it necessary to ask Juanita to drive her to "an important job interview" in Cincinnati. The job interview was to take place in the Netherland Plaza hotel. They were shown upstairs to a suite of rooms, the friend was whisked off to be "interviewed," and Juanita was left to twiddle her thumbs in the living room. A man was sitting in front of the fireplace and Juanita strolled over and sat down in a companionable way and asked his name. "Bud Abbott" he replied. "You mean of Abbott and Costello?" she asked, and he nodded. Juanita launched into conversation only to be brought up short when Abbott, who had been staring at her hat, abruptly asked her to take it off. "My hat?" she asked, "My new hat?" "Yes," Abbott continued undeterred, "You should never never wear a hat." Though it was a new hat and she was fond of it, Juanita removed it on the spot and never wore a hat again.

By the time her friend came back into the room, accompanied by her interviewer, Juanita and Bud Abbott had become friends. "While she was gone, he had explained to me what a pimp was. He just couldn't believe that I didn't know and made me swear on a Gideon Bible," Juanita said. "He thought that was pretty funny, especially considering who I'd come with." In later years they kept in touch and Abbott sent her tickets to shows.

Juanita was not the only sheep straying from the fold. Dick would leave his wife and mother for extended periods of time while out on the road as company auditor for Travelers. When he got back home, as Juanita explained, "he always had something new to do in bed, which made me think more than twice that he wasn't only auditing."

The only member of the household who was at all content with her lot was, of course, Toots. Delighted that Juanita couldn't have children, she found life with them far more restful than in the house where her other daughter-in-law could not be restrained from producing five, all of whom, Toots thought, had been conceived in a conspiracy to rob her of the peace she needed in which to work her crossword puzzles. When Juanita would bring up the idea of adoption, Toots would say, "The only time I ever have any peace is in this house, and all *you* want to do is ruin it for me!" Juanita had met a five-year-old girl in a Shaker orphanage where Dick and another amateur musician occasionally entertained. Juanita dressed her and brought her toys and dolls and visited her every Sunday for five years, but the child's mother eventually reclaimed her and took her home. "It's funny," Juanita recalled, "that with all the names I can remember to this day, I can't remember hers. I had to put her out of my mind, I guess. I can still see her face when I think about it, but I had to put her out of my mind as much as I could so that I wouldn't go crazy with disappointment. I just loved that little girl and even now I keep thinkin' that if we had been able to adopt her, things would've turned out different."

The crossword puzzles continued, while the seams holding the household together gradually came undone. When the Korean War came galloping over the horizon in 1950, Dick was recalled into active service. They sublet their house in Dayton with everything in it and moved to El Paso, Texas, shipping all essentials in a big pine box that had been custom-made for a whiskey still. The apartment they found was unfurnished, but not for long. Juanita made a couch out of the pine box, setting it on top of Dick's footlockers in the living room. Enough boards were left over for an attractive end table which she covered, as she did the couch, in checked gingham with ruffles around the bottom. A dining room set was devised with masonite suitcases for chairs and an ironing board for a table. In the bedroom, a mattress was placed in one corner, and Juanita completed the decor using a dressing table made out of orange crates and a nail keg as a seat. With a mirror and more gingham, it was both dainty and functional.

Army life began in earnest once more. Never in lockstep if she could help it, Juanita entered the ranks of army wives marching to a drummer no one else could hear. "I was not your regular army wife," she explained with considerable understatement. "I was actually known as an instigator. See, the regular army looked down their noses at the reserves, and since Dick was in the reserves, I made sure to stick it in as many people's craws as I could. I was helping one wife throw a party after a football game and she told me that since I was helping her, I could invite my husband's outfit. So I did. One of the guys was black, but I thought, 'So what? If they can fight together, they can play together.' This wasn't exactly Texas philosophy at the time, though. Things got kinda tense that night, but finally a commanding officer went over and shook the guy's hand and the ice sorta melted after that.

"Another time I was in the bar at the Officers' Club on base, and this General came by and said, 'Boy, you sure are pretty, little lady,' and pinched one of my boobs. Right away I kicked him hard as I could in the shins. He got me thrown out of the place, which was really too bad since it was my favorite drinkin' hole and I wasn't ever allowed to come back. Dick didn't mind, although they told him he couldn't come in either because of me. He wasn't the drinker I was and so it didn't bother him much as it did me. I made the rounds after that in Texas and Mexico, both, but I never had any trouble because I had a real aloofness in those days and could be pretty nasty if I set my mind to it. Not as nasty as I got later in the restaurant business, but nasty enough to keep the assholes away. Long as I acted tough as a boiled owl, they left me alone."

In 1952, Dick Musson was transferred to the Presidio Army Base in San Francisco. He travelled to California by train, leaving Juanita and Toots to follow, bickering, in the family car. Right away Juanita set up another Bohemian household at the base housing near the little town of Sausalito, whose residents were not given so much as a word of warning that she had arrived. Life for many of them would never be quite the same again.

Cronkhite Beach, where the military housing clung like white barnacles to the sandy hills above the Pacific Ocean, was pleasant, except for Toots, and warm, except for the fog.

For some reason, the small settlement had been christened the "Pig Farm," perhaps in honor of the area's previous residents. Juanita would beachcomb every day, or drive over to Sausalito to meet with the local fishermen at the old Sausalito Boat and Tackle shop where they taught her to tie knots and make crab nets. She followed their directions about how to crab, putting a lot of junk food into the net and then dropping it into the bay where crabs would get tangled up

39

in the net while trying to snatch themselves a hunk of hot dog. When she felt a crab plucking at her net, she was taught to pull the net up, pry off her prey and toss it in a bucket where it would remain ticking like a time bomb until it was thrown into a pot of boiling water. She took to the waterfront life with typical gusto and became almost as avid a fishermen as her husband was.

Juanita soon made her customary indelible mark as army wife. She was put in charge of the flower arrangements for a luncheon in honor of the wives of the men in Dick's division. One hundred women were to sit at three long tables, with the ranking officers' wives at the middle one. Impressed by the masses of calla lilies growing in the marshes near Fort Cronkhite, Juanita decided to gather all she could lay her hands on for a truly sumptuous effect. After mounding armloads of lilies up the centers of the three linen-covered tables, Juanita stood back to admire her handiwork only to realize that they resembled nothing so much as three enormous caskets at a funeral. It was too late to attempt something more festive in appearance, so Juanita decided to lighten up the lugubrious setting with a military tableau. In the center of the head table, she moved the calla lilies to either side of a large copper tray she filled with sand. On this miniature desert she arranged bits of tumbleweed she had brought with her, for some reason of her own, from Fort Bliss. Then she went downtown and bought a box of toy soldiers which she placed in various hostile attitudes under and around the tumbleweeds. This was, as she explained then, designed as a kind of testimonial to the Colonel who had made Dick's division, as she said, "hang out in the sand all the damn time." As it was in the center of the table it was also before the eyes of the Colonel's wife, who was well aware that her husband was not all that popular with either his men or the women who had to wash the sand out of their hair and the pockets and cuffs of their uniforms.

"No one ever asked me to do any decorating again," Juanita said sadly. "Maybe it was because the calla lilies all kind of wilted before the luncheon started, or maybe they took my testimonial wrong. Actually I think the Colonel's wife secretly thought it was kind of funny. She knew what a jerk the guy was. Not long after that she divorced him—not that I had anything to do with *that*, only maybe she found out just how disgusted we all were that the Colonel kept our boys up to their necks in sand and mud all the time."

Even with such entertainments as ladies' luncheons and after-noons tying knots with fishermen, Juanita still had more time on her hands than she felt altogether comfortable having. A job would bring in more money and besides, she figured, it would ensure her absence from the house Toots insisted upon filling with equal parts smoke and innuendo. She applied for a position with the Vincent Whitney Company in Sausalito and was soon part of the corporate family that manufactured dumbwaiters, among other uplifting equipment. Headquarters was in a building on the waterfront, conveniently close to her favorite stamping grounds. "How many didja catch today?" she'd yell out the window when the little boats docked several hundred feet away. On her lunch hour, she'd go down herself to see how good the morning's fishing had been, returning with enthusiastic reports no one else was interested in hearing. A fellow employee was a dried-up vegetarian who shivered with unconcealed distaste at the slaughter Juanita was only too delighted to relate in detail. It must have been a sad trial to someone unprepared by red meat to brave the shouting, the body counts and the lengthy lunchtime absences.

Things went swiftly from bad to unbearable. One day, according to Juanita, the president of Vincent Whitney asked her to take down some dictation since his secretary was sick at home. Propping a pad on her knee, Juanita complied. At the end of the dictation, her boss asked her, naturally enough, to read the letter back to him. "I wish I could," she replied, "but I don't know what I've put down here." Both were puzzled. Juanita knew shorthand. Her boss knew that she knew; it was one of the prerequisites for her job. She suggested to him, in an effort to be helpful, that perhaps her brain had "gone fishin.'" Her boss went off to write the letter by himself. It was a mystery. However it was also part of the "secretary syndrome" from which she had suffered before. According to Juanita, "Sitting at a desk cut off the circulation in my ass and when that happened, it also cut off my thinking, too, for some reason. After that problem with the dictation, I decided to try and explain it to my boss and he said the problem was that Dick was an introvert and I was an extrovert, and I might as well be locked in a closet as sit at a desk in a small office. I didn't know what the hell he was talkin' about so I looked the words up in a dictionary and decided Dick was the S.O.B. in the family and

I needed a lot more people than the three or four I saw everyday at work."

Everyone concerned was unanimous in deciding that she would be happier in another line of work. After all, she'd lasted about three months and considering that she'd had no circulation during most of that time, she'd done pretty well. Maybe it was the puniness of the vegetarian who first gave her the idea; more likely it was the fishermen who gathered in her kitchen on early weekend mornings for breakfast. Maybe it was simply that she was tired of sitting down. Whatever it was, the Sausalito Bait and Tackle beckoned to her and when Dick was off on business in Utah, Juanita made her move.

There was already a small café called the Barnacle on the premises, though nobody called it anything but "the bait shop," making it the matter of a moment to buy both a cup of coffee and a jar of fish eggs. The owner was an enterprising woman by the name of Florence. It had gone through a series of short order entrepreneurs who had been, according to Juanita, long on hope and short on skills. At the same time Juanita found herself adrift, Florence was talking about shutting down the café altogether. "Oh, you can't do that!" Juanita told her. "Where will the boys get their breakfast? They'll get seasick if they don't eat first." The alternative, that of having all the fishermen in town up to her house for breakfast every day, did not seem at all practical even to Juanita. There was Dick to consider, after all. Though he found three or four friends agreeable weekend company, he could not be relied upon to think twenty or thirty, in boots and macintoshes, a reasonable number grouped around the breakfast table every morning.

"I'll rent the place from you," Juanita told Florence after a brief meditation. "I've always loved catering to men," here speaking the famous words for the first time, "and the only way I can do it legally is to feed 'em, I guess." Be that as it may, she quickly liquidated the Mussons' meagre assets—primarily the grocery money Dick had given her before leaving on business—and became a restaurateur. When Dick returned, it was to find his wife slinging hash down on the waterfront.

Juanita knew nothing about running a restaurant, so she did the prudent thing and hired a young girl named Anne who professed to know everything there *was* to know about running a restaurant, including short order cookery. Thus it was that on opening day, Juanita ushered her with gratitude and anticipation to the grill. Like Prissy in *Gone with the Wind*, however, Annie hung her head and confessed that she actually knew nothing whatsoever about running a restaurant and had, indeed, never worked in one. Furthermore, she admitted, she didn't know how to cook, either. "So what *can* you do?" Juanita asked, understandably annoyed. "I can wait on tables," Anne offered uncertainly. "Maybe I could learn how to make change."

Withdrawing from the immediate line of fire, Annie left Juanita alone in the kitchen with a grill that seemed to grow before her eyes into something vast and unmanageable. But there were tables of fishermen waiting to be fed, so she pushed up her sleeves, turned on the gas, and got to work, shouting over her shoulder for the men to pour their own coffee since she was just too damned busy to do it for them. "And you'll have to look for the cream!" she shouted. "I can't do *everything*, ya know!" Right away she discovered the difficulty of cooking pancakes all the way through and so, in a desperate burst of inspiration, began making them very small and then piling them up in ziggurats on the plates.

Barefooted and with her hair straggling damply around her face, Juanita bellowed when orders were ready and Annie lunged with them over to the counter and the few tables, barely keeping abreast of the incoming tide that threatened to engulf both women in a flood of tiny flapjacks. The fishermen, meanwhile, hungry and eager to fish, got their own silverware, cleared their own tables and put what they owed in the cash register. A few of the more impatient among them began bypassing the befuddled Annie and calling their orders directly to the cook. Finally Juanita slapped her spatula down on the counter and yelled, "No way am I gonna remember all these fuckin' orders! Write 'em down on paper towels!" Not that this made much of a difference, since Juanita was not only very slow, but also an easily bewildered short order cook who did not improve her performance by frequent nips at the Jim Beam she had hidden in a vinegar bottle. On the first day and thereafter, these restorative swigs at the vinegar bottle signalled a change only the most feckless customer would dare to ignore. Liquor was to Juanita as kerosene is to flame, and one misspoken word or misinterpreted gesture could land a hapless customer on a pyre of his own hash browns.

At the end of that opening morning, all the fishermen had been served at last and Juanita, greasy, dishevelled, but not in the least disheartened, shoved her feet into her sandals and told Annie, "To hell with it. You do the dishes. I'm going fishin'!" Down the pier she shambled after the last of her customers, calling, "Hey! Wait for me!"

Art Hoppe, Columnist

My wife and I lived next door to Juanita and her husband in Sausalito. We bought our first television set – it was used and cost next to nothing, as I remember – from Dick, and he installed it, too. In the early days, Juanita was really a kind of ordinary housewife and not flamboyant at all. Both of them seemed to be a very nice, average couple. She was quite a bit thinner then, too, and quieter. Just a plain, old-fashioned housewife, nothing fancy. We saw her occasionally at her restaurants in later years, but by then she was not ordinary at all, of course. Although she was larger and rather noisier, she was still as cheery and happy as she had seemed in earlier days. Just more *of* her, that's all!

3

"Juanita - Panic with Pancakes"

– Marin This Month

Oldtimers remember the Barnacle with affection. A far cry from the chic seaside bistros of today, it remained during Juanita's tenure pretty much what it had been before; a bait and tackle shop clinging with ramshackle charm to the end of a pier. A hole in the floor was left uncovered so that a line hung from the ceiling could hook the occasional minnow. A bell attached to the line signalled a catch, at which time an assortment of stray cats would assemble to partake of the feast. This procedure was often of more interest to the restaurateur than such mundane matters as refilling coffee mugs. "Oh, get it yourself, you got legs!" she would shout, hauling up the line and calling, "Here, kitty, kitty!" in a voice no cat feared nor disobeyed.

Juanita began at this time collecting fawns whose mothers had been killed on the highway near town. She named them all "Sissy," one after another, and brought them up on bottles of milk and cuddling. They slept anywhere they pleased, under a table or under the grill in the kitchen, and were more or less housebroken, depending on how long they had lived under Juanita's benign tyranny. Every once in awhile a customer would be startled by a fawn awakening from its nap by his feet and deciding to have an exploratory nibble of his shoelaces.

From the very beginning, Juanita put a whole new spin on running a restaurant. "I never charged prices high enough to take bullshit," she always said. "I always used to say that I'd make men glad they had the wives they had at home and to think twice about leaving 'em. When they saw how awful I could be, they stayed put all right." Soon there was a sign on the wall that read, "Home cooking complete with argument."

It may have been served with slaps and insults, but what a breakfast! People still remember the platters heavy with ham, with eggs, with hash browns and muffins, with flapjacks and syrup and jam. Real butter and real cream and crisply browned bacon and ham fat all earned her the distinction of being, as Herb Caen would later write, "the West Coast distributor for cholesterol," adding, "The American Medical Association has put her on its 'Wanted' list."

If the customers appreciated her largesse, so did at least one of her early employees. One morning Juanita found a cardboard box labeled "ham scraps." It proved to be full of choice center cuts of ham and worth upwards of twenty dollars. Without saying a word to the would-be thief, she gave the box to one of her favorite deputy sheriffs, Boyd Burnham, for his dog. When he discovered later in the day that the box did not contain scraps, and believed Juanita to have made a mistake, he returned it. "Just take it," Juanita hissed at him, giving him a push. "I want to see the look on my cook's face when he finds out where it's gone."

"We ate ham for a month," Boyd Burnham remembered, "and the dog got some too."

While Dick helped out in the kitchen when Juanita was between cooks, he could only be depended upon when he had nothing to do for Travelers Insurance. Other employees, of all ages, sizes and personal habits, came and went with a variety of explanations and excuses. Some worked for years and were wonderful. Some stayed just long enough to steal a week's groceries or a month's rent. Some worked ten minutes and quit in horror. Working for Juanita could be heaven or hell, depending on one's ability to withstand a constant torrent of advice, abuse and wearing apparel. She would, and did, give to someone she had just spent ten minutes haranguing, the very shirt off her back and whatever she had in her pants pocket. She befriended them, mothered them, and slapped them around. While this treatment was the emotional undoing of some, it was the making of many more young people who were adrift in the Fifties. The San Francisco Bay Area was and would continue to be like a river during spawning season; a destination for the culture's disenchanted. There were many who had never been away from home before, and it must have seemed to them as if they'd never left once Juanita set them to peeling potatoes in the kitchen.

"A lot of these kids didn't know when they were supposed to *stop* peelin' potatoes," Juanita said, "and when I'd go check on 'em, sometimes they didn't hardly have anything left but peel. I used to start laughin' so hard I couldn't get mad at 'em. I guess a lot of times they'd just peel a potato until there wasn't anything left and then throw it all away in the trash."

Around this time, Juanita befriended a man who would remain her faithful employee and dependant for the remainder of his life. Hughie had come West during World War II to work in the Sausalito shipyards and had just stayed on after the war was over and the shipyards deserted. Preferring the bottle to the battleship anyway, Hughie descended the occupational ladder until he was willing to take any sort of odd job in order that he might go wassailing up and down the railroad tracks where he often would be found, a bearded but unbound Pauline, perilously spreadeagled across the ties. According to Juanita, he eventually found a more or less full-time job as general handyman for a wealthy Sausalito couple. For a salary of a sandwich and a bottle of cheap wine, they graciously allowed him to sleep on an old mattress under their house. When winter rains made a swamp of his bed, he dug a trench around it to keep his mattress dry.

When the couple moved thirty miles into the country, they took Hughie along in the back of their truck like one of their dogs (which were, by comparison, treated like royalty). When summer came the couple decided to spend a month in Europe. Hughie was left with orders to feed all the animals on the place and it was arranged that the couple's daughter would drive up once a week with feed for the various dogs, cats and cows living precariously—and they did not know until later just *how* precariously—on the isolated ranch.

Unfortunately for all concerned, the daughter promptly forgot. The month went by without any supplementation of the ranch's provisions. Dutifully, Hughie fed the animals everything he could find that was both available and edible, until the farm freezers and grain bins were empty. When the fuel arrow had fallen all the way to the left, Simon Legree and his consort returned. Furious that Hughie had not been able somehow to pull alfalfa from his hat, they fired him.Warned for some obscure reason not to take the main road to Sausalito, Hughie stumbled off down the old road which meandered through pastures and over hills, and was overgrown with poison oak, blackberry vines and nettles. As it was August, the heat was fierce. Hughie crawled over fences and drank from slimy water troughs along the way, curling up that night beside the old roadway. By the next afternoon he was exhausted. When he finally reached the railroad tracks outside of town, he collapsed with heatstroke. A man who knew him drove past and, recognizing Hughie, bundled him into his pickup and then wondered what on earth he was going to do with him. Knowing, as most people did by now, that Juanita was a soft touch where the down and out were concerned, he drove over to Juanita's Galley and asked her what to do.

"Take him over to my house," she told him, "and give him some of Dick's clothes. And give the poor bastard some cold beer," she added. When she got home, there he was; showered and neatly dressed, as grateful and as grumpy as he would forever after be to her. "If you start taking care of this guy," Dick privately warned her, "you'll have him for the rest of your life."

And that's exactly what happened.

In the years to follow, Hughie would often find himself the happy possessor of hooch and would, upon consuming same, beat a retreat from Juanita's scolding tongue down to the familiar turf of the railroad tracks where he would spend whatever was left of the day or night in a storm drain. "Where in God's name is that asshole Hughie?" became a familiar refrain. Someone gave Juanita a stray dog named "Nibs," but she was so busy flipping flapjacks that the little dog elected himself chief sidekick to Hughie and would tag along faithfully to whatever storm drain Hughie had chosen as his hotel room for the night and then hightail it back home to tattle to Juanita. For eleven years Juanita would throw on a sweater and follow Nibs to where Hughie lay snoring in a drain and hustle and harangue him on home.

As Juanita always would be the first to admit, however, Hughie was not the only one to get frequently shellacked. Since she was a lively drunk, given to throwing bottles and punches and insults, all with deadly accuracy, she quickly became as well-known to everyone in the judicial system as she was to the fishermen on the other side of her grill.

The first time she was arrested for being 85 proof in public was by a cop named George who then went from bar to bar boasting, "I busted Juanita tonight!" This was most unwise, as it turned out, and caused no end of trouble for the "boys in blue" who, after that night, might as well have read their Miranda Rights to a rhino. All it took was for a blue serge suit to approach her with the query, "How are you tonight, Juanita?" for her to slug him. Juanita recalled one eventful night this way:

"I was in the City Hall council room where six cops were tryin' to corral me and take me to jail. I was holding all six of 'em off pretty good, runnin' around the chairs and with them chasing me. When one of 'em would get close, I'd whack 'im alongside the head. Finally they had to call in deputies for assistance and the minute the highway patrol came in, with their brown uniforms, I just stopped stockstill and said, 'Hi! How ya doin', guys?' I went to jail anyway, but that was all right. I deserved it. I just didn't want to go with anybody dressed in blue."

"Juanita's Blue Jeans Turn Judge Purple"
– San Francisco News

One year Juanita got busted five times, each time giving the police such hell that one wonders why they didn't all go into some other line of work. One particular policeman especially was more than Juanita's ample flesh could bear. One night he arrested her as she was on her tipsy way into Sally Stanford's Valhalla. Over her objections that she needed to see a man about a horse before she could accept his gracious offer of a ride to the county jail, he locked her in the back of his patrol car. Scrunching herself up as close to the screen partition as she could, and lowering her drawers, Juanita took aim at the car radio and commenced firing. With a crackle the radio shorted out. Usually of a forgiving nature, Juanita was not able to let bygones be bygones. After her release, she went to Vic Tanney's gym for a few lessons in fisticuffs. According to the way she tells the story, she challenged her sworn enemy to a duel on the Sausalito streets, but he never showed up. "The big baby," she said, smiling rather smugly.

In a bar in neighboring Mill Valley, a young woman, more than a little tiddly, called Juanita a "Sausalito lesbian." That was her first mistake. Turning her back on Juanita was the second. In a moment, Juanita had hold of the woman's zipper. In another, she had yanked it from hood to rumble seat, exposing to the bibulous throng a great deal of upholstery in between. Fired with manly outrage, her boyfriend socked Juanita in the jaw and she went down like a sack of mashed potatoes. Although it would seem that in this case Juanita was more sinned against than sinning, she was still driven off to the county jail where the matron welcomed her favorite guest and put fresh sheets on the bed.

One day a few of the regulars at the Four Winds bar got the bright idea of travelling in a sort of caravan to the horse races, stopping at each oasis along the way. By the time they got to the track, Juanita, for one, had all but forgotten the reason for the journey and settled herself for the duration in the racetrack bar. This was as far as memory went. When the curtain of consciousness rose once more, she was in the back seat of somebody's Buick, stark naked. She also didn't know where she was.

Scrambling into her clothes, she walked to a pay phone and called a friend named Tiny who drove a taxi in Sausalito. As it often is with people nicknamed Peanut or Slim or Shorty, Tiny was fat—but resourceful. Culling the directions from Juanita, he called a friend in San Francisco to go rescue her, with the promise that he would meet them at an all-night restaurant on Geary and, incidentally, pay the fare. All went smoothly and in the morning, after several refreshing stops along the way, Juanita met her irate husband in the living room of their home. Thinking that he might not take the news of her adventure with a merry laugh, she had arranged for Tiny to wait outside until she signalled to him that all was well. All was not well, however. Indeed, all hell broke loose and before long Juanita came trundling out, armed with her checkbook, her husband's observations about her character, habits and general world view echoing in her wake. Tiny drove her to the San Francisco Airport where she caught a plane to Los Angeles, a time-honored venue for those who have found it advisable to be out of town by sundown. After a week, she returned forgiven. "At least life with you is never dull," Dick told her with the resignation of one who knows the salsa will give him heartburn but still can't face eating chips without it.

After this episode, or perhaps because of it, Tiny decided to go on a diet. "He just dieted himself to death," Juanita remembered sadly. "He was the reason I never would go on a diet, except for once when I ate a hell of a lot of grapefruit—but that was before Tiny was dead."

Life—at least for others—went on. One night, for some reason, Toots accompanied Juanita to Sally Stanford's Valhalla for dinner. "Sally always liked to keep the good drinkers in the bar as long as possible," Juanita explained, "and by the time our table was ready, I wasn't interested in eatin' anymore." Sally told her she needed to eat something, but Juanita steadfastly refused, throwing down glass after glass of Scotch. As she said, "It takes a long time for someone to become a true alcoholic, but not if you try to drink it all at once. Somehow I had the idea that Johnny Walker was goin' outta style and I'd better drink it while I still *could*."

Just as she reached the stage where Toots had sprouted two heads, a city councilman plunked himself down on the stool next to Juanita and gave her a cheery smile. "Hi!" he said, his smile fading at the baleful look in her bloodshot eyes. "Hi, yourself, you asshole!" she growled, seeing only the blue suit he was wearing and not the friendly civilian face above it. "Take *that*!" she shouted, throwing her glass of Scotch at him. As he backed up off the stool and out of firing range, Sally, who had witnessed the unprovoked attack, yelled, "All right, that does it! Get the cops here right now and get that woman outta here!"

With that, Juanita slipped to the floor and wrapped her legs around the barstool, vowing never to leave. "They had a hell of a time gettin' me outta there," she explained. "It took two cops and one of her employees. Sally just stood there and yelled the whole time, 'Now don't hurt her! Don't you *dare* hurt her!' while I was kickin' as hard as I could at them. Could've hurt them bad, too, but I guess I didn't." Toots called for a cab and went along home. Juanita went to jail.

"One time I got arrested and the bail bondsman was bailin' me out and my attorney was there in the jail with us," as Juanita reminisced about another spirituous incident, "Next thing I know, this deputy is serving me with a subpoena for something *else* I'd done. He hadn't been able to find me, so he figured he'd serve me right there in the county jail the minute I got out.

"Well, it just made me irate! I took out after him, runnin' all through the jail, knocking papers off desks and people off their chairs, yellin', 'It wasn't *enough* that I got in here already, but now you have to serve me a damned summons, you son-of-a-bitch!' He was runnin' for his life until the cops got me surrounded and threw me back in a cell. It was lucky, though, that my bail bondsman had stuck around because he had to bail me out all over again. I was charged with disturbing the peace, but the case was thrown out of court. The judge said, 'How can you disturb the peace of a county jail?' and let me off. So I was lucky *that* time."

Juanita was known not only for brawling outside her place of business; she gave her restaurant a certain cachet by frequently brawling inside it, as well. The fight could be triggered by her drinking, by a patron's choice of perfume (patchouli was a surefire way of going hungry, or worse) or by her finely-tuned sense of justice. One evening, after she had decided to stay open most of the time, a large Texan came strolling in and, while waiting for his order, called another customer a "nigger." Juanita could call anyone she chose anything she wanted, but no way would she allow some stranger to come in and abuse her clientele.

Snatching up her rolling pin, she took out after the man, yelling at the top of her considerable lungs, "You wanna start a riot down here, calling these niggers, niggers?" Apparently he lost his appetite because he hightailed it out of there with Juanita close behind, brandishing her rolling pin and shouting colorful and obscene personal insults. "I would've *loved* to have a tape of that night!" she recalled, enjoying the happy nostalgic glow. "A real rowdy night that one was, whoooeeeee! I sure was tempted to throw that asshole right out the window, but I thought better of it because it was Saturday night and when could I have gotten the glass fixed?"

In the very early hours of a Sunday morning, as one newspaper reported, "Juanita, clad in one of her fetching Polynesian muumuus, was napping in a car outside when she was roused by an argument at the cashier's desk." With her usual diplomacy, Juanita suggested that the customer who was raising the fuss remove himself from the premises without further delay. This request was, of course, accompanied by graphic gestures and an inspired litany of suggestions, personal observations, and doubts about the customer's matrilineal descent. According to the aggrieved customer, whose name was Otis, it went downhill from there.

Shouting all the while, Juanita began to shove Otis and his cohorts toward the door. Apparently they were not making the sort of progress she wanted, because she hit one unidentified man on the head and then, considerably encouraged by the effect, picked up a chair and brought it down on Otis' head. At that point, the article continued, "He grabbed her by the muumuu and the two started wrestling on the floor." Otis sustained injuries to his jaw and wrists, as he later claimed, while Juanita gained an impressive black eye.

"Warming to her work," the story went on in a faintly approving tone, "the husky restaurateur pushed him and several people out of the door and bade them farewell with a loaded jam dish." Apparently her excellent aim was thrown off by her one-eyed condition, because the jam jar sailed past the lucky Otis and smashed out the headlight of a Chinese laundryman's car. Charges of assault and battery and malicious mischief were filed against her but, according to Juanita, the Chinese laundryman later had a change of heart. She went to jail, anyway, but was released on bail. The article appeared the following day, along with a photograph of Juanita, black eye and all, framed by a lifesaver reading "Pour Your Own Coffee" and brandishing a rolling pin. She was pleased with her press and agreeably flattered by the photo.

Employees were often inspired to get in on the act. One cook was so enraged by the defection of his lover on the arm of another man that he hurled a platter of raw hash browns through a plate glass window as they left.

People who remember Juanita when she was "just a housewife" report that she had been as quiet and mild-mannered as Clark Kent. "She just decided after she opened her first restaurant that she wanted to be like Sally Stanford," one old friend reported. Juanita disagreed with this, at least in part. "Oh, I liked how successful she was, but I never wanted to be like her, and I never have been, either. After I started working with the public, they just about drove me crazy. That's why I started sayin' things like, 'Home cooking complete with argument,' or 'Food guaranteed, but not the disposition of the cook.' I like people—it's the public that's such a pain in the ass."

A large red Coca-cola machine was installed near the kitchen as a kind of partition. Whether it was its color or the fact that it obstructed her view of the boats outside, Juanita hated it. "Every time I'd turn away from the stove, I'd see that damned thing and I'd just be mean to everybody." She would have painted it a less infuriating color. ("I've just always hated red, honey! It was like wavin' a red flag in front of a bull.") Hamstrung by a contract that forbade her from painting the machine pink, she had her employees move it into the farthest corner where it still annoyed her, but not as often.

As the months passed, Dick Musson saw less and less of his wife and what he did manage to catch a glimpse of grew both larger and noisier as time went by. Her voluptuous but slender figure had remained voluptuous, of course, but the girlish slenderness was now erased, in all but memory, by flapjacks and Scotch. Dick loved her dearly and was a patient man, but even the most patient and loving of men poop out. It wasn't that the scenes frazzled him so much. For example, one morning he was talking to a table full of highway patrolmen when Juanita, who was mixing up a big bowl of batter, decided that his idle conversation had gone on entirely too long. Many wives would have been content to merely sigh and look aggrieved. Not Juanita. Balancing the bowl on one hand, she launched it directly at the source of her aggravation. It slammed into a post and shattered. Batter went everywhere; all over Dick, all over the patrolmen, all over everything. Without another word, Dick returned to help at the grill and the patrolmen meekly picked the batter off their uniforms. "I guess they were all afraid to say anything," Juanita admitted, "in case I might do something worse." Happy that everybody was now where she wanted them to be—where they were *supposed* to be—she gave them all a winning smile and began to clean the batter off the floor.

It may be true that "The fruit derived from labour is the sweetest of all pleasures," but Juanita needed a break now and then from the humdrum life of the Galley. Such a break occurred when she was invited for a day of boating on the bay. As Juanita remembered the occasion:

"We were in this big boat out in the Raccoon Straits when all of a sudden we heard a crunch and realized we'd gone aground. Somebody started yellin' 'Everybody aft! Everybody aft!' Only by then mostly everybody was passed out. I didn't know which way aft was, but I went runnin' to see what was going on and passed by this woman who had a little baby. The baby and me were the only ones that weren't drunk, so I grabbed it and went to the back of the boat where I acted as ballast and the boat came off the reef.

"The baby's mother came up and said she wanted her baby back but I told her there was a hole in the boat and asked her if she could swim. She said no, she couldn't, so I told her the baby would have a better chance with me since I could, and that I wouldn't let her have the baby back until we were ashore. She didn't like that but I was a lot bigger than her. Once we were back on land it turned out the girl and the baby had been stranded by this guy, so they came to live at my house for awhile until somebody gave her a room on a barge nearby.

"I felt sad about not being able to keep that baby, since its mother then upped and married this other guy with a schooner and when he told her he had plans to go to the Bahamas, she pulled out the petcocks and sunk it. That sorta put their marriage on ice, but as it turned out, she was already married and had umpteen other kids besides. I told her how I'd sure like to have that baby, but she gave it away to some other people. Turned out, she wouldn't give it to me because she thought I was havin' an affair with one of her husbands— which I wasn't since I didn't have time for that kind of thing at all. When your nose is on the grindstone all the time, your sex life just sorta peters out."

Joe Foley, Bartender

I met Juanita in Sausalito before she went into the restaurant business. She had just moved to town with her husband, Dick, who shared my love for abalone and was a real avid fisherman. I was a bartender and met them at the bar where I worked and, what with one thing and another, we became friends.

Juanita asked me to dinner soon after we'd met. She'd bought these great big steaks and while we were all having a drink, she put them on the grill over charcoal. For some reason, she started cleaning up the living room right then and picked up a bunch of newspapers and without thinking, I guess, shoved them under the meat. So the first taste I had of Juanita's famous cooking tasted just like the Sunday paper.

The second time I went to her house for dinner, I was sitting with Dick in the living room while Juanita was cooking in the kitchen. All of a sudden there was a terrible explosion and in she came running and yelled,"The goddamned oven blew up!"

Her food changed from then on, of course, although Juanita was never what you might call a good short order cook. She was always real slow and got confused when she had too many orders. Not only would she get confused, but the customers would too, so that nobody would be able to remember what it was they'd ordered. It was the most haphazard system you've ever seen in your life, with everybody writing up their own order and Juanita on a tear in the kitchen, yelling and dropping things and slapping people with spatulas. Sometimes everybody at a table would get served except one person, but if that person complained about it, he'd end up real sorry he did! She didn't take too graciously to complaining. "Eat it or wear it" was one of her favorite expressions. Once I saw a policeman complain about something at breakfast and she just eyeballed him and said, "Eat it or wear it!" and he just shut up and ate it. People always did.

One thing she hated making most of all was scrambled eggs because she'd have to cook them separately in 3-egg pans. When I was bartending in Sausalito, before I went to work for Juanita, we'd get in lots and lots of people who'd come in for a drink and want to know where "Juanita's" was. I'd tell them where to go and then say, "Make sure you order scrambled eggs, they're her specialty." I'd send dozens and dozens of people to her place and they'd all order scrambled eggs and get in awful trouble. Juanita would slap her hands on her hips and bellow, "Scrambled! You expect me to stand back here and SCRAMBLE eggs?!"

And yet, no matter how busy she'd be in the kitchen, even if she was just swamped with customers, if there were kids at a table everything in the kitchen would come to a complete stop so she could make them special pancakes. It would take her a long time, too, making all these pancakes with smiley faces on them, but nobody, including the parents, could have a thing to eat until she'd gotten those pancakes done. She loved kids just like she loved animals.

She'd hire a whole flock of high school kids who, together, could hardly accomplish the work of one professional with his hand tied behind his back. All these school kids were always standing around peeling potatoes until they were the size of walnuts. I think she did this because of her own childhood, because these kids were from poorer families and needed jobs. For all her faults, Juanita is still the best-hearted woman I ever knew. From the very beginning she was part of my life and I was a part of hers. There's a lot about life that can be kinda disappointing, but where my life is concerned, Juanita gave me pretty much all the happiness I ever had.

Nan Fowler, Artist

I began to hear stories about a new place in town called "Juanita's Galley" and I decided to go over one afternoon after work for a beer. I rode my bicycle over, parked it outside and went in. The kitchen was right behind the counter, so you could see all the cooking going on. The place was right on the water, a small place with a row of stools inside and several long tables outside where you could take what you had ordered and eat; a real little coffee shop, cold and drafty, and you could hear the water sloshing against the pilings below your feet.

It was a sunny Sunday afternoon and Herb Caen, the columnist for the *San Francisco Chronicle,* was walking around pouring coffee for the people sitting outside. A woman I knew by the name of Joyce was working there and I asked her for a beer. She opened the can and handed it to me and I took it outside and drank it, then went back in and ordered another one, which Joyce also opened and gave to me. However, when I then went back in for a third beer, this fat woman in blue jeans came roaring out from behind her grill and screamed, "Why are you buying beer one at a time? Why don't you buy a six-pack and stop wearing out my employees?"

Now all of this was in front of everyone and I backed away to the door, not exactly standing up to her but not leaving, either, and I said, "But I didn't know ahead of time how many beers I was going to want." She threw a fork at me! I was really terribly embarrassed, but I took my beer outside and drank it and then pedalled on home. Later that night I went down to the Four Winds bar and ran into Joyce who said, "You don't realize it, but you really stood up to Juanita when you didn't run," and then she went on to say, "She'll be here in a little while and she wants to buy you a drink." Which she did. She came in, saw me and started laughing. "Boy! I really had you scared, didn't I?" We became friends after that. I often went to Juanita's and I'd always take my friends there, and though I saw her give other people a hard time, she never gave *me* one again.

Boyd Burnham, Deputy Sheriff

For many years I worked the graveyard shift from midnight to eight a.m. in Sausalito and the surrounding area. In those days there were only two men in patrol cars during the night and since it was a pretty large territory to cover, we were spread pretty thin. Juanita had the only restaurant down there that was open all night for coffee, and since she liked us and took good care of us, we ate there often. She had one special table set aside in a corner and she would tell people, "That's for the cops, because when they come in here to eat, they don't want to listen to people whine about traffic tickets."

Juanita hated the blue uniforms and she loved the green. There was nothing cops could do right and nothing the Sheriff's Department could do wrong. One night she'd been doing a little drinking and had gotten herself arrested. She wasn't about to let the cops take her to jail and they couldn't wrestle her into a car, so they were all shouting and fighting out there in the middle of the street outside the police station near the town park. It was a real knock-down, drag-out and nobody could do anything with her. About this time I drove by and saw what was going on and stopped to ask what the trouble was. One of the officers said, "Look, will you take her up to county jail and book her for us?" and I said, "Sure. Come on, Juanita, hop in!" I opened the door and she jumped in and away we went, no handcuffs or anything.

Actually, I gave Juanita quite a few rides over the years, including the times she'd ask me for a ride home from her restaurant. One time she had a baby deer with her when she asked me to drive her home, and when I said yes, she said, "Well, what about Sissy?" and I said, "Okay, bring her along." It was a real short drive – she lived up behind the old distillery in those days – but that deer managed to make quite a mess of the back seat and when I pointed this out to her, she said, "Boyd, you know what I think of you, and now you know what my *deer* thinks of you!" I didn't tell them back at the substation that a deer had been riding around in the back of my patrol car. I figured they wouldn't really understand something like that happening even in Sausalito.

One Halloween night in about 1959, I went by Juanita's to get a cup of coffee. People were bulging out the doors and windows so I figured I'd just come back later when things had quieted down a little. I was just driving off when Juanita came running out yelling, "Boyd! Stop!" and I thought, "Oh God, what now?" She told me she had some friends she wanted me to meet and that I had to come back with her right then. So I parked the car and went along. She walked me over to a booth and said, "Here are a couple of friends I want you to meet." They were the most beautiful girls I'd ever seen in my life, dressed in evening gowns. Just to be polite, I sat down and told them all about the dangerous and exciting things I'd done in my life and was just having a wonderful time showing off, until I got a look at the time and decided I'd better get along. I didn't want to leave because those girls had been hanging on my every word. I stood up to go and Juanita came over and said, "Boyd, maybe you know these friends of mine are female impersonators from Finocchio's." Kind of embarrassing that they were men, but I thought it was pretty funny, too.

I was called out to San Quentin for crowd control the night Caryl Chessman was executed. There were lots of people gathered behind a barricade we'd erected some distance from the east gate and they were divided into two groups: the people with lighted candles who didn't want Chessman to make the trip, and a whole bunch of bikers who were yelling "Fry 'im! Fry 'im!" Things were getting more and more unruly, until we started wondering if we were going to have a riot on our hands. All of a sudden, there's Juanita, walking around right in the middle of all this mess, handing out coffee and sandwiches to everybody. She didn't care what side anybody was on, she was just interested in feeding whoever was hungry out there. Nothin' ever scared her.

Another time I was called up to the courthouse to testify against her about some problem. I was sitting there waiting to speak when Juanita came in and sat down beside me. We started talking, of course, like always. I was called to the stand and so I gave my testimony, and then went back and picked up the conversation. When she was called to testify, she did and then came back and sat down, like she wouldn't have considered doing anything else. This is something real important to know about Juanita: if you're doing what you're supposed to be doing, if you're doing your job, she has no problem with it. She knew it was my job to testify against her, and after our case was over, we got up and walked out together. As she started off down the hall she called out, "See you tonight, Boyd!"

4

"Juanita Has New Headache"

— San Francisco Chronicle

After six months of raising hell at the Barnacle, Juanita got wind of a new enterprise ambitious enough, and sufficiently haphazard and ill-planned, to merit not only serious consideration but also considerable investment. "Juanita's Folly" was the name she gave the ill-starred adventure, and folly it certainly was. The news was that the federal government planned to build a military installation on Angel Island, not quite two miles off the mainland in the San Francisco Bay. A great number of workers would need housing and meals. Juanita parted ways both with the Barnacle and with Florence (they were not on the best of terms by then anyway) and pursued her new venture as boardinghouse keeper with her usual gusto and lack of concern for such a trivial matter as having anything on paper.

She went shopping, buying kitchen equipment from a restaurant that was going under, and purchasing dozens of beds for the boardinghouse she would run. Too late, she learned that plans had changed and that the workers would be ferried to and from the island every day. Before she could open its doors, Ma Musson's Boardinghouse closed. It had never been Juanita's habit to fret over things that might have been. Looking on the bright side, she unloaded the beds and went looking for a suitable site for her next restaurant.

Down Gate Five Road were the Marinship shipyards, birthplace of the famed Liberty ships which had provided Hughie with a paycheck during World War II and which, like him, had fallen into disarray. Down near the slips was a modest building that had been a paint locker—and, in effect, had remained one since the lockers were all there, complete with a few cans of curdled Battleship Grey. The building was small and dirty and almost windowless. It was perfect. With saw and sledgehammer in hand, Juanita cut larger windows, hauled out the paint lockers, spruced up the interior and when Dick got home from another business trip, surprised him with the "Ferry Slip." By this time one might think Dick would have become hesitant about going away on business trips since his return so often seemed to be met with unexpected surprises, but, then, staying home had its perils as well. Juanita asked him to install the kitchen equipment acquired during her abortive boardinghouse venture, and he did.

In the Ferry Slip, Juanita figured as how she might as well stay open for lunch, since customers stuck around so long waiting for breakfast that it was the lunch hour by the time it arrived. Lunch sort of staggered on until dinnertime. Juanita opened more or less when she wanted to and closed when the spirit moved her, sometimes deciding the sink was so full of dishes that she might as well go fishing. Since there was a leak in the roof over the dishwasher, the job of doing dishes in winter became more than usually disagreeable.

Her beloved highway patrolmen complained to her that there was nowhere for them to get a cup of coffee in the middle of the night, so Juanita gave them a key. Every night found them at the Ferry Slip, happily making pots of black brew and frying up a couple of eggs if they were so inclined. Though she usually opened up at 4 a.m., fishermen would often arrive early and the helpful highway patrolmen would telephone her house with the news that customers were on the doorstep. Then they would open the doors and everyone would sit around drinking coffee until such time as Juanita had bundled herself into jeans and a shirt and bedroom slippers and had come on downhill to cook.

Seasoned customers always waited to see what the morning mood was like before ordering, since the wrong order could cause all hell to break loose. Poached and scrambled eggs were the worst, to be ordered only if Juanita had not been celebrating overmuch the night before. It got to where she knew everyone who came in, by face if not by name, and if their boat was leaving and they didn't have time to eat, Juanita would run down the pier with platters in her hands so that they would not be faced with hunger on the open sea. All of this running dishes down the pier slowed work in the kitchen even more than it was already, but nobody complained about it. Not if they were smart.

Employees came and went, but since most left just as regularly as they arrived, Juanita was often hard pressed to get food on the table while the customer was still there to eat it. One day a private boat docked, as they sometimes did, and a short, round and voluble Italian came ashore. "I will have ten hamburgers," he announced. "But I only know how to cook two at a time," she explained. Without further ado, Caesar Cardini, inventor of the Caesar Salad, squeezed himself in behind the grill and proceeded to instruct the neophyte chef in how to manage ten hamburger patties and twenty bun halves all at the same time. When he had finished, he paid her for what he had cooked, marched down the pier to his vessel, and set forth to sea once more.

Juanita stored this valuable information for future use, although she never would be known as a "short" order cook since everything she made took such an inordinate amount of time. With frequent hits at the vinegar bottle, things slowed down even further. Still, business was brisk.

Actually, there was only one cloud on her horizon and that was the absence of a bait shop nearby. She worried that the fishermen were being inconvenienced by having to buy their bait at one end of town and eat breakfast at the other. So she talked to the owner of a bait and tackle shop in San Francisco about opening a small place near the Ferry Slip, and he soon did, much to Juanita's satisfaction. This addition to the waterfront might have been meat to Juanita, but it was poison to Florence who, until then, had all the local bait business trapped in her own net. With the pioneering presence of Juanita in the nearly-deserted shipyards, followed by the invasion of a competing bait shop, Florence decided it was time to build her own business on the other side of the Ferry Slip in a sort of pincer movement.

Flanked by bait and tackle shops, the "Ferry Slip" flourished. Herb Caen got wind of things and mentioned this new and unusual addition to the Sausalito waterfront in his column—a surefire way for such a business to be put on the map as a place people simply dared not miss. And people didn't. Soon Juanita was forced to hire extra help. Crowding in at all hours of the day and night, lured by the food no less than by lurid tales about the owner, Juanita's clientele became wildly diversified. One night when she was complacently observing her favorite spectacle of lots of people chowing down, she realized that the Ferry Slip had become a favorite hangout for the type of young man who might find the name of the restaurant objectionable. Whacking down the Ferry Slip sign, she replaced it with the name beneath which she would henceforth fry eggs: Juanita's Galley.

One incident of this time nicely illustrates some of the lively entertainment available, on an improvisational basis, at Juanita's. It is best told by Juanita herself:

"Well, one night I saw these two MP's goin' into the restroom and I heard all this action goin' on because I was washin' the damn dishes nearby. I opened the door real fast and yelled, 'I don't allow no shithouse romancin' around here!' Pretty soon they left and pretty soon after that I got a call from the Chief of Police, sayin', 'Juanita, there are two MPs here that want me to arrest you.' I said, 'What for?' and he said, 'Because you hit one in the head.' I said, 'If I hit him in the head it was with the doorknob, and whaddya think his head was doin' down near the doorknob?' But he says, 'Well, I'm afraid you're going to have to come on down here,' and I said, 'Bullshit, I'm workin'. If you wanna arrest me, you come on down here and *get* me.'

"So down they came. I was still doin' the damn dishes and keepin' the coffee goin' cause we had a big crowd that night. The Chief of Police, he goes, 'These men want to make a citizen's arrest, Juanita,' and so I said, 'Do your thing, whatever.' So while I'm pourin' hot water into the coffeemaker, the Chief turns to the first MP and says, 'Do you want to arrest this woman?' and the guy says, 'Yes, I do.' Then he turns to the second MP and he says, 'Do *you* want to arrest this woman?' and this guy also says, 'I do.' And so I put down the coffeepot real quick and yelled, 'Then I pronounce you man and wife!'

"Oh, the whole restaurant just laughed fit to bust. But I had to go to jail, anyway. Max Factor's nephew was there that night, and Walter Keane, who with his wife did those pictures of those big-eyed raggedy children you saw everywhere in those days. Anyway, they went up and bailed me out, the only time I ever got arrested and didn't have to pay my bail bondsman. When I got back to the restaurant that night, I gave 'em their money back and finished the damn dishes.

"The end of the story really is that those guys both got shipped off to Timbuctoo, only in opposite directions. The C.O. from the Presidio came to check the place out to see if the Galley should be off-limits to the military, but he decided it was okay. I was real glad he did, too, because a lot of military people came in and I've always felt pretty military myself."

People of the gay persuasion gravitated to the Galley where they were warmly welcomed either in drag or out, as long as they didn't do anything Juanita considered improperly rambunctious. One early evening, she received a call that a sizable contingent of her customers had just been arrested for dancing naked on the sand of a nearby beach and had been carted off, hissing and snarling, to the county jail. One of the revelers had escaped and the only person he thought might be willing to spring the lot of them was Juanita. Without a second's hesitation, she got into her station wagon and roared off to bail them all out. When questioned later why she had been willing to post bond for so many, she replied, "I wouldn't have had any business next day if I hadn't!" Which, if it wasn't true, was perhaps true enough.

Everything was going along so swimmingly that it was inevitable for the seas to again grow choppy. A nephew of the building's owner decided to go into the restaurant business himself, and since Juanita did not have a lease, she was out on her ear, lock, stock and barrel, and more lock and stock than the owners foresaw, since Juanita was so aggrieved by this sudden turn of events that she stripped the place bare. "I took every damn thing whether it was nailed down or not," she said, "all except the windows. And I would've taken them *too* if I could've."

As luck would have it, Florence had meanwhile decided that two bait shops so close together merely divided the available customers in half, so she moved her second base of operations closer to the main drag, near where the ferry from San Francisco docked. Juanita asked to rent the empty building and, this time, got the agreement in writing. In an interesting turn of events, considering what would happen in years to come, Juanita asked the Sausalito Fire Chief to co-sign for a bank loan to improve the property. Dick was, naturally, out of town at the time.

The ink was no sooner dry than Juanita began the process of transforming the 21' by 21' bait shop into a café. A carpenter was hired to help her enclose another twenty square feet of patio for the kitchen, gathering some of the materials at a lumberyard next door after business hours. When they ran out of two-by-fours, Juanita would clamber over the fence and toss the needed lumber over into her own yard, leaving behind an IOU. When the framing was completed but not yet raised and nailed to the uprights, Juanita waited until a flock of college students came by for lunch and dragooned them into hoisting the framework into place.

When the concrete for the kitchen floor was poured, so was a new patio which quickly developed an unsavory reputation as a gathering place for Communists. "I didn't even know what a Communist was!" Juanita protested, "but these people with spyglasses on the hill kept calling the Chief of Police to complain about all the Communist activity goin' on at Juanita's. When he would sit there havin' a cup of coffee, he would say, "Well, Juanita, I guess I must be a Communist now."" People said a lot worse, of course, but nothing quite so puzzling to the object of their gossip.

Physical labor is, naturally, thirsty work. At night after the carpenter went home, Juanita would drop anchor in the Four Winds bar where her friend, Joe Foley, was bartender. A man who appreciated a hearty drinker, Joe would keep the Scotches coming until Juanita either staggered out to greet the new day or was laid out in state on top of the bar to await, with a strange kind of dignity and in a most unusual silence, the return of consciousness. During these deep meditations, Joe would never allow anyone to touch or speak to her, primarily because Juanita had a war veteran's tendency to awaken with fists flailing. One night someone thought it would be funny to splash a cold drink in her face and she arose with terrible curses and threw everything she could get her hands on at everything within striking range. Mirrors were smashed, bottles broken, and glasses lay in glittering shards all over the floor. "I don't think I hit anybody...but I may have," she admitted.

Through the red haze of hangover and despite mounting debt, the Galley was finally shipshape. When the building inspector got wind of the sub rosa activity, however, he showed up with orders to return everything to its original state. "If you want it torn down," Juanita told him, "you'll have to do it yourself." Faced with such a thankless task, and no doubt having already become acquainted with the decibel level of Juanita's voice, he made a quick retreat, leaving her in possession of the field. "I never much believed in getting permits," Juanita remarked, "so I only got 'em when I had no choice."

Juanita's Galley was now open all day and all night, every day of the year. Even during wintry high tides, business would continue as usual, with customers in rubber boots eating buttered muffins while the bay eddied around their ankles. Despite the scruffy appearance of the place—or, as likely, because of it—celebrities of every type and description began to frequent the little restaurant on the waterfront. It became "the" place to see and be seen.

The last person to be impressed was Juanita. "I didn't know who most of them were anyway, at least at first," she admitted, "because I never had any time to watch TV or go to shows in San Francisco." When someone pointed out to her the presence of a stellar individual, Juanita saw that he or she was not bothered, just the way she made sure her beloved highway patrolmen were left to their eggs in peace. After shows at Enrico Banducci's hungry i or the Purple Onion, after the charity balls on Nob Hill, when Julius Castle or the Papagayo Room in the Fairmont Hotel had given last call and the stages of the Geary and the Marines' Memorial were dark, cars would turn off Bridgeway onto Gate Five Road and pack the parking lot outside the brightly-lighted café. Roars of laughter rang out into the night, people staggered in and staggered out, stray cats and dogs wove their way through the shadows.

Once inside one never knew what, or whom, one would find. Sometimes Jonathan Winters would be there—or his alter ego, Maudie Frickert—holding fellow customers spellbound with extemporaneous craziness. Folksingers like Josh White would be entertaining the crowd while Noel Coward, Joan Sutherland, Bill Cosby, Jose Feliciano and Phyllis Diller looked on. Mort Sahl worked on his material there, although Juanita wouldn't let him perform it in front of her patrons because she was afraid, she said, that one of her less liberal customers might stick him with a steak knife. Anton LeVey, the notorious occultist, could sometimes be found dressed in a gold cape and munching french fries. He gave Juanita a voodoo doll, perhaps figuring that she might have reason someday to need one. He was right.

Dominating the scene with all the noise and color of a Barnum and Bailey ringmaster was, of course, Juanita. Wearing high-heeled gold wedgies, her hair gathered into a fishnet with feathers and squid lures dangling from it, and dressed in the blue jeans she called her "fightin' pants" because that's what she so often did in them, Juanita went clacketyclack, hollering between the kitchen and the dining room, maintaining a fine state of disorder. When there were English muffins to be "forked" (it was Law at Juanita's that muffins had to be split with a fork, never cut with a knife, and to disregard this dictum was to beg on bended knee for a thwack from her rolling pin) there would be a whole table of customers, forks in hand, splitting dozens and dozens of muffins. For this job Juanita drafted anyone—Admirals, cops, drunken scriptwriters—all of whom would meekly fork muffins until she told them they could stop. One of her best muffin-forkers was one of the young handicapped men she occasionally brought over to her house on weekends from the Veteran's Home. "This one boy had no arms or legs," Juanita explained, "because he had the kind of disease where doctors have to keep on amputating everything until there's nothin' left. He had these handles attached to his shoulders and he could fork muffins faster than anybody!" She figured the activity gave everyone the chance to pick up a useful skill along the way.

By this time, Juanita had removed herself from the house in which Toots lived, setting up a separate residence where Dick was welcome to come if he chose, as long as he didn't complain about what he might find on the premises and didn't, of course, bring Toots. On weekends there might be young men in wheelchairs, cats dining from saucers on the windowsills, an assortment of employees or customers too drunk or exhausted the night before to drive home, and such personal decorating touches as a large stuffed gila monster on the refrigerator or a plump and cheerfully alive turkey roosting on the back of the parlor sofa. (The turkey was given to her by a friend one Thanksgiving. That year Juanita didn't dare serve roast turkey, she said, for fear people would think she'd cooked her gift.) At home, with the turkey perched on her lap and an array of animal and human life wandering in and out, Juanita was happy enough. But she was truly in her element at the Galley where there were so many more beings to feed and push around.

A dapper old gent in a stetson hat was being a little too particular about his breakfast one morning and Juanita, still lit from the night before, decided she'd had enough. "For some reason he was just rubbin' me the wrong way, or somethin'. Could've been any number of things since I was gassed at the time," she explained. "Didn't always take that much to set fire to me. Anyway, I threw him out. Next year I saw this little old man in a big hat wandering around the parking lot and so I went out and said, 'You can come in, honey, we don't bite!' And he said, "You sure did last year, you threw me out!' I asked him why I would've done such a thing and he told me that he sure didn't know either, that all he'd been doin' was looking for his son, Kimberly Penney. That's when I found out he was J.C. Penney. I was sorry then that I'd thrown him out since he seemed like such a nice old man, not picky at all, and so I told him I wasn't nearly as cantankerous anymore—at least I wasn't that day—and to come on in. After that we were friends and he'd call me every once in awhile up until the time he died. He appreciated the fact that I was friends with his son and kinda watched over him a little."

James Cash Penney, builder of one of the largest mercantile enterprises in the United States, continued his calls and visits until 1971, when he was called upstairs to corporate headquarters.

"All drunks are perfectionists,"Juanita has said, and nowhere was this perfectionism more apparent than in the Galley's galley where eggs so often fanned the fires of her volcanic discontent. As she said of those days, "All those damned scrambled eggs! You'd get in one asshole who'd order scrambled eggs and then everyone after would order the same damned thing, like sheep. You have to watch 'em and push and pull 'em around until you're half crazy fussin' with the damn things! I wanted people to order the *right* things, like basted eggs or over easy or the best kind, which is Okie eggs where you just break the yolk and cook 'em hard and to hell with it. Other than eggs like them, all the others got my dander up!"

Other kitchen catastrophes—as far as Juanita was concerned—were things on the order of cooks flattening hamburger patties on the grill. "Now that would really make me mean," she said, scowling at the memory, "because they'd just squash all the juice out of the things. No matter how many times I'd tell some of those assholes not to do it, they'd do it anyway just to get my goat." One day her goat was throttled and though she warned the cook not to flatten the burgers again, he immediately did so. With swift justice, Juanita snatched up the two patties and smashed them against the cook's ears. "He threw his apron right at me," she explained about the end of the incident, "and by that I knew he wasn't never comin' back, because I sure as hell wasn't ever goin' to *hire* him back." Early on, it somehow developed that the way employees threw their aprons at Juanita indicated whether they intended returning and whether Juanita would accept them back when they came. Balled up and thrown with force indicated a summary severance of their relationship. Lobbed loosely into the air, something like a handkerchief tossed in surrender, left options on both sides. It became rather a fine art in later years when a few employees quit or were fired on a regular, even daily, basis. It could even be the source of much merriment, sometimes occasioning an immediate restitution of employment.

Differences of opinion were always settled quickly, most often in Juanita's favor since she operated under the strong conviction that even if she were wrong, she was *still* right. "There's a right way, a wrong way, and Juanita's way," she always said. You could argue and you could plead, but if she thought things should go her way then, by God, that's the way they were going to go. "That asshole should know better than to get me riled!" she'd say, half in anger and half in explanation.

Even though a hungry customer might wait an hour without so much as a pickle, if he dared leave the restaurant before his order was plunked down on the table, he stood in grave danger of wearing his flapjacks. One day four cops came in and ordered hamburgers, then waited until they could wait no more. Seeing them return to their patrol cars, Juanita grabbed the half-cooked hamburgers off the grill, ran outside and threw them in the open window of one of the cars. "Here, you gotta eat!" she yelled, returning with a sense of her mission accomplished while the cops stanched the flow of catsup on their pants. A criminal attorney was in the Galley that day and when Juanita came back in, panting, he asked her if she had the services of an attorney. When she told him no, he said, "Well, I can tell you're gonna need one, so I'll be your attorney from here on." Harry Wainwright had an admirable reputation as a tiger, a very successful tiger, in the courtroom. But he lost all five cases when Juanita was his client, probably due to the unequivocal nature of the complaints.

Another cop, off duty and a little the worse for drink, gave up on the steadying possibilities of a hamburger and left. After he had gotten into his car, Juanita arrived at his open window, reached inside, unzipped his fly and shoved the hamburger inside. "Eat it or wear it, buster!" she told him just as she would advise a multitude of people down through the years. It could have been the same cop who was cruising past the Galley one day when Juanita came bellowing out the door behind a fleeing customer, brandishing a butcher knife. "Better not do that, Juanita!" he cautioned as he drove on past.

When renovations were underway on the last of Sausalito's Liberty ships, chief engineer Harry Morgan would go to Juanita's after work. "She had plenty of customers from the waterfront," he said, "and they weren't what you'd call genteel. Nobody changed his clothes to go eat there—you just came in your work clothes, and maybe you didn't take your hard hat off either. But safety gear was no problem to Juanita...she used to say, with the hard hats, if she couldn't do any good hittin' them over the head, she'd just swing up under their chins. I never saw a real fuss in the place myself, but we all knew she wouldn't hesitate to stop one." Or start one, for that matter.

A wealthy attorney had the irritating habit of parking his very expensive Cadillac in front of the Galley, blocking the view of the waterfront. Juanita asked him repeatedly to park it elsewhere, but he would not. Aggravation getting the better of her patience—as it was sure to do—Juanita emptied a bagful of ham scraps all over the hood and roof. When the attorney returned it was to find that his car had become a diner for a flock of seagulls which had spent hours decorating its shining exterior. He never parked there again. "All he needed was just a little lesson in manners," she explained.

Employees were, of course, also the objects of Juanita's rough-hewn style of etiquette training. As if the Galley were a sort of one-room schoolhouse, they were instructed in front of everyone else. Some people were not as adaptable as others to this form of education and, more than once, ran from the restaurant in tears. Others knew her bark was generally worse than her bite. Juanita truly exemplified that poem about the little girl with the curl in the middle of her forehead who "when she was good she was very very good, and when she was bad, she was horrid." No one could be more irascible, or as much fun, as Juanita.

Something happened in 1958 at Gate Five that was later to be remembered by many—incorrectly—as the first time one of Juanita's establishments burned down. That this building did not, in fact, burn down is forgotten by those who prefer to believe that Juanita literally blazed a trail as she travelled north. What actually happened, as far as Juanita herself knows, is that during the three hours she sometimes took off in the middle of the night, somebody broke into the Galley and nearly succeeded in setting fire to it. Juanita had left the grills and exhaust fan on, as always, so that cops in the night and fishermen in the early dawn would not have to wait for the grills to heat up. After smashing most of the new crockery, they took the huge bowl of butter she had left on the counter to soften and spread it all over the grills, which they then turned on to the highest setting. Apparently the vandals didn't think about the exhaust fan, or couldn't find the switch, because they neglected to turn it off before they left. Fortunately for Juanita, a deputy sheriff arrived not long after in search of a cup of coffee and found the place ransacked, but standing. Juanita always believed that the doers of the dirty deed were emissaries of a large Fishermen's Wharf restaurant which resented the fact that she was using dishes marked with the restaurant's logo and were unhappy when she refused to desist. Certainly the crockery bore the brunt of the rampage. What hadn't been broken in the restaurant had been left, for some reason, at a nearby bus stop. There was hardly a whole plate left. Compared to what might have happened, however, Juanita was grateful the whole shebang hadn't gone up in smoke.

Despite all of the work and the increasingly long hours Juanita was not finding herself much richer by the end of the week. Money seemed to disappear as quickly as the English muffins. She had installed louvered windows in the bathrooms so that employees would not be able to toss large parcels of food outside for later collection, but it was brought to her attention that flat packages of steak and ham could, and did, fit neatly through the narrow openings into hands on the other side. After one particularly busy day, she found herself with scarcely more money than it would take to pay the day's meat bill. She had always kept a cookie tin full of money in the oven at night into which employees could dip if they were momentarily on the rocks, but when longer hours required the oven full time, she installed a large piggy bank on the counter into which people could pay their tab, if the cashier was elsewhere at the time, or from which people could extract a loan and leave an IOU. Too often the piggy bank was suffering severe malnutrition without even on IOU to stave off hunger.

"All right, I've had it!" Juanita yelled one night. "From here on out we're on the 'Pay Now, Eat Later' plan!" As soon as order forms could be printed with the Galley's newest motto, customers would walk in, punch their orders in a time clock so that they couldn't whine about someone being served out of line, and then pay the cashier. Only then could they sit down and begin the patient process of waiting for a breakfast that might not appear until lunchtime. One devoted customer confessed later that he usually ate breakfast before leaving his house to have breakfast at the Galley. "I got it worked out so that by the time my second breakfast rolled around, I was hungry again." Most people agreed it was worth the wait. (One enterprising waitress found that she could increase her tips if she kept an eye on where a customer's order was on the cook's order rack. If she was willing to hassle the cook a little, her tips would be increased even more. After asking him several times for updates she would be in danger of being next in line on the grill, so she would take up an old bombsight—a coneshaped funnel with fur around the large end—and peer through it as one would a set of binoculars for the order in question. One day the cook had had enough. Waiting until the waitress had raised the bombsight to her face, he grabbed a handful of hash browns and hurled them into the cone.

The "Pay Now, Eat Later" plan was, for the most part, successful. Those who routinely skipped out on their checks were now forced to ante up. Juanita often gave food away and frequently undercharged for meals, but that was when she wanted to. Medical students came in hungry droves to be fed and she wouldn't accept a cent. "Pay me when you're a doctor," she'd tell them, loading up the young health care practitioners with caffeine, fat, salt, and butter.

Despite the improved economic policy, the day's receipts still wouldn't add up. Month in and month out they came to several thousands less than Juanita thought they ought to—although she had absolutely *no* idea what she should expect—until her longtime cashier went to Las Vegas for a month of gambling. Coincidentally, that month's receipts were up several thousand dollars. Juanita couldn't figure it out. Dora was a friend, and yet... Perhaps Juanita still wouldn't have said anything, even with this proof that Dora was a little lightfingered. Then Dora made the mistake of sashaying in one day wearing a full-length mink coat. She departed the premises with considerably less elegance, and the receipts once more improved. Another time, a cashier disappeared with the weekend's take but thoughtfully sent her erstwhile boss a postcard from Yosemite reading, "Having a wonderful time, wish you were here."

To be honest, Juanita's financial difficulties were also due to her addiction to spending money one minute after she had tucked it into her brassiere. "Antiques" of any vintage and of sometimes questionable worth accumulated around her like the flotsam from a major shipwreck. Around her ankles rose a tide that never ebbed: celluloid dolls, plaster lamps, tarnished silverware, photographs of ancient non-relatives, baby clothes, flattened hats, pieces of discarded farm equipment and trophies from obscure competitive events often claimed the contents of her embosomed bankroll before such minor bills, such as withholding taxes, were paid. The IRS, for one, was unamused and often "hired on" one of its agents as her cashier for as many days as it took to collect what she owed them.

In a conversation many years later, an ex-dishwasher volunteered the information that the only time he ever saw anyone reputable at the cash register was one night when someone in a suit was there making change. "There was a lot of money in the till that night," he told Juanita. "I've always wondered why you didn't hire him on permanently."

"He was with the IRS, honey," Juanita explained.

"Ah, *that* was why there was so much money," he said thoughtfully, "nobody stole it."

"Depends on what you mean by 'stole,'" Juanita replied.

As finances ebbed and the tide of thrift shop treasures rose, Juanita hit upon the idea of offering books of scrip to be purchased at a discount, the little homemade tickets to be used, like food stamps, for meals at the Galley. One could buy twenty dollars worth of scrip which would translate over time into twenty-five dollars in hash browns and hamburgers. In theory, everybody won. In practice, only Juanita made out all right, since customers would often be told by the harried Juanita, "Look, I'm really low on cash right now. Will you please just pay this time? *Next* time you can use the scrip." A customer would feel embarrassed to refuse and thereby would be rewarded by one of Juanita's radiant smiles.

Even at such a rocky pass, Juanita never hesitated to feed anyone who was broke and hungry, or think twice about clothing them or taking them home with her if they needed shelter. It was as if she just assumed that anyone with money could afford to part with some of it, and anyone without it deserved a little. "My grandmother always taught me that you should 'Do unto others as you would have them do unto you,'" Juanita said, then paused and added thoughtfully, "Sometimes people get that wrong and their motto is, 'Do unto others before they can do it to you.' But that wasn't my way. Well, it wasn't my way very *often*," she admitted at last, "only when my dander was up."

People have long wondered how Juanita could have gotten away with what she got away with, without any punishment more severe than a few hours in jail or a modest fine. There have been rumors—where Juanita is concerned, gossip flourishes like crabgrass—that she somehow compensated members of the judicial system for their lenience toward her. There have even been whispers that she rewarded members of the highway patrol with gifts of a warm and intimate nature. Juanita scoffed at the very idea. "Oh, honey," she said, "I was workin' too hard or drinkin' too hard, one or the other, to even *think* of sex." Then her eyes took on a reminiscent gleam and she added, "Most of the time."

Perhaps the answer is that Juanita was always as disarmingly honest as she was cantankerous. She embodied Auden's observation that "Goodness is easier to recognize than to define." Recognizing her for what she was, lawmen and magistrates gave Juanita lots of room to pick herself up, dust herself off and start brawling all over again. And if the powers-that-were in Sausalito gave her a berth wide enough for the Queen Mary, maybe that was partly because Juanita once saved the Sausalito waterfront. She really did.

Mort Sahl, Comedian

It was real different in the old days. Dave Brubeck was at the Black Hawk and I was over at the hungry i, where Enrico Banducci would put you onstage and leave you there for a month until you could find out who you were and where you were going. And, more importantly, if a comedian had nothing to offer he wouldn't put him on at all. Today they'll put on anybody because it's cheap. Used to be people could make up their own minds about what they were seeing; you didn't need to open up a place and call it The Comedy Store. The audience went in and you would say what you wanted to say and the audience could decide whether or not you were going anywhere. Very independent-minded. Now it's all convention. Extremely orthodox. Instead of news, we've got gossip.

People weren't *trying* to be characters then, and there were a few of them in San Francisco because that used to be the place where you could be who you were. That's all gone from from the city now, although there have never been too many of what you'd call real American originals. Juanita was, though. We used to go to Juanita's, Paul Desmond and Enrico and I, after the show. I remember there was always lots of food and you had to bus your own table and pour your own coffee. Juanita was always fiercely in charge, like Tugboat Annie. It was a great place to go and Juanita never treated us any different from everybody else. I miss that kind of place, now that restaurants are all "theme joints" and every place looks like every other place. You might as well be in St. Louis as San Francisco, now that everything's gotten so yuppified. I hope that Juanita is still hanging around, still giving 'em hell. We need her now more than ever.

Enrico Banducci, Entrepreneur and Restaurateur

Juanita's was a great place to go and relax after the show at the hungry i when you'd feel just too beat up to go anyplace else. It was Mort Sahl who took me there the first time, back in 1955. One night after his show he said, "Hey, I know a hell of a place across the bay called 'Juanita's Galley,' where you get great pancakes and hamburgers and coffee and you can talk all you want to without being harassed." So we started going there just to sit around and talk. She'd open up at about four o'clock in the morning, which was the time we'd usually go over for breakfast.

One time she said to Sahl, "You come in here a lot, Mort." He said, "Yeah, I like the place," and then she said, "Well then, why don't you ever eat anything? You think my food's poisoned?" He got sort of nervous and said, "No, no, I'm usually not hungry after a show." He told her he did a lot of thinking in her place and wrote a lot of material, and that seemed to sort of pacify her.

After that first time, I started taking all the artists who performed in my place over to Juanita's with me: Sahl and Don Sherwood and Jonathan Winters and the folksinger, Josh White, were just a few of them. The singer, Odetta, sang there one time. Jonathan Winters would entertain better at a place like Juanita's than he would on my stage, for heaven's sake! I remember one time Johnny was putting on a show and these people kept talking and making noise, so Juanita went up to them and yelled, "If you open your mouths one more time, I'm gonna throw you outta here!" Winters whispered to me, "Is she serious?" and I said, "You bet she's serious!" If she didn't like the look of a customer she'd just point to the door and say, "You, out!" I tell you, if we didn't behave, she'd tell us to shut up or she'd throw us out, too. No favoritism at all. Once Shelly Berman and her got into an argument. I had brought him with me, so I warned him that he'd better take it easy 'cause she was starting to look at *me* funny and I didn't want us *both* to get kicked out. He cooled it, then.

Juanita's was one of the first real coffeehouses, the kind of place where you could go and relax and talk shop, and as long as you acted nice, things were fine. That's all she asked of you. She didn't care who you were or how you looked, and I used to say that at Juanita's all the sables and flannels got along just fine. However, if you acted up and got yourself thrown out, you could come back in five years and she'd take one look at you and yell, "You, out!" She wouldn't like you any better the second time.

Some people were afraid of her and you'd hear them telling each other, "Don't complain about it," or "Don't ask her where your eggs are, for God's sake," because everybody knew that if you asked her one too many times you'd get your eggs, all right, but not on a plate. The service was really slow most of the time, but we all adjusted to that. However, sometimes somebody would come in who didn't know what was what, like the time this guy started yammering about how long he had waited for his pancakes. His voice was so loud that Juanita heard him. "You want your pancakes?" she yelled, "*Here's* your pancakes!" and she came over and slapped them right in his kisser.

Sometimes she just didn't feel like cooking at all – she'd be hungover or something – and if you ordered pancakes, for instance, she'd say, "There's the grill, cook 'em yourself." Sometimes she didn't come in early in the morning and so people would make their own breakfasts and afterwards the honest ones would open up the register and put their money in. I mean, that was the kind of relaxed attitude people had about the place. And yet, you always had the feeling that things were just at the point of becoming outrageous. When you walked in you felt that you were in for something special; that "something's going to happen here"... and it usually did. Juanita herself created that aura; the place *was* Juanita. Full of life – not just a buncha deadheads sittin' around. You know "Elaine's" in New York? Well, Juanita's was the Elaine's of the San Francisco Bay Area. Artists would come in from the East for the first time and right away they'd say, "I want to go to Juanita's." To tell the truth, the hungry i and Juanita's were both really one-of-a-kind places, and we'll probably never see their like again.

Bill Forshay, Entertainer

The first night I was at her place down by the waterfront, these two flyboys came in. Juanita had unmarked doors to the johns and they started toward the wrong door. She yelled at them, but they apparently were a little swacked and didn't notice. She came flying across the room and decked one of them, backhanded him so hard he went down like he'd been clubbed. The other fella turned around and said, "Hey, you can't do that!" and wham! she lowered the boom on *him*. Then she grabbed them both by the seat of their pants and dragged them behind her to the door and threw them outside. They immediately swore out a complaint against her for assault and battery and the cops came to take her to jail. It was late at night, just when the other bars were closing and people were converging on Juanita's from all over. At 2:30 she was at the police station and by 3:30, Walter and Margaret Keene and Vargas, the artists, and Herb Caen and half of Sausalito were up in arms about her being taken off to jail and everybody got together and sprung her. She came right back and started serving everyone breakfast, just like nothing out of the way had happened.

William Hensley, Real Estate Investor

I'll never forget the first night I met Juanita. At the time I was a close friend of Sally Stanford's and had been at her restaurant, the Valhalla, until it closed one Saturday night. I'd heard about Juanita's and decided to go see it for myself. I wandered down to pier five and suddenly found myself in this strange place, like Alice falling down the rabbithole into Wonderland. There was a sign on one wall that read, "Pour your own coffee," so I did, taking it over to a secluded corner where I soon tried to make myself invisible because this fat woman was yelling and carrying on and, all of a sudden, threw a plate full of ham at somebody. I scrunched way down in my chair so she wouldn't see me. No waitress had turned up to work that night and Juanita was in an absolute frenzy. As usual, the place was crowded and chaotic. I'd never seen such carryings-on in my entire life! Everybody wrote up their own order and on the top they'd write the most outrageous names, so there was Juanita screaming at the top of her voice, "Doctor Fuk! Where's Doctor Fuk?"

Suddenly she looked over at me and yelled, "Well, who in the hell do you think *you* are? Can't you see your mother needs some help? Get your ass over here and put an apron on!" I was afraid not to do it, so I got up and put on an apron and started serving up breakfasts, calling out these horrible names at the top of my lungs so people could hear me above the din. After the late night people finally left, the fishermen started coming in – a whole different story. The two o'clock crowd were outrageous and wild and the fishermen were so straight and sober. I worked that first day until seven o'clock in the morning and it was the experience of a lifetime. I had an absolute ball because it was the sort of place where you could get away with saying and doing things you wouldn't dare do or say anywhere else.

I began working there every Saturday and Sunday night, just for the fun of it. Next thing I knew she had me behind the stove cooking, although I'd never cooked before in my life and didn't know the first thing about it. She was an absolute perfectionist where eggs were concerned – she prepared some things so ritualistically that you'd have thought it was some kind of Japanese tea ceremony – and in time I learned everything there was to know about cooking the perfect egg.

This was about the time she started wearing muumuus because she'd injured herself hauling railroad ties around outside the restaurant and wanted something more comfortable than the blue jeans she'd always worn. Of course muumuus quickly became her trademark and were all she wore. I mean, *literally* all she wore. There was a contingent of rowdy troublemakers who would come in and cause trouble but wouldn't dare say a word when Juanita was around. I discovered that they would drive up and then just drive away if they saw someone in a muumuu behind the stove. So when she wasn't there I took to wearing a muumuu and the rowdy guys left us alone. Eventually it got so I was one of the "sights" at Juanita's. She wore these sandals with high stiletto heels that would continually get stuck in the grooves between the wooden slats of the flooring in the kitchen. We had the same size feet so I started wearing her high heels, too. After awhile I was generally known as "Little Juanita."

You just couldn't put in print some of the outrageous things we did. People would come from all over for the show, and we'd really give them one! Occasionally I'd dress in drag, and one night I was sitting there behind the cash register wearing toreador pants and high heels and full make-up and all. These newspapermen came in with this rookie and though they knew I was in drag, the rookie didn't. Letting me in on the gag, they bet this guy five dollars I wouldn't kiss him. I went over and after a brief flirtation, gave him a little kiss and then said, "How does it feel to kiss a man?" Do you know that he rushed out into the night and never returned to work? He quit his job and moved south and to my knowledge never returned.

I was working for a well-known institution at the time and one night one of my very good clients came in with his family and there I was behind the stove, wearing a muumuu and high heels. I have to give him credit, he didn't say a word. He just sat down and had dinner and nothing was ever said. However, one night somebody did develop an attitude and said something offensive to me and Juanita came roaring out, "You son-of-a-bitch! You don't even know the connotation of the word you used!" She grabbed him by the back of the neck, slapped him three or four times across the face and then proceeded, still holding onto his collar in a death grip with one hand, to grab him by the seat of the pants with the other and throw him out the door. She didn't like people getting picked on and would beat the hell out of anybody who harassed you, especially if they were bigger than you. Everybody knew that, so we smaller people could get away with all kinds of stuff – if Juanita was there!

One night after she'd had too much to drink, Juanita thought she'd better go lie down in her car, which was parked out front, and she went and passed out on the front seat with her feet sticking out the open door. These five black guys came along and thought it would be funny to give her a hotfoot, which they proceeded to do. Well, she came out of that car like an *explosion*. The guys all jumped her, but she beat the hell out of them. Of course they should have known better than to do something like that to her; she was really Rambo the First. She picked up the big glass jars of jam from the outdoor tables and started hurling them at these guys as they ran, and though they ran off in every direction after she lobbed the first one, Juanita was so mad she just kept going. I think she ended up smashing three windshields and scratching a bunch of cars before she finally calmed down.

As great as her cooking was, that's how bad a businesswoman Juanita was. So many people just walked out on their bills – not to mention the employees who would steal from her cash register – that I suggested she institute the "Pay Now, Eat Later" plan, which she did. My God, the take went up several hundred percent! The service was generally real slow, and when Juanita was cooking things would be slower than usual and more than usually unpredictable because there was something about the act of cooking that seemed to lash her into a frenzy of rage. Sometimes people wouldn't get served at all and we'd get complaints that our new plan was really "Pay Now, Eat *Never*." Anyway, one night some highway patrolmen came in, and we always tried to serve them promptly because we knew they were on a tight schedule. Juanita was behind the grill that night and things were chaotic and finally the cops decided to leave. Juanita saw them go and so she grabbed up four raw hamburger patties and slopped them with mustard and catsup and then ran outside to their car shouting, "You gotta eat!" and threw them in the window, rubbing one all over this patrolman's tie and jacket. Even then she didn't get in trouble because they all loved her and just accepted that this was the way Juanita was. She'd do things like that, do whatever she felt, whether she was drunk or sober. It didn't matter. She gave the patrolmen keys to her place so they could make themselves coffee, and no matter what they ate she'd only charge them fifty cents.

I had occasion to be real happy that the patrolmen liked her and knew all of us, because when I'd be driving home after work I'd often be so tired I'd nod off. I'd almost always have to go home, but the employees who were too tired to get further than Juanita's house up the hill, they'd all just tumble into her big Victorian bed like a bunch of puppies and Juanita would be lying there in the middle with her arms around those on either side of her. These were people she might have been yelling at all day, too, but it was a real sweet sight.

You know, I've had friends among the rich and famous, and poor and notorious, too. Josephine Baker, Mae West, and Carol Channing, among others. But there were never two more interesting women than Sally Stanford and Juanita. Domineering and difficult – and absolutely divine.

Darrell Reed, Theatrical Wardrobe Supervisor/Dresser

One spring day in 1959, I was hitchhiking in Sausalito and this guy who looked like a cowboy and whose name was Orville picked me up. I mentioned to him that I needed a job and he told me that if I didn't mind doing dishes and working weird hours in the boondocks in Sausalito, he knew of a place that might need me called Juanita's Galley. "The owner screams a lot," he told me, "but you'll like her." Right away I pictured Juanita as being real tiny, with kinky hair and wearing rimless glasses and having a high, screechy voice.

I showed up for work at two in the morning and started doing dishes at the dishwashing area which was right in the middle of the restaurant, right in the middle of all the action. A few minutes later I heard this noise outside the restaurant that sounded like the bellowing of a moose. Suddenly the door burst open and in came this gigantic woman with long, flowing hair and with this huge muumuu on, and she put her hands on her hips and glared at everybody and yelled, "Jee-zus Christ! I paid two hundred dollars for a goddamned

neon sign and you stupid queens haven't got the brains to turn it on!"
I was speechless with shock at first, but we ended up talking a lot after
my shift that night and liked each other right away.

I worked until about three or four in the morning and then
Orville took me home and then came back for me at 9:30 a.m. because
no one had showed up to wash dishes. It was raining that day and
there was a leak in the roof that landed right on top of my head. It was
like Chinese water torture all day long.

The next day I saw Juanita again and she'd done something she
rarely did anymore: she'd gotten drunk and was passed out in her
station wagon outside the restaurant. About three o'clock she woke
up and came crawling out of her car with her muumuu all wrinkled
and her hair tangled, looking a real mess and ready to eat nails. God,
she was mad! She came thundering in and found this poor couple who
hadn't punched their order in on the time clock and she started giving
them hell. "What do you think this place is, one of them uptown
joints?" They got real offended by that and walked out, but she
followed them, yakking and cussing at them. She'd give people hell
pretty often and sometimes they'd leave, but she'd always say, "So
what? Lose two, get four!"

I remember once there was a bunch of obnoxious kids sitting
around a table one day and bitching about how long they'd waited
and Juanita started yelling at them, "Well, for Christ's sake, if you'd
get up and do some dishes and bus some tables, maybe you'd get
waited on a little faster!" Another time this cop came in and ordered
a hamburger, but after awhile he decided he didn't want to wait any
longer, so he left. Well, Juanita wrapped the hamburger up real nice
and followed him outside to his car, pulled out the front of his trousers
and stuffed the hamburger inside his fly. "Eat it or wear it!" she
screamed at him, and he just drove away.

I started doing sketches of her, little cartoons, just to record the
wild things she did. I wasn't sure what she'd think of them, so I
thought it a good idea not to show her. However, I would show them
to the cooks who howled over them. One day, before I could stop
them, they showed several of the cartoons to Juanita. I was really
nervous, but she loved them right away and rolled them up and
shoved them down the front of her muumuu where lots of other
things tended to disappear. After awhile I put all the sketches into a

notebook that I would pass around among all the customers, who would often steal them. One time this group of young people were looking at the book and saying things like, "I'll bet he just made this up. This couldn't have happened," and things like that. Well, a name was called for an order to be picked up, and it didn't happen to be their's, but they said it was and began eating another table's breakfast. When Juanita found out what they'd done! Well, the next scene looked like this: coffee mugs were tipped over, orange juice was everywhere, chairs were knocked over and the young people were running for their lives to their car with Juanita in hot pursuit behind them. "Don't you ever come back, neither!" she was yelling.

After a few months I started working with a nightclub act and then went into theatrical wardrobe, travelling with actresses like Carol Channing and doing shows like *Chorus Line* and the *Man of la Mancha*. While it was hard work and great fun, it still wasn't like life with Juanita!

Joe Kane, Co-Founder United States Leasing Corporation

Juanita was nice to everybody – well, at least she treated everybody, from all walks of life, exactly the *same*. An example of this was something that happened in Sausalito about twenty-five years ago, when blacks were just beginning to come into the forefront socially and everybody was a little bit uneasy about how to handle things. The procedure at her restaurant was that as soon as you got there, you put your name and what you wanted to eat on an order form, and then you punched in the order form on a time clock, which made the food service a little more orderly. That is, if it ever came at all. One day a beautiful black couple came in and sat and sat and sat and it got more and more embarrassing for everybody until Juanita finally noticed and went up to them and said, "Goddamn it, can't you see you're no different from anybody else? Go over and get an order form and punch it in the goddamned time clock!" We nearly died, we just couldn't believe it, but that was the way she was. Democratic.

I used to tell her that people were stealing her blind and that she ought to have some kind of controls in her restaurant, but any time we got her to put someone in to control things, she'd kick them out with the excuse that they were interfering with her business. For instance, her method for wine selection was that you just helped yourself to whatever bottle you wanted, put it on your table, and she'd trust you to put it on your bill. Her wine "cellar" was accessible to anyone with sticky fingers, of course, but that never seemed to bother her.

What did bother her was the quality of the food she served. She was ruthless that meals always be served to customers piping hot and with butter and lots of jam and everything, but actually getting the food would take forever. She never could keep to any kind of schedule, so her customers quickly learned they couldn't either. One day two policemen came in and placed an order for breakfast. It didn't come and it didn't come until finally they walked out and got into their police car. Juanita saw them leave and so she grabbed up their breakfast off the grill into a frying pan, ran outside and threw their eggs and ham in the car window, yelling, "Okay, so wear it!"

Lots of times in Sausalito we'd get together a benefit for her, to pay back taxes, but once she thought of something really ingenious to earn some money. She sold books of scrip. You'd pay in advance for these meal tickets and you'd get a discount; like you'd buy $20 worth of tickets for $18. The problem was that whenever you wanted to cash them in, she'd say, "Well, honey, I can't afford to have you do that right now. I need the money, so pay me cash." And we did. She wouldn't *deny* that eventually she would make good on them, she would just say, "They'll be good sometime, just not right now. So why don't you buy another book?" We ended up with a bunch of books when she moved north and when we asked her what we were going to do with all of them, she cheerfully suggested that they would be nice to paper a wall with.

During the lean times, Juanita would often live rent free in some of the places I owned in Sausalito. I let her live in them without paying because we all liked her so much and she was fun to take care of because she was such a character. And then she probably wouldn't have paid us, anyway.

As a young woman, having come from prim and proper England and moving to Sausalito, Juanita was this incredibly colorful woman; an almost unbelievably different sort of woman. Around someone like her you feel as if you're always somehow dressed in *grey*.

I was working at that time as a fashion model for I. Magnin's and Juanita came in one day looking for a special nightie to give Sally Stanford, who was in the hospital and needed cheering up. She swept in with her hair all done up with a comb and her muumuu, and she wanted a real performance, with models prancing around. I was called down to the lingerie department and soon there I was, whirling about in black negligees and nighties all open at the front and back and thinking, "Oh, dear me!" because I'd never modelled anything like that before, and to be modelling something to be given to an ex-madam was pretty funny. There was a ruckus on the floor because it got around that Juanita was there buying Sally a nightgown, and a crowd soon gathered. It was really something.

One evening a few days later, I went with some friends to the Four Winds bar to have a drink. Juanita had obviously had a few snootfuls too many and there she was – reposing on the bar where they'd laid her out, looking very grand and with her hair all spread out around her and her hands clasped and ankles nicely together. Joe Foley was tending bar and he wouldn't let anyone touch her or move her, although nobody who knew her would've dared to do something like that since she was famous for coming up fighting if someone had the temerity to wake her up. Everybody had to make room for her and set their drinks where they could alongside her like some kind of Irish wake. We had a drink and talked and other people came and went, and she just lay there, dead.

5

"Lady Bountiful"

– San Francisco Examiner

It was a hot summer day. Juanita stepped outside the Galley for a breath of fresh air, only to inhale a lungful of benzene. Across the street a gasoline truck was being filled with such dedicated thoroughness that it had overflowed onto the pavement in a noxious little stream ambling off down the gutter toward town. Juanita began to scream, but since Juanita screaming was not an unusual occurrence, nobody paid her any attention. As Juanita tells it, "I know that everybody was just thinking, 'Oh, there goes that crazy woman again!' while gas was just pourin' all over the blacktop."

"Now gas and blacktop just don't mix; the blacktop goes all soft and the gasoline explodes and nothin' is the way it should be. If anyone woulda lit a cigarette, the whole waterfront would've gone up, boom!" Eventually someone realized what "that crazy woman" was actually yelling about and the Fire Department rushed clanging to the rescue and washed the pavement down. A newspaper story the next day credited Juanita's infamous lungs for saving the waterfront and there were hash browns on the house that night at the Galley to celebrate the lack of hash browns all over every house in town.

Almost nothing escaped Juanita's keen eye and her ears were always tuned to the calamity channel. There was rarely a local mishap in which she did not, sooner or later, make her presence felt. "My curiosity was *somethin'* in those days. There wasn't hardly anything that happened I didn't get involved with one way or another. I used to stop at all accidents and chase all fires and it got to be kind of a habit. After I had the restaurant, I'd always take sandwiches and coffee to every single fire or natural disaster we had."

Her first concern was always for the highway patrolmen and the firemen, but she was an equal opportunity benefactor and fed the guys in blue suits too. When storms would knock down power lines, it was always Juanita who would show up in her galoshes, laden with coffee and victuals for the repairmen. It wouldn't matter that rain was arriving in buckets and the wind made garottes of her hair, there she would be, yelling "Come and get it, guys!" in a voice that made the wind sound tinny by contrast.

One night sirens began to scream at the firehouse. In a flash, Juanita was up, breadknife at the ready and coffee already percolating by the time her turkey wandered in to see what all the commotion was about. Shoving everything—everything but the turkey, who was a spectator, never a participant—into her station wagon, Juanita set forth toward the flames. It turned out, ironically, to be a major fire at the old American Distillery and while Juanita stood handing out the grub, whiskey ran down the street and pooled around her ankles. "I didn't even take one drink," she claimed with modest pride, "not even when a vat of booze exploded nearby."

In addition to all of these civic catastrophes, she took part in less dramatic, but potentially more explosive occasions. After one of her many tipsy mishaps, Juanita made the acquaintance of Ernest C. Zunino, a Municipal Court judge. He had pioneered a program whereby local merchants could hire convicts in a work furlough program to aid in their rehabilitation. When he broached the idea to her, Juanita was, of course, delighted to take part.

The day before Easter—a very important day on Juanita's calendar—she had in her employ a resident of San Quentin whose responsibility that morning was to hardboil sixty dozen eggs. As Juanita caught a little shut-eye in preparation for what was to come, the work furlough participant carefully lowered all twenty dozen eggs into an enormous stockpot and set it to boil. By the time Juanita came yawning onto the scene, the eggs were boiled hard indeed, many of them so thoroughly that their yolks were purple. Immediately, Juanita's cheeks assumed the same shade. "What the fuck do you think you've done, you asshole!" she shrieked at the six-and-a-half foot, hulking murderer, slapping him soundly with the back of her hand. "Now you're just gonna have to do them all over again, and *this* time you better fuckin' get it right!" Charging off to the grocery store, she returned with another gross of eggs to find her mother's little helper had flown the coop and gone back to the relative safety and serenity of the slammer.

This experience did not deter Juanita from trying again with a ragtag collection of other jailbirds, few of whom stayed long enough to learn the proper way to fork a muffin. Not that Juanita abused them. She merely always believed that if a job was worth doing, it was worth doing well. Whether her student was a teenager, a Baptist minister or a paroled killer, they all had to learn to do things "Juanita's way." Though strict as a drill sergeant, she was still such an effective teacher that those who stayed learned enough to ensure them excellent jobs at their next place of employment, though that was cold comfort for some.

The Sea Scouts often dropped by the Galley after their meetings to help Juanita out with the day's leftovers. Moaning over their enchiladas one night, they told her that they had planned to sell hot dogs at an upcoming boat regatta but that the Chief of Police had nixed the idea. "We need a radio for our boat," they chorused sadly, "and now we don't know how we're going to make the money."

With a sudden conspiratorial glitter in her eye, Juanita reassured them, "Oh, you'll have your wienie stand, don't worry!"

She was as good as her word. Never one to get in a pucker over something so trivial as police permission, Juanita supplied the Scouts with a flatbed truck, her property to put it on, and a cooler for the Cokes. She also loaned them the money for the dogs and the buns. By the end of the day they had enough to pay her back *and* purchase the coveted radio. The opinion of the Chief of Police about all this is not known, but more than one official has found it easier to throw up his hands in surrender when faced with such vocal and corporeal opposition. Juanita and the Sea Scouts had subsequent adventures together, and if Juanita had done them a good turn, they would in time do her an even better one.

In record time, Juanita became one of the "sights" any visitor to Sausalito had to see for himself. Soon tour buses would pull up outside the Galley and she would trundle on out to greet the folks and welcome them to California. For as long as she lived in Sausalito, Juanita was as popular as the famed Muir Woods and considerably more entertaining than the excellent scale model of the San Francisco Bay with its reenactment of the ebb and flow of the tides. She would clamber up into the bus and deliver herself of a whole speech she would invent on the spot, full of the wildest inaccuracies so much more enthralling than mere fact. Tourists loved her. She was exactly what they had expected Northern California to be when they dreamed about it in their La-Z-Boys back home in Iowa. A ride down outrageous Polk Street in "Frisco" and a stop at Juanita's added just that exotic touch so delightful on a journey to foreign lands.

When Juanita was not at her restaurant, bus drivers would usually push right on up the hill to her house and honk. Out she'd come with her turkey on one hip and a fawn by her side, all of them staggering together up the bus steps and onstage. "But if I was havin' my period, or somethin'," she explained, "I'd just stand on the porch and wave until they went away."

In addition to pleasing the Chamber of Commerce, she did her part for international relations. A group of Japanese tourists descended on the Galley one day for lunch. During the course of it, Juanita gave one of the visiting gentlemen her patented "ear muff treatment," and wrapped her super-economy -sized breasts around his head from behind. Each of the men politely requested that he might also experience this odd, but charming, American custom, while his friends snapped photographs. On many walls in Tokyo and Yokohama there must be hung a most obscure picture of a large smiling woman embracing, from behind, a small, headless man.

In spite of all of this international glamour, Juanita did not forget the folks at home. Often she would march across the street to the waterfront beauty shop, laden with plates of spaghetti and garlic bread which she would hand to the women sitting under the dryers. With her hair tied up in the fishnet and the gold high-heeled wedgies on her feet, she must have seemed to those not already acquainted with her a bizarre apparition indeed. "Now eat it all, honey!" she would fondly urge the bewildered women, "cause you're gonna need all the strength you can get, sittin' under a hot dryer all day long." Since she herself did not require the services of a beauty shop, she felt an inordinate pity for those women who were more or less enslaved by their tonsorial addictions. Sitting under a dryer seemed a terrible waste of time which only good food, and lots of it, could make bearable.

It will never be known how many strays, both human and animal, Juanita has fed, clothed and housed over the years, but they surely number in the hundreds. Some have written to thank her for the light she shed in a dark hour. One such letter reads, "Hi Juanita,

You know me, my name is Casey W...the piano tuner, hope everything is fine with you, sure know a lot of people that have been to your place from all over. Well what happened, I got two drunk driving charges against me, and the judge recommended that they put me in the alcoholic ward, thats where I am, had my driver's license taking away from me so I couldn't also get around to tune pianos. I remember in the past how good you were to me, didn't know whether to ask you or not, ended up broke in here no money or cigerettes, all my folks are dead, didn't know who to ask. What I needed was some cigerettes and a little change to get me by. When I get out will work over all your pianos for nothing if you have any pianos and will also pay you what I owe. Hoping to here from you."

Whether she had any pianos or not, Juanita would always send the money, answering a call for help from one of the children she never had.

Teachers sometimes brought their classes over to the Galley for breakfast. It was a peculiar sort of field trip, perhaps, but Juanita and the children had a wonderful time. Before the much-anticipated event, one young diplomat wrote to her, possibly to avoid a problem in advance: "Thank you for letting us come over for breakfast and I hope you got a bunch of stuff. And my teacher told us a bunch of nice stuff about you and when we go I hope you won't get mad if somebody leves some of there food." Out of a similar concern, another young boy wrote, "Dear Jaunita, I want to Thank you for letting us come to have breakfast at your restront. I hope it will taste good because I hate almost anything I eat. Sincerely yours, Eric."

Juanita's reputation may have been that she was someone to reckon with, someone who couldn't be fooled that the liver was eaten when it was really hidden under the mashed potatoes, but she really didn't frighten anyone either. At least not for long. Perhaps one woman put it best when she wrote Juanita with this wish, "St. Jude is Patron Saint of the impossible. I hope he helps you as much as he's helped me."

Ernest C. Zunino, Municipal Court Judge

When I first came to Marin County in the Fifties, I started the work-furlough program, the first in the nation, for the county's Probation Department. Juanita was then operating a restaurant in Sausalito and she was one of the first, and one of the few, employers willing to take the convicts I was responsible for and give them a job and keep them working. I was always well assured that if they didn't show up on time, or left early, or showed up drunk, Juanita would straighten them out herself and then let me know about it. She did take a chance with some of the people in the program that she hired, and I've always had a soft spot in my heart for her because she did take that chance. There was more than one work-furlough participant, however, who came back to me a short time after being at Juanita's to tell me, "I'm not going back. I don't want to work for her ever again." The alternative might be sitting on his fanny in San Quentin, but some of them preferred that to working for her.

Juanita had a lot of affection for people in the Justice Department. Every time they'd go out on a search and rescue operation, Juanita was always there with sandwiches and coffee for everyone. On several occasions, unfortunately, she had assigned the duty to someone under my control from the work-furlough program and since they knew to whom the food was going, some of the things they'd do to the officers' sandwiches are unmentionable. I never told Juanita about that because she would've killed them. Just thrown them off her boat.

In the early Sixties she started getting some pretty rough crowds at her place and police were apprehensive about a lot of these people, but she never stepped back from any of them. She really had guts. Things got pretty wild on more than one occasion, but you'd have the hardest time getting her to come forward to say anything about anybody, even someone who'd wrecked her place. She just wouldn't do it. One incident in mind is when some local kids went in with fire axes and tore the place completely apart. It was a serious altercation; she was an eyewitness, but she wouldn't come forward.

Juanita has always been overly protective of everyone with whom she was associated. You never had to question where you stood with her, ever. She was always on the periphery of politics and she knew everyone and everyone spoke to her, so she obviously was in a position to pick up tidbits of information here and there about people. And she was a good friend of Sally Stanford's. But I don't believe she ever used that information, as some people believe, to exert pressure to get herself out of trouble. Never in *my* experience with her, anyway.

She'd talk the same way to everyone, no matter who they were. We used to have a judge here, Judge Haley – he was later murdered in his courtroom – who could have been a priest instead of a judge. Juanita had to appear before him one day on some charge or other and showed up, of course, in her usual muumuu. Now, Judge Haley didn't think ladies should appear before him in his courtroom dressed that way. He started to tell her that, but the way she answered him back only Juanita would have been able to get away with. He only said in his mild way that on her next appearance she would have to dress more appropriately. I don't remember the exact colloquialism she used, but I'm sure he couldn't have thought it very ladylike, either. When the occasion arose for her to appear before him again, she was wearing a muumuu. I think that was when he just gave up. Because that was Juanita.

Marvin Hyman, Former Bailbondsman, Pawn Broker

Many years ago when I was in the bailbond business, Juanita used to call me up every once in awhile to post bail for somebody. I bailed out a lot of people for her over the years, most of them her employees or friends. She took all the responsibility, so if any of them had run away, she would have had to come up with the money. She was a good soul and would take in anyone off the street and give them a place to stay. If they needed food, she fed them. If they needed clothes, she'd clothe them.

Later on I left the bailbond business and opened a pawn shop. I became kind of like Juanita's banker then, and I enjoyed being able to help her out when she needed money. She'd never go into the particulars about why she needed it, just how much she wanted and what she had to pawn. The impression I had was that most of the time she needed money to pay overdue food bills. Considering the size of the prime rib she served, I'm not surprised how big her bills must have been. Actually, I don't understand how she ever made a profit at *all* – the portions she served were huge, unbelievable.

I've never done business with another character like Juanita – not too many people like that around. She used to come in all the time with this squash blossom necklace when she needed money and then, after awhile, back she'd come to get it out of hock. One time there was going to be a roast of a local dignitary and Juanita and I were both invited. She came to see me that day and asked if she could borrow the necklace, since it was still in pawn, because she was going to get all dressed up and that was her favorite necklace. I loaned it to her and that night, after the roast was over, she came up to me and said, "I guess you probably want this back now," and handed it to me with no hard feelings and not embarrassed at all that she had to return her jewelry to her pawn broker.

6

"Juanita Objects - the Galley Shakes"

—San Francisco Chronicle

As her fame grew, so did Juanita's thirst. Waking up naked in the back seat of a Buick was bad enough, but when the curtain rose on a similar scene a short time later, she began to wonder whether she would be able to outlast John Barleycorn after all. On a visit to Las Vegas she was sitting at the bar when Robert Mitchum plunked himself down on the next stool, looking grim. "What's the matter, honey?" she asked. When he explained that he'd run out of chips, according to Juanita, she cheerfully slid a few down the bar to him. This priming of the pump succeeded so well that the duo retired upstairs to celebrate in the hotel shower.

"All I remember was standing there and both of us were buck-ass naked, and then it all goes black," she said sadly. "I don't remember whether all we did was just clean fun, or what he looked like, nothin' at all until I woke up next morning in bed, alone. Now if *that* wouldn't have been enough to stop anybody from drinkin', I don't know what would!"

She did not stop drinking until 1957 when she decided that something had to be done at last. Without provocation she had hit Dick in the head with a telephone.

"I just lobbed it at the poor guy," she said, "and he was took by surprise. Toots wasn't any too happy about it either and, to tell the truth, it's not somethin' you oughta do to a man."

Though the sex was great when she was sober, and the conversation often exceptional, Dick had been worn down not only by the boozy brouhahas, but by his wife's wifely devotion to the Galley. It was as if their children were all the people Juanita fed, and she would not stop caring for them just because her husband wanted to see her without her rolling pin occasionally. When they fought, as they seemed to do more and more often, their two dogs, Jerry and Monkey, ("I gave him that name cause he'd been bitten by a rat ")

95

would stand between them, distressed, looking from one to the other with such painfully anxious looks on their faces that the adversaries would suddenly choke with laughter and have to stop.

The incident of the telephone brought down the curtain on their domestic drama at last. Since Juanita had long since moved out, their separation caused very little rearrangement of their living quarters. Toots was pleased that Dick had at last "come to his senses" and began to suggest he waste not a moment in finding another Mrs. Musson, who this time might be both tidy and mute.

Disgusted with herself and hauled into court soon afterward on yet another charge of being drunk in public, Juanita decided enough was enough. When the judge asked the arresting officer, "And what was the blood alcohol level of Mrs. Musson at the time of the arrest?" Juanita called out, "100 percent!" Taken aback by this unexpected honesty he turned to her and asked, "Do you want to do something about your drinking, Juanita?" She replied, "I sure do. It's gettin' to be sort of a problem lately." As gavel whacked bench, Juanita Musson was sent on vacation for three weeks to a farm for recovering alcoholics in Sonoma County. As Juanita describes it, the trip to sobriety was a wet one.

"There was this bar on the way, the last place to stop for a drink before you got to the farm and your drinking days were over. It was great. The bartender would press a button and air would gush up from a hole in the floor and send some girl's skirt up over her head. They had a speaker in the bathroom, too, and just for a joke the bartender could call in over a loudspeaker, after he was pretty sure she was sittin' down, 'How'ya doin', honey? Need anything in there?' Pretty soon some girl would come out with her face all red and everybody would laugh. It was just a great place! I got some of my better decorating ideas there, like hangin' jockstraps and bras all over the bathroom ceilings. Sort of a fashion tip."

The fun was not to last. After a Scotch for the road, it was on to the hour of reckoning, held in a large log cabin in the redwoods. Assigned to a building that had once been a speakeasy and a cathouse, Juanita stayed the allotted time, drinking copious amounts of milk and meeting lots of interesting people, including priests, policemen and a colleague of the judge who had sent her there. Dick came up for an hour on Sundays to visit, but the rest of the time she spent reading, a pastime her occupation had rarely allowed. "With all the hours I was spendin' sober," she said, "I got caught up with all the news."

Upon her release back into Sausalito society, Juanita decided she needed the sober support of Alcoholics Anonymous. She was lamenting the fact one day that her station wagon had broken down and so she couldn't make it all the way to Tiburon for the meetings. Her problem reached the ears of the highway patrol. "They had a cop drive me over every week and somebody else would give me a lift home. I was the only member who arrived in a patrol car, but I don't know if people thought that was because I was so stylish or because I was such a drunk," she explained, "Really, it just showed me how badly the highway patrol didn't want to keep takin' me to jail and breakin' up fights. Driving me around took a whole lot less of their time and wasn't near as dangerous."

For ten years Juanita was mostly on the wagon, "until," as she admitted, "I fell off with a thud." But that was later, when the world ran out of milk, but there was still plenty of Scotch left.

Sadly, the Musson menagerie was splitsville, although Toots was the only one sporting pom poms. Juanita arrived in court dressed in her customary white blouse and fightin' pants, and the judge thundered from the bench, "Go home and change! That's no way to appear in court!" Juanita told him she didn't own a dress and hadn't gone shopping in so long she didn't even know where a dress was to be had. "Go *buy* one!" he shouted, adamant.

The purchase of a dress was not to be taken lightly, especially since it was the first dress to be purchased in years and was to serve in a sort of symbolic capacity. Shunning the thrift shops that had enjoyed most of her patronage, Juanita went to an expensive women's clothing store where it took her an hour to find the dress that would be just the right fashion statement to make in courtroom number three. It was described, in a newspaper article of the time, as a "light green creation," and because the soon-to-be-ex-Mrs. Musson had overachieved the limitations of a size 18, the coat dress had to be resewn up the back in order to fit, and the belt left unfastened. Looking, as it has been said, every other inch a lady, Juanita went to a nearby bar to fortify herself with a virgin mary, which is where the bailiff found her. With his hearty encouragement, she returned to the courtroom where the case was resumed as if she had never left.

"On what grounds do you wish to divorce your husband, Mrs. Musson?" she was asked.

"Because one time I was drunk and when he tried to get the car keys from me, I stuffed them down my blouse," she replied.

The judge was plainly bewildered. "But what grounds are those?"

"Because when he couldn't get them away from me, he bit me on the arm. I had to call the doctor to see if I needed rabies shots."

"Divorce granted," said the judge, having heard quite enough by this time and probably asking himself why he did not retire while still in full possession of his wits.

Even though Dick and Juanita would always stay friends and sometimes "slept over" at each other's houses in the coming years, they never again lived together as man and wife. They were so content in their unwedded bliss that they neglected to file final dissolution papers, a fact Juanita did not discover until Dick's death, by which time he had remarried and, unwittingly, become a bigamist. Nonetheless, on that August day of 1957, ignorant of the joke Fate would later play on them, Dick and Juanita left the courtroom, arm in arm, ready to face the world of single blessedness with a cheery 'See ya later, honey!' and a great big kiss. The light green creation, having served its purpose, was ditched just in time for a seasonal change of fashion that would remain her style of dress in all the seasons to come, like the leaves of an evergreen tree.

That summer, the manager of the Kingston Trio sent Juanita a muumuu from Hawaii. It was an instant fit. She renounced her fightin' pants forever. Not only was this wonderful new garment endlessly expandable—as was, apparently, Juanita herself—it also had the remarkable capability of camouflaging the direction in which she was travelling. "People just couldn't tell anymore which was me and which was muumuu, and that suited me just fine," she stated, "Since I was always my own bouncer, I needed the right outfit for the job." The muumuu was soon Juanita's trademark and no one, including the feisty Hilo Hattie, ever wore it with more aplomb. Thanks to Caen, she became known far and wide as "that Mau Mau in a muumuu," correctly suggesting the martial nature of her new uniform. Except for the time a woman yanked the muumuu over Juanita's head, temporarily blinding her so that she could get her punches in without retaliation, the muumuu was most satisfactory.

Maybe it was to suit the exotic nature of this new wearing apparel that Juanita started wearing her long hair in a knot surmounted by a mantilla comb hung with an assortment of fetishes, including – but not limited to – fruit, flowers, feathers and small bright banners, achieving a sort of Hawaiian Gypsy effect that was rather odd but most becoming. With the high-heeled wedgies on her feet and a sparkle of mischief or malice in her limpid blue eyes, Juanita was dressed fit to kill.

This transformation from dockhand to social lioness changed nothing but Juanita's taste in dress. Underneath she was just the same as she'd always been, as many customers discovered for themselves. Once the muumuu was made her own, people delighted in giving her more of them, the more exotic the better, and Juanita adored modelling them for her customers in the dining room, slipping off the old one while pulling on the new. She was also to be seen—however indistinctly—wearing several muumuus at once. On busy days when there just wasn't time to remove a soiled muumuu, she would simply throw a clean one on over it, until six or eight muumuus hid her body as modestly as if she had been a devout Muslim.

While all this added more padding to the legend, it also exasperated another notorious woman who tried, in vain, over the years to reform Juanita. Out watering the dirt around the Galley one afternoon to lay the dust, Juanita decided on a whim to spray some teenagers basking in the sun nearby. With shrieks and screams of joy, they wrestled the hose from her and drenched her to the skin. With eyes still sparkling, Juanita went back into the restaurant, pulled her muumuu off over her head and, without taking the slightest notice of her fascinated audience, re-dressed. "I try and try to get Juanita to act like a lady," Sally Stanford said in a voice of weary resignation, "and now just *look* at her!"

It was inevitable that the two most famous women in Sausalito would become either great friends or great enemies. Juanita and Sally Stanford became both.

Sally had as colorful a career as Juanita, and had been the subject of liberal amounts of scandalmongering, much of it true. The consensus seems to be that while she did much shrewd horsetrading and could skewer the unlucky with one flinty glance and one well-chosen insult, she was also memorable for salvaging the unfortunate and being, for some, a dear and devoted friend. If attendance at her funeral is any indication, she was both loved and respected by the community in which she had, for years, been Madam Mayor.

"Madam" was a title Sally enjoyed. For years she had run a brothel in San Francisco where "the girls" would linger in enticing poses next to a fountain and fish pond in the old-fashioned parlor. Her next establishment had later become a watering hole called The Fallen Angel, where Juanita distinguished herself by getting uproariously drunk on frequent occasions with a paraplegic friend, both of them becoming so loud and obnoxious that other customers would pay waitresses to move them to a more distant table. It was at the Valhalla, where Sally went to pasture, that Juanita made the ex-madam's acquaintance and where she was usually welcomed with open arms for her gargantuan liquid appetite. When Juanita opened the Galley, Sally was an infrequent guest, although both women had a fondness for the kind of midwestern cooking that included plenty of mashed potatoes and hot fat.

"I used to say that Sally's was the first place when somebody hit town and mine was the last, and since I wore a ponytail, everybody could tell what side of the horse Sally was on," Juanita explained. "My customers used to tell me, 'Now, that depends on what side of town you come in on. You're the horse's *head* the other way!'"

Though people have confused the two women over the years, accusing Juanita of having been a madam and Sally of having been loud (both accusations vehemently denied) the only areas of comparison were that both were formidable in personality, tireless in industry, and completely lacking in self-consciousness. Both enjoyed good food and good liquor, although Sally's appetite for both was nowhere near that of her fellow entrepreneur. As an example, Juanita recounted the following story:

"Once Sally and I were havin' a fried chicken dinner at her place on Pacific in San Francisco. Before the chicken was done, all the electricity went out so we got out a kerosene lantern I'd given her and finished fryin' the chicken on that. Suddenly we realized the kitchen was on fire, so we called the Fire Department. By the time they arrived, we were sitting at a table, eatin'. The firemen told us we had to get out, but we told them no way were we gonna move after spendin' all that time fryin' that damned chicken and we didn't want it to get cold.

"'Go on and put the fire out, honey,' I told 'em, 'Don't pay any attention to *us*.' So they dragged their hoses in around us while Sally was snappin' at 'em, 'Now don't you get my rugs all wet!' They put out the fire and didn't get the rugs too wet, and we had a very nice dinner. I always did like firemen."

In 1958, just after her divorce, Juanita went to visit Sally in the hospital where her friend was recovering from a heart attack. Madam Sally was standing at the sink, washing her nightgowns. "You shouldn't be doin' that, let me do it!" Juanita commanded, elbowing frail Sally back to bed. All of her maternal instincts roused by Sally's plight, Juanita would go over to her house in the afternoons to "keep an eye on things and fatten her up." She did Sally's laundry as well as a little freelance home decorating since she had so much time to spare now that she was steering clear of saloons. Decorating was always one of Juanita's primary passions. A desk without a lamp, or an armchair without a doily, or a windowsill minus a potted plant and glassware she always considered uncivilized, a breach of decency she tried to correct as speedily as possible in the "more is better" school of home furnishing.

This domestic tranquility was, sadly, not to last. A flood in Sally's house, due to a severe winter storm, turned carpets into swamps. Sally wanted all the walls repainted and put Juanita in charge. When the painters finished and handed Sally the bill she announced, according to Juanita, "This is all very well and good, but this isn't the color I wanted." Then she turned to Juanita with eyes like icepicks and said, "You *knew* I didn't want this dreadful color!" With that, Juanita turned on her heel and left, shouting over her shoulder, "Don't ever involve me in your damned business deals ever again!" Though she left behind an antique bisque doll and a few dishes, she considered this price for freedom a bargain indeed. Not that their relationship was over; this was merely the first of many skirmishes through the years. Like the Red Queen and the White Queen, they enjoyed alternately subduing and stirring each other up in the Wonderland of Sausalito.

Whether they were in the midst of a quarrel or not, Sally and Juanita kept an eye on each other. Juanita still dropped in at the

Valhalla to check out the action and Sally occasionally crossed the tracks to white-glove the Galley. Sally was a perfectionist, according to Juanita, and just because the Galley wasn't hers didn't mean she couldn't offer helpful criticism, delivered without a trace of either hesitancy or tact. "She was such a clean person," Juanita said, "I've even seen her climb all the way inside her dishwasher because she hadn't scrubbed it right. That's the way she was—course, she was pretty small, too."

As well as having an interest in feeding people, both women shared a love for birds and animals—in Sally's case, the more exotic the better. The Valhalla's mascot was a parrot named Loretta, whose tricks were simple but effective. (When one considers the past profession of the owner, this was but to be expected.) Perched near the bar, Loretta kept the same sort of beady eye on things as her mistress did, helping out the family finances when called upon to do so. Sally would pick her up and coo in her harsh and undovelike voice, "Now flutter those wings, Loretta! I want all the dollars on the bar for myself. I want them to fly!" and Loretta would cause such a draft on cue that the money on the bar would be wafted over to the bartender's feet. When the evening wasn't lively enough, Sally would put Loretta on the bar and say, "Now show me how girls like to lay, darling," and the bird would roll over on its back.

Juanita and Loretta had developed a close friendship by the time Juanita left Sally to wash her own nightgowns. The next time Juanita returned to the Valhalla after that first spat, Loretta flew immediately from Sally's shoulder onto Juanita's. That did it. After a two-minute detente, the battle began again in earnest, with Sausalito's mayor-to-be shouting about unnatural attractions and Juanita, smug as a canary, shouting right back. In Herb Caen's column several days later, he wrote that Sally was so incensed, she was going to sue Juanita for "alienation of affection." As it turned out, the parrot would probably have preferred living at the Galley, however much a come-down that would have been politically, for her life at the Valhalla was anything but heavenly. When Sally was safely off the premises, Juanita found out years later, the waiters and busboys would chase poor Loretta all around the dining room, flicking their teatowels at her. Eventually some well-meaning but witless soul put her out on her perch in the sun and forgot all about her. Since it was 100-degree weather and he had neglected to furnish her with a water dish, she soon plummeted to the end of her chain, a victim of sunstroke. Though Sally eventually forgave the culprit, Juanita—in a rare show of unforgiveness—to this day has not.

In the words of Bill Hensley, a man who was devoted for years to both Sally and Juanita:

"They were both independent, domineering women with good hearts and successful businesses. They were friends, although probably only because they lived for so long in the same town. They were both notorious and loved animals and collecting lots of "stuff" – junk and antiques both – but that's where comparisons between them end. Sally was always trying to tell Juanita how to make more money and make better use of what she had. Unfortunately, Sally just wasted her breath because Juanita had no business sense whatsoever. She would've been a millionaire, otherwise, because her places were always such gold mines. But I don't think Juanita has ever really cared about money the way Sally did, and didn't particularly care if she didn't have any.

"Of course, if living to the fullest is a kind of wealth, then Juanita has always been a very rich woman."

John Despot, Insurance Auditor

My wife and I met the Mussons in the early Fifties. Dick was working for Travelers Insurance as an auditor and I went to work as an auditor-trainee. Dick was one of my trainers. He had graduated from Brown University as an engineer and had been a Captain in the artillery in World War II. He could do anything with his hands. When we also bought a house in Sausalito, he rebuilt a hot water heater for us and rewired the house and did the plumbing. My wife always said that when Dick walked in the room, you knew a *man* was there. Six feet tall, crewcut hair, always fit and trim and never with a pound of flab on him. He never had a qualm about who he was, where he wanted to go or how he was going to get there. He had more self confidence than anyone I've ever met in my life.

At that time Juanita had the most beautiful body you ever saw. She probably weighed 118 pounds and was built like a brick outhouse. She was just a sweet housewife sort of person. Then she met Sally Stanford and, very honestly, I think she decided then and there to emulate her. Right away she went from being a real good-lookin' little gal to being a real tough, hard talkin' kind of gal. She also started to drink and became sort of like a madam. Following in Sally's footsteps, she opened a restaurant on the waterfront. Dick was really in love with her and so anything she wanted to do was okay with him. If she wanted to be like Sally Stanford, then so be it. He helped her all he could and didn't fight her on a thing. Uncomplaining, he did everything she wanted. He never said a word about her drinking or brawling and never acted embarrassed or avoided the subject. I don't think he ever raised his voice to her in all the years they were married.

What happened next made her famous. A young attorney came in one day and after waiting for 25 minutes to be served, he got up and left. Juanita saw him get into his open convertible and ran out with a plate of food and yelled, "You son-of-a-bitch, if you don't wanna eat it, you can *wear* it!" and dumped it all over him. That was when she first hit the papers, the day she was hauled into court for that. The judge didn't approve of her wearing dungarees and told her that she couldn't appear in court dressed that way. Juanita said okay and walked out. Now, the Kingston Trio had brought her back a muumuu from Hawaii, and so she put that on and returned to the courtroom with "This okay, honey?" It was all over the papers. She kept doin' that kind of stuff and it kept makin' the papers and so the word got out that this Juanita was someone you had to see to believe! That was exactly what she had been looking for.

The problem was that the Travelers Insurance Company, which was a good old conservative firm out of Connecticut, wasn't going to put up with this since the newspapers also mentioned Dick's name and the fact that he worked for Travelers. So Dick was given a choice by the company that he could leave San Francisco for Oregon – presumably splitsville – or quit the company. Juanita wanted to stay in Sausalito because of her restaurant, so Dick accepted the transfer to Oregon.

Dick's mother was living at that time and she and Juanita had always gotten along like a cat and dog. Toots was very cold, real thin and real cold. Uninviting. I don't think she ever gave anybody a hug, for instance. But Dick was stuck with the situation because he had given a deathbed promise to his father that he would take care of her, and he was the kind of guy who honored that kind of promise. So he was always stuck in the middle, trying to satisfy both of the women he loved.

But I tell you, Juanita would do anything in the world she could to rub Dick's mother wrong. When Toots arrived, there was always hell to pay! Right after Juanita and Dick had broken up, but before he moved to Oregon, he rented an apartment in San Francisco. Toots came out from the East for her annual visit and when Juanita heard about it, she jumped in her car, drove over to the apartment, grabbed Dick and took him upstairs to the bedroom. About twenty minutes later she came downstairs, looked at Toots and said, "Man, he's just as great as ever!" There wasn't much Toots could say.

Really the best thing for both of them was when Dick left Juanita and went north, although they never did go sign the final divorce papers. I think they always loved each other, right up until the minute Dick died.

Bill Soule, Beauty Shop Owner

I owned a large beauty shop, the Golden Arch, in San Francisco for many years. Sally Stanford and Juanita were good friends – although sometimes they were speaking and sometimes they weren't. Neither usually got her hair done; all Sally would do with her hair was twist it around and stick a pin in it, and Juanita would just wind hers up and stick in a mantilla comb. However, every year like clockwork they would come every week into the city for six weeks, Juanita being the chauffeur. They caused an absolute uproar. My clients would come in and see Sally or Juanita sitting at the front desk making endless phone calls, and this would create considerable conversation. Gossip would flow up and down the street of the neighborhood. They were noisy and grand and fun – and tricky. After the six weeks were up, Sally, who was always running for office in Sausalito, would call up my friend, Joe Kane, and say, "My annual campaign is coming due, can I use one of your buildings downtown at the usual rent?" The usual rent was zero, of course. He'd say yes and they'd both sweep out and we wouldn't see them again for another year.

Juanita was a good friend to Sally, who, incidentally, didn't have as many friends as she deserved to have since she was a lot better person than her reputation made her out to be. Her funeral was so big that it had to be moved to a large church in another town. The priest stood up there and looked everybody straight in the eye and said, "I've had several complaints about why we should not have this type of woman eulogized in a church like this, and I just want you to know that Sally Stanford did far more for mankind than most of you people here." At this, the last to arrive, Juanita came walking up the aisle in her muumuu and with a big shawl wrapped around her, looking as regal as can be, and sat down right in the front row. The priest waited until she'd made her grand entrance and was seated before he continued on with the service. It was a wonderful moment. Sally would've loved it.

7

"Juanita Runs Beanery You Gotta See"

– *Fort Worth Press*

Juanita, wrapped around and around with yards of orange terrycloth and with plastic pumpkins dangling from her upswept hairdo, faced the new decade of the Sixties as a large and spirited squash. But it wasn't only Halloween on the horizon near the end of 1959, it was a double-wheeled ferryboat wallowing a few hundred yards out in the bay. For as long as she had been in the business of feeding people, she had longed to feed them on board the half-sunk Charles Van Damme.

With a history as colorful as Juanita's own, the Charles Van Damme had plied for many years the waters of the bay between the little towns of Benicia and Martinez. Bridges put the old paddle-wheeler out of business, but after a few years it came out of retirement as the Canton Ferry restaurant and was moored, full of chop suey, outside the city of Oakland, near where other derelicts in retirement pulled against their tethers like tired old horses. The restaurant went bust, as they so often do, leaving the Canton Ferry adrift in a financial doldrums the owners did not find agreeable. Due to a tug-of-war Juanita could not explain, the ferry's Sausalito owners were unable to simply drag it across the bay and so were forced to take creative measures to gain the boat's release. At midnight, then, two tugboats set forth loaded with boatnappers. According to Juanita, they released the old ferryboat from bondage and towed it, slowly and majestically, from Oakland to Sausalito, where they scuttled it by opening the petcocks. It sank, that grand old man, up to its gunwales in muddy water. When Juanita's lease was almost up, and the rent raised to an unacceptable $550 a month, she decided it was time to fish or cut bait. Without preliminaries, she went to speak to one of the ferryboat's owners. She wanted it for a restaurant, she told him, and how much would he want for it if she towed it to land? "If you can get a permit to put a restaurant in it," he told Juanita, "you can have the boat rent free for one year." He also told her that, contrary to local gossip, the ferryboat did not have a hole in it but would be perfectly seaworthy once its petcocks were closed.

Accordingly, and full of cheerful anticipation, Juanita presented herself at a meeting of the Board of Supervisors who saw her coming with, perhaps, a less-rosy outlook on what was to come. After all, this was the woman who, at a meeting of Sausalito's City Council, got so steamed up about drains and the lethargic temperament of the council in general that she couldn't be hushed up. Finally, the mayor's patience frayed under Juanita's tart and unsolicited remarks and ordered the policeman on duty to escort her from the room. At that point Dick had leaped up, muttering "shut up, Juanita," and hustled her out into the evening air. Thus, when the Board of Supervisors saw her sweep into the room, they must have glanced at each other with the slightly hysterical dread that she so often inspired in the breasts of those authorized by society to keep individual mischief to a sane, if dreary, minimum. Not because civil servants disliked having to tell her no, but because they often found it easier to give in before the shouting started. In the world where Juanita reigned, rules were meant to be broken, laws to be ignored and permits forgotten. Not that people in positions of authority always threw in the towel. They just did so often enough for her to generally get her own way. This was as it should have been, Juanita knew, since such dull and unimaginative bureaucrats couldn't be expected to share her glorious vision of the future.

After the Board of Supervisors listened to her they agreed, according to Juanita that if she absolutely positively would *not* discharge any raw sewage in the bay, the deed was as good as done. Juanita swept from the room triumphant. A new Galley was born.

Overseeing all operations herself, Juanita had the Charles Van Damme dragged into port during the course of three high tides. It was beached, like a strange and ungainly whale, at the shoreline. After years underwater, much of the lower section of the ferryboat was badly in need of scraping and scrubbing and hosing down. For this work Juanita enlisted the Sea Scouts who charged an hourly rate of three enchiladas and numberless Cokes. While pumps flushed out gallons of fragrant bay water, the Scouts hosed down the boat's muddy innards, becoming as happily filthy as a bunch of little pigs in a mudhole. There were lively games of tic-tac-toe played on each other's backs. There was much boyish roughhousing requiring many boys to fall shrieking into the bay. At the end of each afternoon's work, they all would march uphill to Juanita's house for a shower and a good-natured game of "Tease the Turkey" before marching back downhill to consume heroic quantities of food and drink. Too late, Juanita discovered her error in not removing the wall-to-wall pink carpet in her bathroom.

When a nearby restaurant went out of business, Juanita bought all its antiquated equipment and stuck it in various places out on deck. The old refrigerators and stoves were her idea of perfect ballast. Every day after school, children would help her shove this stuff around on deck as a step toward eliminating the ferryboat's natural inclination to list alarmingly in one direction or another. From the time she began until the ferryboat opened for business, Juanita spent every nickel she could lay her hands on in sprucing Charles up and putting him back to work. "Worth every cent!" she insisted, and who would dare to disagree?

Somehow Juanita managed to locate the elderly craftsman who had put the canvas on the Van Damme decks in 1913, and he agreed to help in the 1960 facelift.

"I will never forget that old man sittin' there with his wooden leg stickin' straight out ahead of him," she recalled, "and with the other curled up under him, sewin' the canvas together and varnishing it, just like in the good old days."

The Health Department—always a thorn in Juanita's side, although the discomfort was mutual—demanded that she have the ceiling lowered in the ferryboat's galley so that fumes would be the more easily sucked out by an exhaust fan she installed. Unbeknownst to future employees, she also installed a periscope to keep an eye on things from her bedroom directly above the kitchen. She included in her surveillance equipment a walkie-talkie, although, as she explained, "It didn't have no 'walkie' to it." Thus she could, while pretending to be napping, overhear and oversee any mutinous behavior.

One day Juanita returned from a wrestling match with the IRS – another thorn – to find trucks full of dirt idling nearby. She asked what was up and they told her they'd brought a lot of clean fill for a man who had neglected to obtain a permit for it to be dumped. "Well, I have a permit!" Juanita shouted, and though the sheriff came to make sure she did—and could be forgiven for thinking that perhaps she did not—he found everything in order. Thrilled with her unexpected good fortune, she shouted for all the truckdrivers to dump their dirt immediately, which they did, relieved not to have to return it, Sisyphus-wise, from whence it had come. The next few days found Juanita driving a tractor with a sheepsfoot over and over the dirt, back and forth, until it was flat enough to become a parking lot.

"That was one of happiest times of my life," she later confessed, "just draggin' that old sheepsfoot round and round in the dirt. I could have just kept on doin' that for *days*, it was so much fun. But I always had to stop so that I could go up to the kitchen to supervise this one cook we had there at the beginning. He'd let all his orders pile up until he had ten of them before he'd get off his ass to cook anything at all. He seemed pretty shiftless to me at the time, but he's an attorney now, so that just goes to show you."

She advertised for more fill and, for a few weeks, had a dump of her very own. Before she would run the sheepsfoot over the past day's offerings, she would sift happily through the debris, looking for treasures. "You know what people throw away?" she said with a shake of her head, "a $1200 Oriental carpet, honey, and a whole box of little glass baskets! Just think of anybody throwing away things like *that*!" Scavenging was almost more fun than running a restaurant.

Girls from an exclusive Marin County private school showed up one afternoon to see the ferryboat and got caught up in restoration fever. They asked Juanita what they could do to help. Since kids were crawling all over the place, washing windows, dusting pipes, scrubbing decks, she told them they could take the chewing gum off the bottom of the tables. Cheerfully these cherished daughters of prominent families set to work with a will. To encourage them in their efforts, Juanita went out and purchased several antique apothecary jars into which the girls put their afternoon's harvest. Parents were curious, most of them, to know how Juanita had managed to get their fastidious offspring to do such menial work and were a little nonplussed the first time they came as customers to have their daughters point proudly to the contents of the apothecary jars. Not all parents were pleased, however. "One father told me years later that he really hated me for having his daughter do such a low-down thing as take gum off tables," Juanita explained. "But after awhile he realized how wonderful it was to have a place for his daughter to go and be of help. He said his daughter told him that if she lived to be a hundred, she'd never put gum under a table again or allow a child of her own to ever do it."

These children of privilege would go skiing and if they broke a leg, they'd always give the autographed cast to Juanita afterwards. She hung them on the pipes in the dining room, to the children's glory. Lots of other personal memorabilia was added over time, like coral to a reef, until the Charles Van Damme was considerably more colorful than it had been in the years when it ferried goats and chickens across the bay or was hung with paper lanterns and dispensed dim sum.

Business continued on a 24 hour basis. Juanita got along by sleeping for fifteen minutes every three or four hours before returning to her chosen mission of serving more people more food than they could ever possibly eat. It took huge, industrial-size rolls of aluminum foil to wrap up the prime rib and steaks people could not bear to leave behind. Taking time off from everything else, Juanita would make these customized doggie bags into works of art, fashioning them into swans or roosters and using far too much foil in the process.

A loudspeaker was installed in the ferryboat so that the highway patrol could come in and miss nothing from their radios. While this added to the cacophony, it also produced a sort of "You Are There" feeling for the other customers who sat assembled in chairs of which no two were alike. The variety in furnishing matched the diversity of the clientele. While patrolmen sat comfortably ensconced over plat-ters of ham and eggs, bikers in black leather converged for secret meetings and people like Phyllis Diller and Erma Bombeck and Glenn Ford felt right at home. When Jonathan Winters was in town he enlivened the atmosphere considerably with his spontaneous, nutsy brilliance, and when Juanita asked him if he wouldn't really be happier left in peace, he admonished her with "But these are my people, Juanita!" There was an upstairs room empty of all but wall-to-wall carpeting, a few benches and a television set. Celebrities tired after a show, kids bored with parental conversation, bikers plotting strategy could go upstairs and lie around all night if they felt like it. The

Kingston Trio was hitting its stride and, after several years of discount dining, they returned to the ferryboat famous and gave Juanita a check for over a thousand dollars in trade for the IOU she had never requested. They also brought her a black muumuu with gold roses down the front which she wore with a strand of pearls on a date with the *San Francisco Chronicle* columnist, Count Marco. "I knew he was famous for hating women to wear black and pearls together, he thought it looked tacky. I just decided to give him a little run for his money—and, besides, I thought I looked real nice."

Count Marco was no less flamboyant in his day than was Juanita, the occasional pebble in his shoe. Feelings ran high when the Count was the object of discussion; outrage and amusement being uppermost. "Beauty and the Beast" was what he had named his column, the headline given international cachet by the addition of a (possibly spurious) coat of arms. Below it, full of wit, spite and proclamation, he would give fashion and beauty tips, chastise childless couples and conduct odd contests, such as the "Fat Venus" weight-loss competition in the early Sixties. To say he was opinionated is to declare the sky blue. Mark Spinelli – his name in the buff – was outspoken, outrageous and, according to Juanita, loads of fun. He took to the vaudeville atmosphere surrounding Juanita like an actor to the footlights.

There were many who did.

When Sausalito or its environs were being used as a movie set, actors and actresses headed on over to Juanita's where, in the bright lights and noisy disorder of the place, they must have felt no theatrical anticlimax. While "Blood Alley" was being filmed, Glenn Ford and Robert Mitchum came in for coffee and wisecracks as did Anthony Quinn during lulls in the shooting of "Portrait in Black". It was on Glenn Ford's earnest recommendation that Erskine Johnson, the Hollywood columnist, accompanied him to the ferryboat for lunch. (Johnson was, himself, something of a card. To protest the eating of popcorn in movie theatres, he once had a four course meal served to him by tuxedoed waiters during a screening of "South Sea Sinner". Neighboring patrons must have been torn between the Grade C action on the screen and the famous Hollywood personality smacking his way through Squab under Glass to Cherries Jubilee flambée.)

"Don't complain about anything or Juanita will throw you

out," Ford warned Johnson at the door. Johnson included in his column about the experience the information that his companion was just winding up twenty-two years with Columbia Pictures with the movie, "Experiment in Terror", but whether he was implying anything is open to conjecture. Johnson appears to have been more impressed by the Galley's owner and decor than by the bill of fare that day, which was corned beef and cabbage. Perhaps Juanita kept the menu simple because in those days she relied strictly on word-of-mouth. "I don't need any menus," she used to say, "because I do all the talking."

Johnson was captivated by the large, loud woman in the blue-flowered muumuu and compared her to Mae West and Texas Guinan. He wrote, "She walked unsteadily, listing to port, on three-inch spiked heels. She was followed by a four-month-old fawn she called 'Sissy.' Sissy later lapped up a soft drink out of a saucer, then chewed on a telephone cord." The two men were told to write out their orders, punch them in the time clock and pour their own coffee. Though he did not describe either the service or the food, he did finish his column with, "A juke box blared out 'Never on Sunday.' A grass hula skirt, a blue hairnet and a pair of boxing gloves, hanging on pegs, gave the room what Juanita called 'flair.' As Sissy went on chewing the phone cord, Glenn Ford repeated: "'This joint you should see at 3 a.m.' At midday it was unbelievable enough."

Noel Coward included in his novel, *Pomp and Circumstance*, a literary bow to the "Mau Mau in a muumuu." Though "Juanita" is in the wings throughout the book, she is referred to several times for her excellent cuisine, shrewd business sense and short fuse. "I know you and I don't see eye to eye about Juanita," one of Coward's characters says with a supercilious sniff. "I'm sure she runs the hotel very efficiently and is supposed to be terribly amusing, but personally I find her appallingly vulgar. I mean, one never knows what she's going to say next. You must admit that she has the most uncontrollable temper and is always flying at people.'" Coward, no stranger to eccentricity and author of such paeans to the singular individual as "Blithe Spirit" and "Private Lives", was so fond of Juanita that he reportedly kept an autographed photo of her beside his bed along with that of his friend, Joan Sutherland.

Joan Sutherland, for her part, became a devotee of Juanita's on her first visit. According to Juanita, she arrived just as Juanita was screaming at her one-legged cook about the way he should prepare eggs. "I'm gonna rip off that fuckin' peg leg of yours and beat you to death with it!" the diva overheard as she stepped aboard. After breakfast she presented her hostess with an autographed photo. "She told me it was the best breakfast she ever ate and she musta liked it because she came back a lot of times," Juanita explained. "See, sometimes a little argument helps pep up people's appetites, makes 'em feel at home."

Tommy and Dick Smothers, and Erskine Caldwell and his wife, were often to be seen with their feet under one of Juanita's oak tables. Charlie Finlay, owner of the Oakland A's, used to come in and, according to Juanita, spar a little with her. "Oh, we used to fight a lot," she said, "especially if he'd been drinkin' and was a little bit on the feisty side. But he was a great guy. The ferryboat was kinda like a playhouse for him and he'd set up parties all the time."

Britt Ekland came in with a very handsome Swedish actor who suddenly threw Juanita's hormones out of whack. "I got all fluster-ated," she explained, "so I dropped a big bottle of mustard. His studio had told him that the Galley would be a good place for him to be seen – and, boy, he was good to see, all righty!" As Ekland looked on with cool disdain, Juanita first mopped the mustard off the floor and then sat in a chair next to their table and cleaned the mustard from between her toes, all the while carrying on a most admiring conversation with Ekland's toothsome consort.

Given her tempestuous nature, not all the big names – or the small ones, either – thought her the cat's meow. Many just thought her a cat. And those who liked her most of the time also had moments in which they gladly would have had her walk the plank. Herb Caen wrote in a column that Jonathan Winters had climbed, in a tiddly state, up the mast of the Balclutha sailing ship moored at San Francisco's Fishermen's Wharf. Juanita, who had once received a letter from Winters explaining that he was also a member of the "soda set," was afraid Caen's public mention of Winter's spirited escapade might bump him off the wagon and was furious. "Don't shoot a guy when he's down!" she shouted at him, being more the "Mau Mau" and less the "lovable tomato" of memory. She could definitely be difficult.

"One time these young men came in, " Juanita recalled, "and while one went to the bathroom, the other started pourin' the Tabasco and pepper and everything else he could lay his hands on into his friend's coffee cup. When his friend came back to the table and started to drink the coffee, I went over and said, 'I wouldn't drink that if I were you. I'd let your good friend here drink it.'" She put her right arm around his shoulders, pinched his nostrils with the fingers of her left hand, held the cup to his mouth and told him to drink. He did. In the normal course of human events, neither would have ever darkened the Galley door again. But, she went on, "Two days later the guy's friend came back in and told me they'd run in the Bay to Breakers Race the next day and the guy I made drink the coffee had won. His friend wanted to know what the concoction was so he could drink it before the next race and I said, 'Just ask your friend, he's the cook,' but he told me that he'd already asked him but he wouldn't tell."

Once Juanita noticed a cockroach in a corner of the restaurant and, to the amusement of some of her guests and the discomfort of others, she yelled, "Let's go catch that sucker and *roast* 'im!" There were probably those who breathed a little easier when the prey eluded her.

Christmas came and went, but a decorated tree stayed bravely on through season after season. Valentine's Day was celebrated with paper hearts and flowers, and then St. Patrick's Day brought its four-leaf clovers and leprechauns, all keeping the atmosphere festive until Easter. By this time the Christmas tree would be showing signs of age, but Juanita would cleverly disguise the needleless condition of the branches with Easter decorations. Then Halloween arrived, followed by Thanksgiving, and finally another Christmas, when the old tree would finally be laid to rest and a new tree put up in its place. Though it was probably not what Juanita had in mind, the casual accumulation of holiday memorabilia from holidays past gave the Galley a timeless air; if you weren't keen on Christmas, you could feel as if you were celebrating Halloween. Or all the holidays at once, if you wanted.

Of all the holidays, Easter was the day Juanita loved best. Hundreds of hardboiled and dyed eggs would be hidden all over the Galley under chairs, beneath the pedestals of the oak tables, in the crotches of pipes and in all corners. Children, themselves dressed like Easter eggs in pastels and spotless white, would scramble joyously under customers' legs, pulling eggs from between their feet like short and disorderly magicians, while Juanita watched with an indulgent smile. No child ever left without at least one Easter egg, even if Juanita had to take it from someone luckier in the hunt. Every year she would see to it that the children not only received eggs, but also got to play with some newly-hatched chicks. "You'd have to keep an eye on the kids, though," she said, "or they'd just squeeze those little chicks flat!"

One year, the day before Easter, Juanita drove to an egg farm and bought several eggs guaranteed to hatch by the next day. She tucked them warmly into her bosom and drove off. As this was during one of her drinking periods, she stopped into a bar on the way home and, while hoisting a couple, felt the unmistakable peck of a tiny beak. Pulling the egg from between her breasts, she peered closely at it for a moment, then popped it back into its nest and announced, "Well, my eggs are hatching, better be gettin' on home." And without further explanation, she left.

The most memorable Easter of all was on the Charles Van Damme when the Vienna Boy's Choir came marching up the gangway. After playing with the baby chicks corralled on a converted ping pong table on the top deck, they assembled to cut a record, their angelic voices for once silencing the racket below decks. A few months after the boys had returned home, Juanita received a copy of the record as a gift. She played it proudly over and over again for anyone who would, or would not, listen. She loaned it to a girl whose father, a minister, had steadfastly disapproved of Juanita and her doings, and the next day he showed up to apologize for ever thinking that Juanita was some kind of sinister Pied Piper, leading the local children astray. (His tune might have changed had he gone to brunch at the Galley on Mother's Day. Juanita always presented flowers to all the women customers and addressed all the fathers, happily and loudly, "And Happy Mother's Day to you, too, motherfuckers!")

Although Juanita was always more comfortable in the rôle of giver, she received interesting gifts, as well. One Valentine's Day she found in her refrigerated dessert case a large beef heart tied with a ribbon. A card attached read, "Happy Valentine's Day to Juanita, whose heart is bigger than this one!"

Animals have most often been the gift of choice among Juanita's admirers. They have been exotic, occasionally attractive and usually, if not literally, pigheaded. Dogs, foxes, feral cats, owls, roosters, monkeys, peacocks, jackasses and rats have, over the years, appeared on Juanita's doorstep with – often without – the giver. If the cat was pregnant, the dog blind, the fox surly or the peacock stupid, it didn't matter to Juanita, to whom all animals are lovable, beautiful and well-mannered. Customers and employees have often disagreed, having been bitten, scratched or peed-upon. To Juanita's astonishment, there are people in this world who do not find a hairless, toothless dog or a snarling cat adorable, nor do they instantly forgive an unprovoked attack by an enraged raccoon. She, herself, experienced few problems of that kind. Once when a rooster pecked her, she took it into her kitchen and showed it a pot of chicken soup. "If you peck me again," she warned him, "this'll be *you*."

One of her pets arrived while Juanita was off on a short trip with a moneyed gentleman who had been pleading with her to accompany him on a cruise to the Orient. Back at the ferryboat, they went upstairs to her bedroom and, anticipating nothing but the usual hodgepodge of knickknacks, were surprised to find a turkey roosting on the headboard of the bed. Obviously it had spent the entire weekend amusing itself with a species of interior decoration and now seemed to be surveying its contribution to the atmosphere with a kind of weary content.

Whether it was the smell, or the notion that Juanita was in the habit of sharing her quarters with turkeys, something sent her lover reeling backward, too overcome to repeat his pleas that she accompany him to Bangkok. Perhaps he feared that Juanita would insist upon bringing the turkey with her. Whatever it was, he never called again. Juanita was sorry because she had been about to give in and go, but not sorry enough to regret having the turkey. It was a beautiful white turkey, after all, and had showed remarkable pluck by not dropping dead of thirst. As soon as Juanita had fed and watered the bird and, crooning, carried it up and down the decks, the turkey felt comfortable enough to lay a few eggs in a phone booth on deck.

"I didn't want any frustrated females on board," Juanita explained, "so I went out and bought two fertile eggs and switched 'em on her."

Two male chicks soon made their appearance: One was, sadly enough, destined to play but a cameo rôle, exiting in a spectacular fashion by falling down the stairs. The other, defying the laws of gravity, hypothermia and the gloomy predictions of turkey experts, lived to the ripe old age of five. "Wattles," so named because where wattles were concerned he was very well endowed, had a terrible fascination with the sea. Coupled with a case of severe vertigo, this might easily have led to an early and watery grave, but thanks to the sharp eyes of those on deck, every time the turkey took a tumble someone would cry out, "Turkey overboard!" While Juanita and her customers kept anxious vigil, someone would be drafted to row out in a skiff to rescue the bird. Wattles would have managed to scramble onto a stick or some other floating object, and by the time the rescuer arrived, he would be surveying the bay with the calm demeanor of a seasoned, shipwrecked captain aboard a sturdy, if diminutive, dinghy.

Juanita would put the turkey on a chair in front of a heater, where he would stand in patient good humor until he was nice and dry. Sometimes he took a header more than once a day. Whether this was by accident or because he enjoyed the process of being rescued, no one knew. "He was almost like a seagull," Juanita explained, "only a lot bigger. And of course he couldn't fly."

Going overboard was not an amusement limited to turkeys. Animals, human and otherwise, ended up in the soup—or the mud if the tide was out—on a fairly regular basis. This livened things up considerably. One day someone came running into the kitchen to tell Juanita that a man had thrown one of her cats overboard. Charging out on deck, she yelled, "What asshole threw my cat in the mud?" A helpful soul pointed out the guilty party and Juanita grabbed the man by the seat of his pants and hurled him off the deck. At that point she was informed that the man who was now up to his eyebrows in slime was an off-duty cop. Not only that, but he wasn't the culprit, after all. "We had a big laugh over that, I can tell you!" she cheerfully reminisced. "Whoooeee!"

Even though the Charles Van Damme was a gold mine, the IRS didn't always end up with its share of the gold. Withholding taxes might have been some quaint Romanian ritual as far as Juanita was concerned, her attitude being that "If they want the money so bad they can just come and get it." They often did. One day a sheriff was given the thankless task of collecting the contents of the till, but by closing time there was only $42. Since business had been brisk, he suspected a siphon somewhere between customers' wallets and the long arm of the law. Next day he came back with numbered order books that he sternly handed out to all of the waiters and waitresses. By midnight his take was much *much* larger. No one, least of all Juanita, could figure out how she made so much money but seemed always to be in debt. Money just disappeared. Sometimes employees would, through a miracle of thrift, save enough tip money to start their own businesses, and some of them would take extended vacations in expensive locales. Sometimes Juanita would spend the day's receipts bailing someone out of jail or buying herself or someone else a trunkful of trinkets. There just never seemed to be enough left over to pay taxes or, on occasion, her enormous meat bills. She would, of course, pay her bills *sometime*, when the spirit *moved* her, but otherwise, like Scarlett, she left the settling for another day. She simply would not fret over details until she was forced to do so. The trouble with this method of doing business is clear: Although it certainly cuts costs in the short run, sooner or later a very large bill, with interest and penalties, will be presented with "Past Due" stamped on it in red. Still, Juanita was an optimist. Bills could get lost. Creditors might develop faulty memories or previously unsuspected reservoirs of generosity. IRS agents might take the wrong offramp and wander, lost, in the wilderness of the Sausalito hills long enough for her to save some money. When they showed up with their unreasonable demands for payment, Juanita would sometimes pull a roll of bills from between her breasts ("the only suckers I trust") and hand it over. "There," she'd say, exasperated. "Now take this and leave me alone."

Money wasn't the only commodity with a tendency to disappear. Since Juanita gave customers free range of her restaurants, even letting them sleep in her bedroom if they seemed especially pooped, knickknacks and jewelry evaporated as well. Once she let two girls sleep in her room and next day, after they'd taken a powder, Juanita discovered they'd also taken all of her antique jewelry. "Boy, was I mad!" she said of the incident, adding wistfully, "I hope they at least enjoyed wearin' it."

119

The theft of Wattles was a worse affliction for Juanita, especially as it occurred on Christmas Day. At first, nobody had noticed the turkey was gone. Then Juanita, in growing distress, ordered all customers and employees to join in a search and rescue operation. They found no turkey in the phone booth, no turkey in the bedroom, no turkey overboard. Somebody said, "Gee, I saw a woman in a fur coat leaving this morning and it looked like she had a white muff under her coat. Maybe it was Wattles." This was a dreadful idea. Through tears, and itching to smack the next fur-coated woman she saw, Juanita said, "Well, at least he was warm."

The year 1963 brought her financial troubles to a head. Even Juanita acknowledged that she owed the IRS many thousands more than could fit in her brassiere. A series of fundraisers began, largely supported by customers and local teens, and a huge sign, "Save the Galley," was tacked to the side of the old ferryboat. The faithful Kingston Trio, Tommy Smothers, Glenn Yarbrough, and a group calling itself "Belchfire Five Plus One," along with many others, performed for free. "They were great, those guys," Juanita remembered, "Some blond gal sold kisses for a dollar and the MC was a neat guy who billed himself as 'the dirtiest mouth in Marin County,' although I think that honor was mine. Anyway, we made a lot of money, I guess, but most of it disappeared. I overheard a couple of kids over my walkie-talkie talkin' about how much they were stealin', like about three thousand dollars, so I canned their asses outta there. Most of the money got squirreled away in the pockets of the kids who were selling Save the Galley tickets, so I decided there wasn't much point in having fundraisers anymore. I mean, somebody benefits, sure, but not always the guy the benefit is *for*. Still, it was real nice to know that so many people tried to help me. Customers tried to pay us in cash so the agent at the till wouldn't get the money, but that didn't end up workin' either." She got a temporary reprieve when she forked over about half the money she owed.

It was not only the IRS that hulked darkly on Juanita's horizon. There was also a notorious motorcycle gang that held weekly meetings, with her permission, on the ferryboat's upper deck. That they frequently planned mayhem was, presumably, unknown to their hostess. Although they had been made most welcome and had been, of course, well fed, they neglected to inform Juanita when their social calendar included a rumble in her dining room. Juanita may have been extremely tolerant and was known to love parties. Nevertheless, it is doubtful that she would have agreed with the party committee about the location chosen for the upcoming festivities.

Beginning with her very first restaurant, Juanita had been her own bouncer. As her weight ballooned, she became someone to reckon with. Eventually, however, she found it helpful to hire an off-duty deputy to stick around on weekends. Brawls were infrequent, but hostile drunks and punks with a little too much testosterone sprang up like weeds and, like weeds, needed to be whacked. One evening she was sitting in her bedroom when an employee dashed in with the startling news that someone was in the kitchen cutting up the cook with a razor blade. Juanita took off like a rocket. Halfway downstairs, she saw the culprit making his escape out the front door and took off after him, clutching her breasts with one hand and her freshly-coiffed hair with the other. She paid no attention to the fact that she had neglected to put on shoes, although the bruises resulting from that night would pain her for weeks to follow.

"I chased that sonofabitch right under the freeway overpass and through the fields and down the streets and right into his house, where I found him pulling his bloody shirt off over his head. I grabbed him from behind," she explained, then paused for a moment in thought, "and I guess if the police hadn't of arrived right then, I'm not quite sure what I would've done next with 'im. Sat on him, maybe. Anyway, as it turned out, a Greyhound bus driver had recognized me runnin' along in my muumuu and he told the police, who were nearby, anyway. Turns out, the guy had already cut open a woman's stomach in Louisiana and I don't know why he'd been let loose to cut up people's employees like he did, but things evened out because he got thrown in jail. My cook ended up being a fire chief, so there you go."

How did she do it? She chuckled. "Honey, it's amazing how fast you can run when you're mad *and* sober!"

Was she scared? Another chuckle. "Not that night. Well, maybe once I was," she conceded thoughtfully, "but I can't seem to recollect just *when.*"

Though a deputy could have handled these situations—was paid to handle them, in fact—Juanita just couldn't stop herself from jumping in and smacking a bunch of rascals upside the head. When she was finally told to desist in using her hands, she exercised her belly muscles so that she walk into a melée and either trample malefactors underfoot or send them careening into walls with one well-aimed thrust of her enormous abdomen. The Sheriff's Department still received complaints about her, however, and so she was sternly ordered to keep her hands and her stomach out of trouble and, furthermore, if she refused to cooperate, her source of off-duty deputies would dry up. "So I promised him I wouldn't butt in anymore," she admitted sadly, "and let the officers handle everything themselves." Therefore, the night the rumble started, Juanita was essentially defanged.

It started quietly enough. Since it was a Friday night, the dining room was packed with the usual mix of dentists, celebrities, drag queens, honeymoon couples and thugs. Men in black leather parked their motorcycles outside and then took their places at the round oak tables so cozily decorated with large glass jam jars and vases of fresh parsley. The object of their hostility was a rival gang of black men with whom they had had words a few days earlier. When the evening was well underway, prime rib arriving by the cartload, and music and laughter and necking youths filling up even the darkest corner, catastrophe struck.

"Nigger!" one of the gang members offered by way of greeting. All hell broke loose. Chairs, tables and vases were overturned, jam jars sailed through the room and out into the night through the smashed windowglass. The air was full of curses and parsley. The bikers wrapped chains around their wrists and the blacks pulled knives from their pockets. An early casualty was felled by a flying sugar bowl. Someone grabbed a fireaxe off the wall and effectively removed one more player from the game. (He was a poor sport, as it turned out. He later sued Juanita for his resulting headache and, unbelievably, won.) Because she had promised only to observe and not to participate, Juanita stood up on the bandstand, arms folded grimly, and watched.

"George was the off-duty deputy there that night and he was a real good fighter. He was tryin' to corral everybody but there were just too many assholes for him to handle." Juanita ordered that the door be locked—presumably by then all peaceful customers had fled—so that no one else could join the melée.

"I was absolutely livid, I tell you!" she continued. "I went into the kitchen and a bunch of them were wrasslin' around on the floor. Since I wasn't *about* to see my glass refrigerator get broke, I decided I had to do somethin'. Besides, it was George who was on the bottom of the pile and one of the biker's chicks was beatin' the hell outta him. Well, I mean, I just couldn't stand by and let that happen, so I grabbed that gal by her hair. She was wearin' it in this big beehive hairdo and it was so full of hairspray that my hand got stuck in it, like she was the tar baby or somethin'. After I pulled her up I remembered I had a big pot of clam chowder on the stove and I thought for a minute it might be a good idea to shove her head down into it, but then I thought, 'Hell, then I'll just hafta make a whole 'nother batch,' so I just put my other hand around her throat and sorta choked off her wind a little bit. I encouraged her to leave the kitchen then, which she did pretty quick."

As for George, his persecution did not soon end. After being pummeled nearly unconscious by the girl, he was hit over the head with a trumpet snatched from the bandstand and then had to suffer the further indignity of having a fishbowl smashed on his shoulder. According to Juanita, "Poor George had to spend days in the hospital, but I'll bet that broad that decked him didn't feel so good the next day, herself!"

Things had settled down somewhat by the time a riot squad of fifty arrived. After a few more skirmishes here and there, and a few more chairs smashing through the last unbroken windows, calm descended over the battlefield. Looking like blood, strawberry jam was in pools on the floor and liberally splattered the walls. A huge map of Alaska on one wall had suffered the impact of a jar of jam right where—as Juanita was later to learn—the Battle of the Yukon had taken place. From then on the rumble was familiarly known as the Battle of the Yukon, although in the case of the real Yukon, it was business as usual as soon as the smoke cleared. Sadly, that is not what happened aboard the ferryboat.

Next morning, the Charles Van Damme sat forlornly in the mud, windows shattered, decks bristling with splintered chairs, the gangway littered with weapons of war discarded by the forces in retreat. Inside, things were worse. Juanita surveyed the battlefield, dejected. There was hardly a table or a chair left unscarred. Platters and glasses and cups lay in pieces everywhere. Surprised by their unexpected good fortune, Juanita's menagerie of tame and feral cats were dining on prime rib while Wattles—this being before his kidnapping—strutted with a turkey's absurd self-importance, pecking at buttered muffins along the way.

All in all, it was a scene that would have defeated the Great Santini. Not Juanita. Marshalling her forces, she barked orders to her staff and seized a mop. By the end of the day they had filled thirty large garbage cans with strawberry jam jars and assorted rubbish. Alice Yarish, longtime friend and reporter for the *San Francisco Examiner*, arrived to do a story, only to burst into tears at the sight.

"She knew how hard I'd worked to get it all together," Juanita explained, "and now she just didn't know how we were going to go on."

While Yarish was there, gathering the sad facts, a woman truckdriver, curious to see the scene of the action, made the mistake of strolling across Juanita's freshly-washed carpet. "Get the hell off, you asshole!" Juanita shrieked. "Come and git me!" the woman screeched back.

"I never will forget how much I wanted to slap her in the head with my mop," Juanita confessed, "but I didn't. We became friends after that."

When Bay Area newspapers hit the stands, headlines were lurid. "A Juanita-Sized Brawl," one shouted, "50 Men Riot Squad." Parents who had let their offspring hang out at the ferryboat now declared the place off-limits. Overnight, the Charles Van Damme's reputation plummeted—at least in the opinion of the less-forgiving —from that of a fashionable, if funky, eatery to the sort of dive where dangerous characters cut their steaks with switchblades and rearranged furniture with their fists. Saturday night, usually the busiest night of the week, was dead. On Sunday, the same bikers who had destroyed the place showed up for the Galley's famous breakfast buffet, thundering up the gangplank astride their motorcycles. Juanita barred the way. "Get off my boat!" she screamed. "But, Juanita," several whined, revving their engines in what they evidently considered a compelling display of masculine charm," we dig this place!"

"Yeah," she growled, "you dug its grave. Now get out!"

Slow to get the message, they eventually rolled back down the gangplank, their muscular female companions making rude gestures from the back of the bikes, where they clung to their seats like mutant limpets.

Juanita missed the teenagers most of all. She had always been careful to help the youth of Sausalito avoid temptation, including refusing to sell booze on the boat and demanding a fifty cent cover charge every time a kid came in so that he wouldn't make too many trips to and from a bottle in the parking lot. She had provided food for the hungry, coffee for the tipsy, and a place for people to sleep if they had nowhere else to go or were in no shape to greet the folks at home. Loyal customers still made the pilgrimage to the best prime rib in town, but word of mouth sent most business elsewhere. Juanita had been somewhat casual about handing over withholding taxes to the IRS; now she was in no position to hand over anything at all. Agents gathered, like buzzards, over the listing carcass of the Charles Van Damme.

As if all this weren't enough, one night a man tried to sell what he said was dope to one of Juanita's dishwashers. The dishwasher dutifully informed a deputy and the dealer was immediately escorted from the premises by official automobile. The next day, newspapers headlined, "Drug Bust at Juanita's." Even though the "drugs" turned out to be aspirin, it was too late. The damage was done. Not only were there vicious hoodlums on board the ferryboat, there were also drug pushers...and heaven alone knew what . Many people were no longer willing to find out what else lurked in the shadows of the old paddlewheels.

"The IRS came around and told me I had to give them $1600 or they'd close me up," Juanita said. "I didn't have that much money since I'd spent everything replacing the jam jars and dishes and chairs and everything. I asked for an extension, but they wouldn't give it to me. So me and twenty-one kids were out of a job."

Adding insult to injury, Juanita's landlord threatened to sue over back rent. He dropped the lawsuit later, either because Juanita was on her way out, anyway, or because he had no interest in performing bloodletting surgery on a turnip.

When a reporter asked why she refused give up, Juanita answered wearily, "I just keep on tryin'."

Next day, the door of the Charles Van Damme was padlocked
by order of the federal government for nonpayment of back taxes and
a broadside was attached to the door announcing an auction in which
the ferryboat's contents would all be sold to satisfy creditors.

It is said that in this, her darkest hour of need, her dear Sea
Scouts came chugging to her rescue. It is said that beds, chairs, tables
and trunks of knickknacks mysteriously disappeared from the un-
locked upper deck in the middle of the night, and were carried off to
undisclosed locations in and around Sausalito. It is said that come
morning, IRS agents were plenty surprised to discover that Juanita's
bedroom was as starkly furnished as a nun's cell. It is said that all of
these things resurfaced afterwards, but how they disappeared and
how they made their way back to Juanita is still only a matter for conjecture. Sea Scouts are loyal and enterprising young men, but hearsay
is hearsay, after all.

According to Juanita, another restaurateur, whom she had
helped start a business in Sausalito, bought her kitchen equipment for
a song and hauled it off without attempting to repay what he owed
her or even agreeing to sell the equipment back to her for what he had
paid for it. In a rage, Juanita fell off the wagon right into the middle
of the guy's restaurant, bellying up to all the tables and drinking his
customers' drinks and then, when she was drunk enough, throwing
everybody out.

She returned to her empty bedroom on the upper deck of the
Charles Van Damme—a room once described by a reporter as 'a mid-
Victorian Cleopatra's barge'—and decided to end it all. She explained, "I thought of throwing myself off the Golden Gate Bridge,
but I really didn't like heights and it was cold. Then I thought maybe
I could stab myself to death, but I figured I'd probably do it all wrong
and get blood all over everything. I knew a gun would be messy, too,
and besides, I didn't have one. Poison seemed like a good idea at first,
but then I thought of how awful it would taste and I might throw up
or somethin'.

"I was just sittin' there, tryin' to figure out how to do it, when there was a knock on the door and a voice said, 'Juanita, I want to talk to you. Open the door.' It sounded like a friend of mine who had a lot of rotten luck recently – a lot rottener than mine – and so I finally opened the door and let him in. He talked me out of killin' myself – that is, if I really would've done it. Whether I would've ended up doin' it or not, I'll always be grateful to that guy for savin' my life when he had his own troubles to worry about."

Another night she paid a call on the fairweather-friend restaurateur and got so obnoxiously drunk that someone called Sally Stanford, who arrived in her pickup truck. "She loaded me in one door and then when she went around to get in her side, I slipped out and tried to run away," Juanita said. "She'd drag me back before I could get too far and load me in the pickup again. Finally I just got too tired to run away anymore, so she drove me to the Valhalla and locked me up in a room and wouldn't let me out until I'd quit ravin'. After I slept it off, I was okay and she let me out. Later on that guy and his wife would go out in their cars and play chicken with each other, so I guess you could say he ended up not makin' out as good as he thought he would."

On her last trip down the gangway, Juanita told a reporter who was there to record the sorrowful event, "Well, that's the end of my mad pad. I don't know what I'll do now—maybe I can get a job as a bouncer somewhere." The idea seemed to cheer her .

"Sometime later I tried to get the ferryboat back," she said. "The manager of the Kingston Trio and his brother tried to help me out, but by then some highflyers had arrived, lightin' their cigars with ten dollar bills, and they bought it out from under us. They decided to cut a door in the bilge during low tide and when the tide came in again, the back part of the boat fell off and it never floated on an even keel again. It was just stuck in the mud for all eternity after that, just fallin' apart. The guys with the cigars went away and just left it there, stuck in the mud. Served them right, of course," she finished on a happier note, "the assholes!"

She had quitclaimed her house to a friend in order to keep it out of government hands, but when she asked for it back, the woman refused. "I never made an issue of it, though," Juanita explained, "and that woman hasn't had a well day since."

127

Though friends advised Juanita to declare bankruptcy, she proudly refused. "I paid everybody back. Well, *mostly*," she said. It took her years.

By the end of 1963, after having sheltered so many over the past eight years, Juanita had nowhere to go. She was homeless.

<hr>

"The Bull", *Biker*

I was a biker in the Sixties and I used to wear a gold ring in my nose, so I was known as "The Bull." Our organization met at Juanita's and she used to cook for us and we'd have our meetings there on her ferryboat. She and I were specially good friends and I used to play with her turkeys and massage her feet. Juanita'd have a rock band there sometimes, some group that needed a place to practice, a place to get heard, and she used to love to stand on the stage and talk over the microphone like a kind of master of ceremonies. One night I walked in with a couple other bikers. I'd brought her a gold nose ring and after I gave it to her, she clipped it on her nose and announced over the loudspeaker, "That's Bull over there. I just love that guy! One of these days I'm goin to make love with him, but then I'll probably only be able to thank him for the tip!"

She gave us bikers the rule of the place. We could come in whenever we wanted to and hang out. The way Juanita was, she'd take people in but then she'd demand loyalty from them. But at that time I was in my early twenties and my loyalty was more for the other bikers than for her. What happened was, a couple of bikers were in the ferryboat one night and some blacks came in and a fight got started. I don't know who won, but it started out as a verbal argument and ended up as a fistfight outside. A week or so later we decided to go back in there and hang around to wait for the black guys to come back in and when they did, a fight started. It looked like one of those Tom Mix movies, with chairs flyin' out the windows and plates sailin' through the air and jam splashed all over the walls. Juanita was standing on the stage and yelling, "Stop! Stop this fightin'!" But it didn't do any good. There must've been about twenty people on each side and nobody was standin' around and waitin'. Everybody, inside and outside, were punching and swinging and throwing each other over the side of the boat into the bay. One guy got hit on the head with a fireaxe – he was almost killed. I think he ended up suing Juanita for that, as a matter of fact, something she would think was pretty disloyal, too. That fight was really the most amazing thing I ever have seen.

A couple of days later I saw her picture in the paper with a chair over her head and she was sayin', "This is the end of my business," which it was, at least on that boat. The income tax evasion people got after her and then the Board of Health, until she actually had to close her place down. Its closing was really the direct result of the fight because once that went down, so did everything else come down on her. Juanita and I became enemies from that time on, until we made up a few years later. But that's another story...

Roman "Bert" Balladine, World's Foremost Male Belly Dance Instructor and Choreographer

Juanita had a restaurant in an old decaying ferryboat that was the only place where you could bring your dog to eat, too. It was a good place for poor artists and actors and dancers to eat since Juanita gave everybody doggie bags which were really supposed to be for dogs, but we always ate them. The bigger your dog, the bigger your doggie bag. I used to think that the only reason I got to eat at Juanita's was *because* I brought my dog with me, since she always gave him more food than she gave me. And served him much more graciously, too. But then, "Love me, love my dog," so that was okay. My dog preferred the Meatloaf Special and it seemed like Juanita served that real often, maybe because our dogs all liked it best.

There were a lot of us hippies at that time in Sausalito, living what was then known as an "alternative lifestyle." People were all trying to "find themselves" – and looking in the weirdest places! At night I was in an act in San Francisco that was billed as The Psychodelic Dance of Love. My partner and I wore nothing but g-strings and Day-Glo paint. It was Great Art, of course, and with an erotic touch both because we were practically naked but also because we danced in the dark under ultraviolet light.

During the day I taught belly dancing at the Sausalito Art Center, where people also made pottery and macramé plant holders. My students were all illegal squatters who lived in little houseboats in the bay docked near Juanita's ferryboat. For costumes they would mostly wear curtains they took off somebody's wall, and if the curtains were ripped they'd call themselves Gypsy Dancers and wear hoop earrings.

When Juanita ran afoul of the IRS, all of us pitched in to help. Our fundraisers were kind of bizarre because we were bizarre and the Sixties were bizarre, too. We did our best but maybe it wasn't enough, since Juanita went broke, anyway. My dog and I both missed her.

Counting change with Sissy.

Juanita's Galley, Gate Five Road, 1956.

Juanita and her Catch of the Day, 1952.

Toots with crabs, Cronkhite Beach, California, 1952.

Sketches by
Darrell Reed

Dealing with the "damned public".

Sally Stanford in mink and Juanita in muumuu, with Wattles, 1960.

The Canton Ferry before its reincarnation, 1959.

PAY NOW and
EAT LATER   №̱ 54488

We are not a
non-profit organization.
Keep this receipt.

Juanita's
GALLEY
GATE 5 ROAD·MARINSHIP·SAUSALITO, CALIFORNIA

HOUSE RULES

1. WRITE YOUR OWN ORDER. Be sure to put
your name on order so we can find you.
2. POUR YOUR OWN COFFEE.
3. PUT CARD IN TIME CLOCK
   AND PUNCH. This is the only time
   you can punch me and I will not punch back
4. HAND ORDER TO COOK. Our food
   always guaranteed - but not the
   disposition of the cook.

NAME:_____
ORDER:_____
_____
_____
_____

CHECK HERE FOR SPECIAL SERVICE*
SLOW ☐   DON'T CARE ☐
DAMN BIG RUSH ☐
* Doesn't mean you will get what you ask for - But
check any one that will make you feel better.

№̱ 54488

address

WELCOME MATES!   JUANITA'S GALLEY

OPEN 24 HOURS A DAY
ABOARD THE FERRYBOAT
CHARLES VAN DAMME

SAUSALITO, CALIFORNIA

Juanita's
GALLEY   GATE 5 ROAD MARINSHIP

HOUSE RULES

1. Pour your own coffee.
2. Write your order. Give name.
3. No back talk to the help.

NAME:_____
ORDER:_____
_____
_____
_____
_____

263   ORDER TIME

CHECK HERE FOR SPECIAL SERVICE*
SLOW ☐   DON'T CARE ☐
DAMN BIG RUSH ☐
* Doesn't mean you will get what you ask for - But
check any one that will make you feel better.

Top left: The famous "Pay Now, Eat Later" plan.

Above: George Schultz, later Secretary of State, helped design this swashbuckling logo for the Galley order forms.

Bottom left: After the paper towels ran out, Juanita got order forms.

Mr. and Mrs. Joe Chancellor, with Juanita, on their wedding day, 1957.

8

"Juanita – Another Try in Another Town"

– Contra Costa Times

After the boat closed, I didn't know where to go or what to do with myself," Juanita explained. "I got Hughie set up somewhere, but I didn't know what I was gonna do without money and without a restaurant and with most of the stuff I had left hidden in warehouses and people's garages all over Sausalito. I figured everything would work out okay, I just didn't know what the hell was gonna happen."

So she went to her old friend, Joe Kane, who owned an empty store on Bridgeway, Sausalito's main street. He told her she could live there rent-free until she found a place, and she gratefully accepted. With a waitress by the name of Bria, they collected enough of Juanita's furniture and knickknacks to make the bare room more homelike, and moved in. Juanita relished the adventure.

"Bria wanted to be a writer and she'd always wanted to live in a loft. She fixed a sort of loft in the back of the shop and hung a knotted rope from the ceiling so that she could climb up to it. When she wasn't in her loft, she was sittin' in my tin sitz bath, dressed in black leotards and smokin' a cigarette in a long holder. She was ahead of her time, really. Tourists would look in the window and think the place was an antique shop and they'd come on in. I'd usually be lyin' in the window in my big bed and Bria would be in the sitz bath, smokin', and these people from Idaho or somewhere would look around and sometimes ask me how much somethin' cost. I'd say, 'I'm sorry, but this is a private home,' and they'd leave. If we needed the money, I'd sell whatever it was they wanted and we'd go to a bar and celebrate.

"Bria always looked half-starved, so she used to go around to the different restaurants and ask for a bone for our dog. Of course the cooks knew the bones weren't really for any dog, so they'd cut a nice big piece of meat to go along with the bone and send that with her, too. We ended up eatin' pretty well! One time I had a little money and was plannin' on being asked out to dinner, so I bought a barbecued chicken for Hughie. When my date didn't pan out, I went up to see if Hughie had any leftovers and there he was, feedin' that whole chicken to his dog! He hadn't eaten so much as a bite himself. Well, I sure as hell wasn't goin' to fight over the wishbone with his damned dog. Mad? Whoooeee!"

Living in a shop window might seem an unpleasant prospect to the majority, but Juanita was not in the least disturbed. "I just always made sure my bed was made before I opened the curtains in the morning," she said, sounding every inch the house-proud home-maker. "I got bored just sittin' around watchin' Bria smoke and bullshittin' the tourists, so I decided to go ask Sally for a job. Now that the Galley was gone, there wasn't any place servin' good breakfast in town, so I told her I'd do breakfast at the Valhalla and she said okay. Herb Caen gave me lots of publicity. Sally started makin' lots more money, but when she handed me my first paycheck and I saw she was paying me $1.40 an hour – a dollar forty an hour! – I told her to go screw herself. I put that damned check in my purse and never cashed it. It's still around here somewhere. I told her that if she was gonna be that goddamned cheap, then I would work for nothin'. So that's what I did."

Juanita was good for business. Not only were the tables crowded at breakfast, but all day well-wishers would buy Juanita drinks. "I was still mostly on the wagon at the time and I didn't wanna drink all the bloody marys people kept pushin' at me, but when I complained to Sally she just said, 'Don't take the shingles off the roof, Juanita,' and told the bartender to mix me bloody marys without the vodka. One night I drank thirty-two bloody marys and next day I woke up feelin' awful and was so swole up it took three days for me to shrink back down. After that I'd drink gin and water – only without the gin."

Sally gave her the night job of hat-check girl in the cloakroom where Sally kept a gallon mayonnaise jar for donations to the Little League. Juanita remembered it well:

"Sally started accusin' me of takin' money from the mayonnaise jar and gave me hell about it. But I tell you that she used to take those gallon jars home and stick them in the safe she had there, which was so stuffed with cash and Little League donation jars that you couldn't hardly walk inside it. I mean, that woman was tighter'n a tick. Not that she didn't give the Little Leaguers money from the mayonnaise jars – she just gave them *some* of it. But why she thought I was stealin' it, I don't know. That was just her way sometimes, I guess. Sally was really like a kid who sees another kid with a piece of candy. All of a sudden that's what she wanted, too, that particular piece of candy, and she'd move her mind so she could get it. That was just her way."

Organizations would arrange private parties at the Valhalla, taking over the entire restaurant for an evening. The festive decorations most often included shapely young men and women who, according to Juanita, ended the evening as party favors for the guests. On occasion, Juanita joined the other "hostesses" on hand for the event.

"I was kind of an entrepreneur," Juanita said, "but you could never have said I 'worked' for Sally, since she left the cathouse business years before I even met her. You might say that Sally just wanted to make sure everybody had a good time and what the boys and girls did in their spare time was up to them. I do remember once this guy rollin' up a hundred dollar bill and then tuckin' it down the front of my muumuu. Sally got real upset when I wouldn't split it with her. That was just a tip, though, because I never got any money for sex, just a good time and good dinner and maybe a nice little tip, which came in handy since I wasn't gettin' one of Sally's miserable paychecks.

"People have always accused me of bein' a hooker. I've always said, 'I never charged a nickel from a horizontal position,' and Sally'd always say that I'd never have made any money as a whore 'cause I had no business sense and would never have charged enough. She was right, too.

"One night there was a real elegant party with a lot of Hollywood stars. Jimmy Stewart was there and Erskine Caldwell and other fancy people. I even had my picture taken with Stewart, but it got burnt up in a fire or got stolen or something. Anyways, I was sittin' there and havin' a great time, when who should walk in but Arthur Godfrey! Now, Sally had asked me to be there as a kind of 'local color' and she couldn't believe it that I knew Godfrey. I walked right up to him and said, 'Arthur Godfrey, do you remember me?' By then I'd put on quite a few pounds, but he said, 'Juanita, your face is so familiar to me, I'd never forget it!' I thought Sally would drop her teeth! That man didn't leave my side for the whole rest of the night. We just sat there on Sally's loveseat, talkin' about every place we'd been, everywhere we'd flown in the old days.

"After that night, Godfrey would call me every time he came to San Francisco. We'd just have the greatest time, usually at the Mark Hopkins. The last time I saw him he was real sick and he died not too long after. He was a great guy. More treat than trick, let's put it that way."

But Juanita without a restaurant was like a madam without a telephone. She just couldn't conduct her life without a place of her own in which to fry eggs and raise hell. She was forty years old, weighed over two hundred pounds and, now that the mourning period was over for the Charles Van Damme, ready to wrassle alligators. She had two options. One was presented to her from a man by the name of John Stinnet, who had started coming to Juanita's Galley some years before, often at a moment of financial crisis. He'd offer help with so much affectionate concern that Juanita was puzzled. Who was the guy, anyway? What was in it for him? "I mean, the guy was so nice," Juanita said of him, "that I was kinda suspicious." He had known her mother, he told her, and had lived for awhile in Oklahoma. "But why did he seem to care so much about me?" Juanita wondered. "It got me to thinkin'." He urged her to come with him to Alaska and run the restaurant he owned along with so many other businesses that he was, quite evidently, a wealthy man. "But I wanted to go it alone, go it my way, so I said no. I've often thought about how my life would've been different if I'd said yes."

Sally offered a second option of a place she owned fifty miles north, in the wine country near Sonoma. It was a derelict little bar and filling station in the town of El Verano (which was also, incidentally, where the notorious madam, Spanish Kitty, ran a bordello in the Twenties). Juanita drove up in Sally's pickup to have a look. The place was a dump. All but buried in weeds, it looked like a service station-cum-log cabin. Gas pumps still out front sported prices a decade old. Inside there was a bar complete with cobwebs and dusty, empty bottles. It was perfect.

Rolling up her sleeves, Juanita dove right in, mowing down the weeds, tearing out the pumps and polishing the bar. Every afternoon she would go to Verdier's, a small resort nearby, to shower and change clothes before driving back down to check coats at Sally's. Mornings would find her in her glory, brandishing a broom. After the place was tidied up and ready to open, Juanita asked the local building inspector to come over and give his approval.

"You gotta be kidding," he told her. "That place has been condemned for years."

"You know what?" Juanita mused, "Sally knew all about it being condemned. When I asked her what the hell she'd been thinkin' of, lettin' me go to all that trouble for nothin', she just said, 'Well, I figured you could get away with it if anybody could.' I was so damn mad I could've shot her. We didn't speak for quite some time after that, until she sent me a fox named Rommel as a make-up present and he bit me."

Back at Verdier's that afternoon, she was still in a rage. One of the employees there said to her, "Why don't you buy this place? It's for sale."

Verdier's was one of the last remaining resorts in the Sonoma Valley. Once famous for the area's hot springs and as a mecca for fog-weary residents of San Francisco, Verdier's had catered to French guests the way Fetter's Hot Springs did to Jewish sunlovers. Most everybody else paddled around at Boyes Hot Springs, the first resort of them all.

Verdier's had seen better days. By the time Juanita gave it the once-over, its garden had become wilderness and the buildings were badly in need of paintbrush and hammer. There was never anything on earth Juanita loved more than seedy old buildings, the scruffier the better. One call to a devoted customer who missed her gargantuan breakfasts brought him along in his sportscar, cash in pockets and pen in hand. Soon, Verdier's was hers (partly) to repair (by herself.) Hog heaven. Apparently the resort had just grown higgledy-piggledy, as the spirit moved its builders. The spacious, once-beautiful grounds, the little cabins and small two-story hotel—everything scaled down to the size of nineteenth century people—were on one side of Linden Street. Across the street were a bar and a dining room, separated by a brick patio. Entrance to the dining room was through the kitchen, which must have delighted the cooks. There was a pool, of course, and a wishing well.

At last there was room enough for all of the animals Juanita wanted. Her old turkey settled right in, followed soon by a rooster Juanita immediately christened "Chickenshit." He was the gift of a kindergarten teacher whose pupils had loved the chick it once had been but not the crowing oldster it had become. Chickenshit was from the very beginning Juanita's pride and joy. "Don't I have a lovely cock?" she would ask her male customers. "Do you think my cock is bigger than yours?" In and out of the kitchen and dining room, Chickenshit rode on Juanita's shoulder, petted, fed on muffin crumbs, and spoiled rotten.

"He was just great with the customers," Juanita recalled. "I guess because he was so used to children squeezin' the daylights outta him, he didn't much mind anything anymore."

Before her doors opened for business, scandalous news spread the length of the Valley of the Moon that Juanita, who "must have been one of Sally's girls," was about to open her own cathouse. Even after the "Juanita's Galley" sign had been hung on the wall, there were those who "knew for certain" that the cabins and hotel were being used for illicit purposes.

"Well, maybe they were," Juanita conceded. "I never paid any mind to what people did in my places. I couldn't have cared less who was makin' out with who else. I've always had people go upstairs and lock the door and either pay me room rent next day or send a check in the mail. What they did behind that door was their own business." For awhile after the restaurant opened, men would ask the waitresses where the action was, and the women told them the names of other restaurants and bars in the valley until they finally figured out what the men meant.

For reasons only known to herself, Juanita decided her new Galley needed more doors. Many, many doors, some of them finished and some merely left as openings in the walls. She explained that she wanted lots of places for people to go in and out of, although she admitted that she was not entirely certain why. Fortunately she left enough walls intact to prevent the roof from caving in on her first daring customers. Inspectors insisted she replace all the original wiring or they would condemn the well-ventilated buildings. As if this weren't enough, the Health Department soon heard of Chickenshit and called Juanita on the carpet in the District Attorney's office.

According to Juanita, the D.A. asked the health inspector if he had seen any chicken or turkey manure on the floor. The inspector admitted that he had not, but since the fowl had the run of the place, it would only be a matter of time before nature took its course.

At this, Juanita leapt in with, "Of course he didn't see any chickenshit on my floor! You think I want to step in it and go slidin' around all over the place?" She said that if they ever did relieve themselves anywhere inside her premises, she would most assuredly clean it up, although she wouldn't go so far as to admit such a thing was likely to happen, anyway, and they shouldn't get the idea that she was. "I told them I didn't let my animals get on the tables or the stove or anything," Juanita recalled with a sparkle of mischief in her eyes, "and they believed me, too."

At the end of the interview, Juanita confided winningly to the D.A., "I just like to keep Chickenshit around so when some old bald fart comes in I can put it on the guy's head and ask if he's ever had a pecker up there before. Good for his circulation." One health inspector remembered years later, "We had to practically invent a new restaurant code, since existing regulations didn't ever seem to apply to Juanita." He sighed when he said this, as if terrible memories of those days were still fresh.

Opening night was a great success and the next night was, suitably enough, Halloween. Half of the restaurant was taken by highway patrolmen and their wives, the other half by a beautifully-costumed party of gay men. Although it was a noisy night, full of ribald jokes and suggestive banter, "It was just like the Kingdom of Heaven, with the lion layin' down with the lamb," Juanita sighed. "Everybody had a great time and nobody got slapped." Juanita attended the event dressed as a pumpkin – evidently a favorite disguise, though hardly camouflage. The night before, at the official Grand Opening, she had appeared in more elegant dress. Radiant and gracious in a black muumuu trimmed with ostrich feathers, she carried, in black-gloved hands, a small, befeathered umbrella. She was mesmerizing on both occasions.

Juanita had a fondness for mavericks and renegades of all descriptions, and was especially amused by the gay men who frequented the Galley both in and out of drag. One evening, a new waitress was forking muffins in the kitchen when in sashayed a young

144

man dressed in a pink polka-dotted g-string with a champagne bucket in one hand and a glass in the other. "Ice," he whispered through perfectly-rouged lips, eyes raised heavenward, "more ice." She saw him later in the evening with his feet hooked around a barstool, leaning over backward like an acrobatic chorus girl, shimmying and singing, "I'm a juicy fruit! I'm a juicy fruuuiiiiiit!"

It was a busy Saturday night in the bar when three young men decided to drop their pants and "flash" the assembled customers. Unfortunately the room was so crowded, and the tipplers so interested in the course of events, that there wasn't room for the rascals to pull their pants back up. By the time a deputy sheriff arrived, conditions were the same except that the flashers were beginning to feel less like the perpetrators of a joke and more like the butt of one. "Shall I take 'em in, Juanita?" the deputy asked, looking on the scene with some sympathy.

"Nah," she replied, "let 'em stay there so we can all see what they don't have." So everyone did.

When none of these hijinks hurt anyone, Juanita not only tolerated but actively encouraged such behavior and demanded that everyone there tolerate it, too. One evening a group of young men were enjoying a modest romp in the bar when a disapproving older woman downed one drink too many and stood up to denounce them.

"You're just a bunch of queers who should be in Vietnam!"

Juanita, who was near enough to overhear, strode up to the woman and bellowed, "For your information, a lot of these boys are just back from Vietnam and have already done their duty to keep bitches like you safe!"

"Oh, yeah?" the woman snarled, rounding on her hostess. "Well, everybody knows *you're* just a lesbian!"

Fists on ample hips, Juanita looked the woman up and down and sneered, "And just how can everybody think I'm a lesbian when it's a well known fact that I'm the best cocksucker in this valley!" Moments before, two highway patrolmen had come in from the dining room and now, seeing what was afoot, took the loutish female by either arm and escorted her outside. "You *tell* her I'm the best cocksucker in the valley!" Juanita yelled after them. Then, good humor restored, she went on about her work.

As had been the rule, Juanita's Galley was a home away from

home for those who had no family to go to on the holidays. Thanksgiving Dinner was celebrated with turkeys both on and under the tables. Christmas Day was made festive both with food and with presents for everyone. Juanita always carted home the ugliest tree she could find and decorated it with candy canes, cookies and ornaments employees and customers made in the kitchen out of flour paste they'd bake and paint. "It was one of my mottos," Juanita said, "that I really didn't want a lover so much as I wanted my very own Santa Claus." Instead, she was Santa Claus. One Christmas she went home to Tulsa and when she returned it was to find that, contrary to her orders, her employees had decided not to open the restaurant but to get drunk, instead. "I fired their asses," she said, "and then had to hire them all back the next day. But boy was I mad! Whooooeee!"

As her restaurants got larger, the problem of getting responsible employees became more acute. "Lots of people she hired made the place look like The Addams' Family sometimes," one long-ago employee remembered. "You couldn't believe some of them could ever get jobs anywhere else."

Since Juanita had the reputation of being unmerciful to those who worked for her, it is questionable how much of the noisy disorder was the fault of the employer or the employee. Juanita's favorite method of giving directions was at the top of her voice. Some hired hands were so unsettled by this that they would start to tremble and drop plates at her approach. "She's coming! She's coming!" some wild-haired youth would hiss as she dashed past. This would only cause greater pandemonium as those too shy, too insane or too stoned to do battle scurried off in search of a place to hide.

As with everything else having to do with Juanita, the subject of how she treated her staff is controversial. Some maintain that she was an ogre who shouted, pinched and slapped at the hapless with spatulas. Others believe with equal conviction that she only gave people a hard time when they were slacking off and that most of the shouting was mere theatrics, designed to improve employees' tips. One woman who worked as a waitress at the Galley for many years described how "Sometimes we'd work our buns off, and still the tips would be lousy. So what we'd do is, we'd draw straws to see who would have to go into Juanita's bedroom and wake her up. She'd always wake up cussin' and tryin' to slug someone, so if you were the one who had to wake her, you'd have to shake her and then run for your life. She'd start yellin' and come stormin' into the dining room, raising hell about everything. Like magic, tips would just start to flow because everybody would feel so sorry for us, bein' abused like that."

Juanita was the first to admit she could be a curmudgeon, but she knew all along that her outbursts were a boon to a waitress's bank account. The general consensus is that she would have shouted anyway since, to her, shouting was the most effective form of encouragement. She often shouted at customers, and she would throw them out on a whim, whether they deserved to be or not. Sometimes, especially after she started drinking regularly again, she would decide that she didn't like the look on a customer's face or the smell of her cologne or the fact that she had just nibbled at her dinner. ("Ya think I'm tryin' to poison ya? Get the hell out!") Often she had a more substantial reason, such as an employee neglecting to ring up sales or a customer "forgetting" to pay his bill.

One of the many peculiarities of the Galley in El Verano was the fact that the "wine cellar" was outside the dining room where anyone who wanted wine with dinner would be directed to choose the bottle himself. One evening Juanita noticed a smallish man who seemed to have put on a little too much weight at dinner. "I went up and pulled open his jacket and the little squirt had tucked bottles into his waistband and pockets. I told him to put them down on his table, which he did. Then I picked him up like a wet rag and threw the little bastard out the door." In describing the incident, Juanita acknowledged that it seemed "like bowling, only not so smooth."

On the subject of fighting—in which she continued to be an eager participant—she also had this to say: "I like fightin' men. I don't like fightin' women, see, because they fight dirty—they fight *back*." Hughie moved to El Verano and Joe Foley, erstwhile bartender at the Four Winds in Sausalito, also followed his friend and fellow barfly north. Juanita was happy to have him because he was a courteous, dependable man, and one who could be trusted. That he was also a practical joker buttered her bread on both sides. He brought with him his basset hound, which was "five times the size he ought to have been," a contemporary said, "so that his belly dragged along the ground. Both Joe and his dog had about the same expression, and they looked kind of alike, too."

147

Joe liked to surprise people by hiding his tape recorder so that passersby would be amazed to hear noises issuing from inappropriate places. Sometimes he hid the recorder inside a bush and played a tape of a baby crying. Alarmed, people would search everywhere in increasing anxiety before someone finally brushed away the right leaves. Joe made a tape of Juanita on the warpath and would play it at full volume when Juanita was away and the restaurant lacked atmosphere.

Not that Joe wasn't sometimes the butt of a joke, himself. Juanita recalled the time he passed out on his bed in his cabin on the grounds. Since he had neglected to shut the door, he was visited by all the animals on the place. In Juanita's words: "I had another fawn by that time and she got to playing with Joe's basset hound and a sheep somebody had just given me. They were all runnin' after each other, like children, in and out of every open door on the property. They'd run in Joe's room, and the fawn and the sheep would jump over the bed where he was layin' unconscious, and then run out the door again. They went round and round like that for a long time and Joe never knew a thing about it."

While animals kept coming and staying, employees mostly came and went. Some people were halfway between someplace and someplace else and the Galley was a convenient waystation. Sometimes they were single mothers who waitressed in order to keep their children fed. Many were flower children on the fringes of a despised society. Quite a few were artists of varying talents who sang in the dining room or painted outbuildings or forked muffins for room and board. One enterprising artist painted a manger scene for Juanita, making the principal players white on one side of the board and black on the other. Even the sheep, the chickens and the mule underwent the same transformation. Juanita was mightily pleased with it and kept it propped up on the lawn for months.

"I don't remember hiring anybody you'd call strange," she said, then added, upon reflection, "Maybe they were *all* a little strange. But only one was a real degenerate and I got rid of him but fast." What sort of perversion he practised and how she found out about it, she wouldn't say.

It was not always necessary to work for Juanita in order to become a member of her extended family. Some people repaid her with cash and devotion; others took whatever wasn't nailed down, including Juanita's clothes, animals and cooking utensils. Joe Foley once found a pair of "hippie-types" lowering the Jacuzzi from an upstairs window on a rope. One former employee stole her car. "But it wasn't that he stole it that made me so damn mad," she said, "but because I was workin' and he was havin' such a good time!" When the culprit blithely returned the Chevy, Juanita met him with hammer in hand and smashed out all the car windows. "But why did you do that, Juanita?" she was asked. "It was *your* car." "Well, I figured it was a better idea to smash my car than to smash *him*."

Characters often showed up with untidy – and hilarious – life stories. Once one did not, and Juanita remembered him with guilt and pain.

"This guy had been a customer for a long time. His mother died and his brother sold the house and kept the money so this poor guy had nowhere to go and no money to get anywhere, anyway. I told him he could live in one of the cabins. I kept takin' his food over to him, me or somebody else, but since he was so sour and grumpy, nobody liked to have anything to do with him, including me. I guess it was his asthma made him so mean, because he didn't used to be like that in Sausalito.

"One day I told him he'd have to come to the kitchen to get his own food. At the same time he asked me for some money and since I figured he was just goin' to spend it on booze, I told him no. Turned out he wanted it for medicine, but he hadn't told me that. He hadn't told me he was suicidal either. One morning he didn't come outside and when we went in to check on him we found that he'd blown his brains out with a shotgun. Blood all over everything. I never have forgiven myself for gettin' tough with him and won't until my dyin' day. I just always keep thinkin' that if I'd known he was so upset, there would've been somethin' I could've done for him. He was just like a dog nobody wanted to pet anymore."

Children and teenagers, whether they were employees or not, were treated as if they were Juanita's own. If they were still in school, she insisted they do their homework at the big table in the kitchen where there was usually someone willing – if unable – to lend a hand with fractions. If they were caught hanging out with the wrong crowd or smoking or with a beer in one hand, they heard about it. If she caught a child running after one of her animals, she would yell, "Your legs are longer than his!" and that would stop the little persecutor dead in his tracks. "Kids have gotta be civilized," Juanita explained, "and if it takes a little yellin' or a nice kick in the butt, then that's the way it is."

One employee took up bicycle riding for exercise. Juanita told her, "You'd better stop that because you're makin' your ass too big." "I don't have a big ass," the woman replied, stung. "You do, too," Juanita retorted. "Just look in the mirror!" Though she insisted she was only trying to be helpful, that remark put a damper on their friendship for years.

"I just don't think exercise is all it's cracked up to be, is all," she confided. "You're a whole lot better off just stayin' home and pullin' weeds."

Most people Juanita hired in El Verano had never worked in a restaurant before and didn't know the difference between a rolling pin and a curling iron. That was okay with Juanita. She loved to teach. It can safely be said that her students found it difficult to forget their culinary education at her hands. For example, one day she walked into the kitchen to find an new employee smashing hamburger patties flat between two plates.

"I told her not to do that again because the hamburgers were too thin. Next time I looked she was doin' the same damn thing. So I said to her, 'Look, if you do that again, you're gonna *wear* them patties!'

"Well, right away she smashed another one just to spite me, so I walked on over and took up the squashed patty and rubbed it in her face. She got mad then and yelled, 'Okay, okay, then you fight me!' But she was so short that I could hold her off while she just flailed away at me and yelled. Finally she got tired, I guess, and backed off and threw her apron at me. I said, 'Ha! You didn't throw your apron right! You'll be back.' And she was—but she didn't smash hamburgers again."

Many employees found themselves not only on the receiving end of Juanita's scolding, but of her home decorating skills. "I've always had to keep an eye on her," Joe Foley said, "or she'd put bookshelves full of bric-a-brac in my living room and posters all over my walls. If she could get away with it, she'd fill up somebody else's house with stuff just like she filled up her own. It's like a compulsion with her. She sees an empty place and just can't be happy until it's filled up with something. She was all the time buying stuff and finding stuff and then trying to force everybody to take it. She was a mighty generous woman, but she carried it a little too far sometimes."

Joe recalled the time Juanita set out to make good on an overdraft at the bank and ended up being bushwhacked by shopping fever and coming home with a trunkload of antiques she'd bought with the money instead. "You see," he explained, "money has never meant anything to her. She always made big money, but she never looked ahead. If she had money on the 15th, she'd spend it all by the 17th and think nothing of it. I'd tell her, 'You don't need that stuff you bought, why don't you save your money?' and she'd just answer, 'Oh, something will come along.' And you know what? It usually did. Even if it didn't, she just loved buying and collecting things so much that it didn't matter how much it cost or what it was.

"She met this guy in El Verano who had a pickup truck. They'd load the truck up with junk and take off for the dump. I'd wave goodbye to them as they drove away. After awhile, back they'd come with the truck still all piled up with junk. I'm a city boy and never knew anything about dumps, so I just figured they couldn't ever manage to find out where the dump was. It was kind of a mystery to me how they could drive off so happy every time in search of a dump they never were able to find. Well, it turned out that they'd found the dump all right. But what they were doing was just switching junk. They'd unload what they had and then go hunting around and find things like half a chair or a bent birdcage stand, and they'd figure that somebody someday would come along who could fix it, so they'd throw it in the truck. Home they'd come, smiling and happy about all the great stuff they'd found. I couldn't believe it when I finally found out what they'd been up to."

What with all the publicity and the rural charm of El Verano, the Galley was as busy as it had ever been in Sausalito. Though Juanita herself was always to overshadow both food and decor, those were also provocative and part of the growing legend. Arlene Dahl and Joan Sutherland came for lunch and afterwards a proud Juanita gave them the grand tour. As she was pointing out the various splendors, Joe Foley, who was tagging along behind, saw Sutherland turn to

Dahl and whisper, "Looks like a bunch of junk to me." Fortunately for the world of opera, Juanita did not also overhear.

Amid the chickens, the ancient mangles and the Christmas decorations, Juanita set out a buffet that her customers remember with tears in their eyes. She insisted that the food always be arranged exactly the same way so that the blind could load their plates as easily as anyone else. The buffet was also low enough for people in wheelchairs.

There were several kinds of salads and dressings, flanked by bowls of olives and green onions, all of which had to be kept full at all times – or else. A mirror served as a tray for stuffed eggs which slid over its surface like skaters on an icy pond. There were platters of fried chicken, chiles rellenos, breaded pork chops and a huge, carve-it-yourself ham. (If Juanita didn't like the way a customer was carving it, he or she was sure to receive a quick, and very public, lesson.) Watermelons carved like rabbits held diced fruit and there was a chamber pot for the baked beans. Everything was surrounded by a mountain of ice and a forest of parsley. ("One day some fool woman ate it all. Just walked around that buffet and ate the whole damn lot just like a cow.")

This buffet constituted the first course. Huge steaks or three pound slabs of prime rib came next, accompanied by baked potatoes and English muffins, all oozing butter. One dinner was enough to serve three ravenous lumberjacks, but Juanita never reduced the size of the servings. She liked it when people ate heartily and then took home foil-wrapped leftovers the size of a newborn child. When employees tried to institute cost-cutting measures like slicing thinner portions of meat, Juanita hit the ceiling. People came to Juanita's to eat and, by God, they would! Dainty appetites indicated a serious spiritual defect. Juanita would as soon have shot a cat as suffer a picky eater. "Eat it or wear it!" remained her rallying cry. All in all, dining at the Galley could be a risky business.

There were peaceful times, usually when Juanita was sleeping, but most customers felt cheated if dinner did not include at least one glimpse of their hostess in full cry. Since her bedroom was just off the dining room, customers often began their dining experience greeted, à la Madame Recamier, by Juanita, lounging in bed, having her toenails polished by any one of several young men or women who also undertook the duties of ladies-in-waiting by brushing her long hair or massaging her feet. "Hi, honey!" she would call out when a customer peeked around the edge of the door. "Come right on in!" One of her purchases included the huge four-poster she installed in the room, an antique "bishop's bed" which provided plenty of room not only for Juanita, but for her menagerie as well. ("I think the Bishop would've liked that, don't you?") She often extended a gracious invitation to customers to dine in her room ("We'll just put up a card table!") and would sometimes remain in bed, occasionally asleep and snoring, while they dined.

Balladeer Barbara Tabler tells the story about the time she brought members of Planned Parenthood with her to lunch. They had come to San Francisco for a national convention. "Fifteen of us walked into the place and Juanita, who was in bed, saw us through the mirrors she had set up so she could see who was coming in the door. She called out, 'Barbara, are those the Planned Parenthood friends you told me about?' I said, 'Yes,' and just as we got to her door, she called out, 'You know, I sure do like those people! They make fucking fun!' Well, you should have seen their faces. Just that one moment was worth the whole trip to them!"

Juanita was also known to greet arrivals from the large, claw-footed bathtub in the yard, and one woman remembered her greeting customers from her bathtub inside the restaurant one night. She was reclining, wearing her tortoiseshell comb and up to her breasts in bubbles, but gracious withal. Juanita has denied this, however, on the grounds that the bathroom was too small for a gathering place. However, she admitted that she often enjoyed a well-earned nap in the garden tub where she frequently found merrymakers passed-out from the night before. The tub was also a handy receptacle for wine grapes, which Juanita and customers took turns stomping just for fun, and for the satisfaction of seeing their feet turn purple.

Center stage was still the dining room. "Ever have a pecker on your head?" she'd ask a man after setting Chickenshit aloft. "Know anything better than a good cock, Honey?" she'd ask a sweet young thing. "If you treat a cock right, it'll do whatever you want it to!" she'd advise, laying the chicken down the table and stroking its belly.

One evening, golf great Jack Nicklaus found himself the sudden object of attention when Juanita came up behind him and pressed her breast against one of his ears and Chickenshit against the other. "Ever have a bust in the mouth and a birdie on your shoulder?" she cooed.

As Juanita's menagerie swelled to include skunks, rabbits, pigeons, foxes, pigs, iguanas and squirrel monkeys – most of them liberated from a life behind bars – so did her headaches increase with such humorless people as health inspectors and those who had been nipped, snapped at and crapped upon. It must be said that most people, including some long-suffering employees of the Health Department, enjoyed the zoo atmosphere of the Galley, even though most could be forgiven for wondering just how much of themselves the animals gave in Juanita's kitchen. Some people never came twice, but many found themselves addicted to what one customer described as "a three ring circus, complete with lunch and lion tamer." Showing a fine disregard for authority, Juanita installed a sign out front that read, "Approved – New Hampshire Board of Health." ("You have to be accredited by *somebody*. Certainly California wasn't going to!")

"I had some bad luck with some of my animals, though," Juanita said, "especially when I started out. See, people would just drop off all these animals and I didn't always know what was good for them. Somebody gave me an iguana, and one day I thought he looked kinda peaked, so I put his cage out in the sun. I didn't think about that he didn't have any way of getting into the shade. I guess he got sick and tired of the heat and died. Poor baby. I did it to a possum once, too, who shouldn't have been out in the sun in the first place, since he was nocturnal. I tell you, you learn a lot about animals when you have them!

"Poor Jo-Jo, my squirrel monkey," she continued, "he liked to hang around with the cats and they'd run all over the place together. One day someone shot him with a .22. I tell you, I'd have shot somebody who did somethin' like that, soon as look at 'em!"

Most of the birds and animals, however, led well-fed and merry lives, swinging in the oak trees or swimming in the pool, harassing each other and the customers with a democratic sense of fair play. Childless as she was, Juanita cared for them as if *they* were her children. Even the least tamed among them rarely nipped her, and then usually in the excitement of some catastrophe. She talked to them as if they understood her, and perhaps they did. When she went to bed she was always accompanied by a little marching band of furred and feathered friends, all of whom snuggled down around her in the bedclothes or perched on the headboard of the bishop's bed. Cats gave birth to kittens in the sheets. Chickenshit greeted the dawn from on top her chest of drawers. If an animal was too blind or deaf or lame to come along, she'd scoop the creature up and carry it. There was never any reason to sleep alone at Juanita's.

She collected a few antique pieces of furniture that masqueraded in the dining room as tables, benches and buffets but which were, in actuality, beds. Unbeknownst to either the Fire or Health Departments, she could have these beds lowered or swung out or otherwise transformed in order that the drunken or weary might catch forty winks. The finest of them all had a door in the front, a toilet somewhere inside, a closet for clothes and a ledge for writing letters. Several resembled grand pianos and one looked like a roll-top desk. It is amusing to imagine how the room must have looked after lights out, changed from dining room to dormitory.

As the Sixties passed by in Day-Glo boots, festoons of flowers and love beads, the Galley's fame steadily grew as "the" place to go. Even tours arranged for overseas tourists often included a must-see visit to the Galley. Newspapers including the *New York Times* and magazines like *Australian Vogue* and *Playboy* carried you-gotta-see-it-to-believe-it stories. That the place was overrun with chickens and iguanas and blind, surly dogs only added to the adventure of dining in a little town undiscoverable on most maps. Success meant little to Juanita, except that it brought more money to buy oddities for her antique collection and food for her animals. Her fame meant little or nothing to her. She was still pretty much the "Okie" she had always been, making dressing tables out of apple crates and slaw out of cabbages. Her only concession to her position of eminence was to wear wilder and wilder muumuus and to adorn her upswept hairdo with an increasingly complex assemblage of decorations. Though she only got gussied-up for the evening—and went barefoot and wore a sort of raggedy undress otherwise—Christmas, as an example, would find her in a red and green muumuu like a psychedelic circus tent, her huge tortoiseshell comb the anchor for glass balls, little Christmas trees and homemade cookie ornaments. There were times she seemed more apparition than woman, sailing into the dining room, glittering with ornaments, a rooster on her shoulder and a fawn by her side, bestowing kisses and curses as she paraded by. Kissed or cursed, most customers loved the show—even if they might have one apprehensive eye on any creatures clambering over their heads and dinnerplates.

Dick Musson had pulled up stakes and moved to Portland, from which damp clime he kept in touch with his not-quite-ex-wife. He always stopped to visit when he was in California, the two of them enjoying their frequent brief honeymoons considerably more than they had their marriage. Without Toots outside the door, romance blossomed.

Juanita also kept in constant contact with her mother, Louise, who had at last married Joe Chancellor, owner of a bar in Tulsa. Joe had been married five times previously, but he had always returned to Louise when he found himself again in a bachelor state. Juanita had been fond of him for years, not only because of his financial generosity to her as a young girl, but for his kindness to her mother who had finally accepted him on his sixth proposal of marriage. Juanita flew to Tulsa to be on hand for the nuptials and was delighted by her mother's happiness.

Oklahoma was then a dry state and it was necessary to bring one's own bottle into a bar and then pay for a setup of glass and ice. Visiting a bar in downtown Tulsa, Juanita pulled her money out of her bra to pay the bartender and then nonchalantly tucked the remainder back inside. Unaware that she was being watched by none other than the town hood, she threw back a couple of Scotches and then paid a call to the ladies' room. "Give me your money," the hood demanded as she left the bathroom and, pulling a gun out of his pocket, levelled it point blank at the only two suckers Juanita trusted. "Well," she replied, "you'll play with hell tryin' to get it!" "I know where you keep it," he said by way of encouragement, "and if you don't give it to me I'll blow your tits off." Persuaded, Juanita handed over the cash. With that, he pistol-whipped her until, as she said, she was "bleedin' like a stuck hog."

With the cool contempt of his kind, the hood went back into the bar, perhaps figuring that the incident was over and the uppity female effectively muzzled. As most of Juanita's customers could have told him, she did not shut up so easily. Marching into the bar, she walked right up to the hood – who sneered – and kicked him in the balls. "This asshole stole all my money!" she shouted, then turned and tried to kick him again.

Intimidated by the thug's evil reputation, nobody called the police until he had clunked Juanita on the head with the butt of his gun and sent her staggering backward, her face covered in blood. Though Tulsa police caught him, they somehow figured Juanita was at least half to blame and let both of them go with a warning.

"I never got my money back," Juanita explained, "but I did get a hell of a lot of satisfaction kickin' him in the nuts. Gave him a little somethin' to remember me by. Mother was afraid that Joe would go gunnin' for the guy and that I should hightail it outta town, so I did. I went on up to Portland to see Dick, but when he took one look at me, he wanted to beat the crap outta that cheap little hood, too. I wasn't comfortable riskin' all these men's lives, so I went on back home. Joe was hurt that I hadn't said goodbye, though."

After her return to El Verano, it was to another sort of scuffle, one involving a Hollywood columnist who had visited the Galley and then written, among other things, that it was "a cross between an Army barracks and a 'Send your kids to Camp' project." According to Juanita, Fil Perell – known to his readers as "Flip" – cooked up the idea of inviting her down for a battle of the banquets, perhaps as a diplomatic precaution against open warfare.

Juanita, Lee Rae Mullins and another waitress were all invited to stay at Flip's house. What the columnist did not realize was that Juanita was also bringing Chickenshit. Preparations for the journey included new clothes from Frederick's of Hollywood for the women and a pedicure for Chickenshit. Lee Rae not only painted his toenails an attractive shade of red but glued rhinestones on his comb, giving him an air both rakish and regal. Though he was forced to travel incognito in a large wicker handbag while on board the plane, the rest of the journey was made with him perched prettily on Juanita's shoulder.

"TERROR OF EL VERANO INVADES LOS ANGELES!" screamed Flip's headline when Juanita and her entourage hit town. "Juanita…well-known restaurateur from the north, armed with her trusty muumuus and accompanied by an army of THREE, stormed into our beautiful city of the Angeles, all fire and brimstone, seeking revenge for one of my past columns that was somewhat critical of the north." Though it was more sizzle than sirloin, both Flip and Juanita made the most of the media event. What Mr. Perell thought upon making the discovery that his houseguests included a rooster he did not confess in his column, only that the morning after their much-heralded arrival, he was awakened before dawn by Chickenshit crowing in his bathtub. They all attended several parties and ate at a number of L.A.'s most elegant eateries, including the Black Forest Restaurant where Juanita spotted Ray Charles at a nearby table. She waltzed over and placed the rooster in Charles' lap. "I used to say after that that Ray Charles felt my cock," Juanita explained. "While we were there, Chickenshit crowed and a guy at the bar said, 'I think I need another drink—I just heard a rooster crow.'"

Chickenshit behaved admirably throughout. At first, the columnist was somewhat distressed over the rooster's liberal decorating ideas, but when Juanita reassured him that "it's only chickenshit, after all, and nothin' to get all worked up over," apparently Flip threw in the towel – in more ways than one.

One night the women met up with some attractive men who invited them to go on down the coast to a place called the Oarhouse. They all piled in a car and headed down the freeway at 85 miles an hour. When Lee Rae mentioned nervously that they were going pretty fast and might get pulled over, the men all laughed and told her not to worry about it. At the end of a raucous evening, the men presented their business cards: all were with the Los Angeles Police Department, and one claimed to be Chief of Police. "I didn't have any tickets needed fixin', so it didn't do me any good," Juanita lamented, "but he was a nice guy, anyway."

On the way back from the San Francisco Airport, Juanita recalled, "I decided it would be a good idea to go up to the top of the Mark Hopkins, since Rae had never been up there. I especially wanted to cheer her up because even though she'd had a real good time, she was disappointed that she hadn't been able to speak to Ray Charles. See, she was such a fan that she got stagestruck, and so there was this guy who was blind bein' introduced to someone who could only make these choking noises. She got his autograph, but she was feelin' kinda disappointed in herself. So I thought drinks would be nice.

"We ordered dinner and then this waiter came up with a big silver platter with a dome on it and when he lifted up the dome it was full of little hot, steaming washcloths. When the guy offered me one

I said, 'Do you really expect me to pick up this fuckin' hot boilin' fuckin' towel?' Chickenshit woke up right then and started scramblin' around inside his basket and makin' little crowing noises. People were startin' to look over at us and so I said to the guy, a little quieter, 'Well, asshole, you can't expect people to burn their fuckin' fingers on these fuckin' towels, do you?' Tryin' to say it real nice because people were really startin' to look at us then."

Impervious to the tsk-tsks and arched eyebrows, Juanita requested that the platter of little hot towels be removed before, as she said, " I do somethin' you and I *both* are gonna regret." The women were served with a dispatch uncustomary in so swank an establishment and then, with Chickenshit on Juanita's shoulder, they flounced out.

On the heels of their triumph in the south, Juanita was asked to be a guest on the Gypsy Rose Lee talk show. This charming and good-natured program ran daily between 1966 and 1968 and though it was filmed in San Francisco, it was nationally syndicated. The striptease artist-turned-television-personality rode herd on an eclectic group of the known and unknown who would discuss a variety of subjects including cooking, clothing styles, kitchen gadgets, unusual inventions and the homelier aspects of each other's lives. According to Gypsy's son, Eric Preminger , the show usually featured some kind of product demonstration conducted rather haphazardly as the program progressed. "Once my mother had Woody Allen on the show with some other people, and she demonstrated camping equipment. I also remember one time Shelley Berman was a guest. Mother demonstrated an inflatable life raft. Shelley got into the boat with her and recited poetry. Another time she showed guests what she was sending me in Vietnam where I was stationed. There were a pair of leopard bikini pants, as I remember. The show was usually outrageous and typical of my mother."

Juanita warned the show's producer that she was sure she would get stage fright; he assured her that she would do just fine. "Well, I'll bring my cock," she told him, "just so I'll have somethin' to hold onto."

When she arrived at the studio, Gypsy was running around backstage in her slip and brassiere, chattering away to her guests. "I was kinda surprised that was all she was wearin'," Juanita admitted, "but since she'd been a stripper, I guess she was just more comfortable the less she wore."

Ensconced in her dressing room, with Chickenshit perched on her dressing table, Juanita was made up while Gypsy ran breathlessly in and out. Juanita remembered that it was a cozy atmosphere, much like a girl's dormitory, with whispers and laughter and experimenting with each other's lipsticks. The same good-natured bonhomie continued on the set, where everyone took their places before a live audience. When Gypsy introduced her guests she did not omit mentioning Chickenshit, whom she rechristened, "Mr. C.S. Smith". The first time, Joan Rivers was also on the show, but it was Mr. Smith who stole it right out from under the nearly-famous, wisecracking blonde. "I was so proud of him," Juanita said. "He didn't crap once on the set – not even during commercials."

Her second time on Gypsy's show, the subject was the jewelry grieving Victorians made from the hair of the dearly departed. Though it seems a remarkable coincidence, Juanita insisted that she "just happened" to be wearing a hair ring Sally Stanford had given her. While Chickenshit Smith strolled amiably up and down the back of the studio couch, the women discussed the guest collector's large assortment of hair rings, hair lockets, hair watch fobs and—which seems almost too much of a good thing—ornaments made of hair to be worn *in* the hair. Juanita's ring got a thumbs-up, too.

The third and last show Juanita graced was made memorable by the guest whose talent consisted of—and was apparently limited to— the balancing of martini glasses on her breasts as on a tray. With a sniff and perhaps a little professional jealousy, Juanita commented, "She didn't have what *I* had. Just real good uplift, is all."

Juanita brought to the show a gift she had found for Gypsy at a garage sale. It was a shopping cart she thought might be useful for Gypsy to drag along on her frequent travels. "I told her that since she had to drag so much crap on and off planes, it was just the ticket for her. She thought the world of it, too, and kept retracting the little wheels right there on stage."

Though Juanita was asked to appear on other television shows, she generally gave them a miss. "I had a hell of a lotta cookin' to do, honey. I didn't have time for all that bullshit."

As for Chickenshit Smith, he appeared to have enjoyed his

Warholesque fifteen minutes of fame. His appearances on Gypsy's show were to be, in terms of immortality, his swan song. Although most animals arrived at Juanita's and never left, some travelled sadly in the "reverse English" direction. Just as Wattles had disappeared that Christmas Day disguised as a muff, so did poor Chickenshit Smith make his exit under mysterious circumstances. One day he was on his perch outside the kitchen door of the Galley, and the next day he was gone. Heartbroken, Juanita drove up and down the streets looking for him. "I thought maybe somebody had gotten drunk and kidnapped him, then flung him outta the car somewhere. But we never found him. The word got out that someone had stolen my cock, and we even put up a sign telling that there was a reward for returnin' Chickenshit to me, but he was gone. After that I had more roosters, and I named them all Chickenshit, one after another, until I got one I named Sir Cock, just for a change."

The next Mr. Smith came to a bad end when he was run over by a car. An off-duty policeman remembered the scene.

"Juanita was out in the road, drunk as hell and clutching the rooster by the neck. Every car that went by, she'd stagger after it, waving the rooster in the air and screaming, 'The last of the Mohicans, you son-of-a-bitch!' She was mad as hell and would kick at the cars, too, as they slowed down. If one of them had made the mistake of stopping, I think she would've decked the guy."

In return for Juanita's visit, Louise came West to view her daughter's new domain. She was pleased with the sylvan setting and proud that her daughter was doing so well. Saturdays and Sundays the place was packed, S.R.O., everybody waiting in the bar so long before being seated that by the time their names were called some were too loaded to remember who they were. Money poured in and money poured out. Usually Juanita gauged how well the Galley was doing by the size of the roll of bills in her brassiere.

Unlike many captains of industry, however, Juanita let her personal life slop over into her professional life, insuring a steady supply of catastrophes. A brawl erupted, under somewhat hazy circumstances, ending with one of the participants hurling a large rock through the window of the cabin where Louise was staying. It struck Louise's favorite chair—although she was not sitting in it at the time—and at the very thought that her mother might have been injured, Juanita exploded. A police officer arrived on the scene to find her beside herself with fury. Marching up to him, she said, "You better take me to jail right now, because if you leave me here I'm gonna kill that son-of-a-bitch!" Since Juanita was guilty of disturbing the peace, the officer was probably going to make the suggestion himself, but he must have been relieved to find the Terror of El Verano going along so willingly. "I sure didn't want to go to jail for murder," she explained, "even though it would've given me a hell of a lotta satisfaction to throttle that bastard!"

On another occasion, she gave a hand to the police by capturing a burglar. An employee saw a man leaving a cabin that did not happen to be his own, with a purse that did not happen to be his, either, and ran to tell Juanita. Hitching up her muumuu, she took off, chasing the man across a field to a fence which she scrambled over as swiftly as he had vaulted it. If he looked back, he must have been unsettled by the sight of a three-hundred-pound woman in a muumuu thundering along behind and gaining on him. When she caught him, she threw him to the ground and sat – hard – on his chest. Until the police arrived, she remained where she was, yanking at the hair in his armpits whenever he struggled to get loose. "I'll sue you!" he cried, to which Juanita calmly responded, "But I'll squash you first."

Deliverymen sometimes found themselves thrown into a fray. A driver delivering the week's meat order placed the boxes of steak on the floor in front of the freezer because it wasn't in his union contract actually to put the meat into the freezer. This was what he always did. However, on this particular morning, he made the mistake of piling the boxes so close to the freezer door that Juanita couldn't open it. So she did the only reasonable thing: she began hurling the boxes after the man as he beat a hasty retreat to his truck. The boxes broke and so, without missing stride, she scooped up the steaks and kept on running, throwing the meat into the cab of the truck and all over the seats, broadsiding the driver with a T-bone to the jaw.

As the deliveryman desperately threw his truck into gear and started to drive off, Juanita ran around to the front of the vehicle, threw herself onto the hood and held on gamely to the hood ornament until she fell off into the road. The driver, still stunned by this unexpected turn of events, slammed on the brakes and—probably with an interesting mixture of hope and foreboding—found

Juanita underneath the truck with the wind knocked out of her. Amiably, her anger spent, she crawled out and requested a ride to the hospital where she found she had fractured nothing but her dignity. It is not known how the driver fared, but it is possible that the early application of steak to the injured area soothed the bruises resulting from its impact.

Perhaps it should come as no surprise that a rumor circulated in the late Sixties that Juanita had died in her sleep. A friend called to inform her that she was on the grapevine's casualty list. The news made Juanita laugh. "Honey," she said, "when I go it won't be from natural causes!" Which was, of course, exactly what her friends feared. If there were many who loved Juanita, there were also a few who would not have braked for her any more than had the driver who encountered the second Chickenshit Smith. She was far too cantankerous not to have enemies.

Sears Point Raceway hired Juanita to cater the racetrack's Grand Opening. They also invited her to be their Queen for the Day, an honor she graciously accepted. On the day of the event she appeared in a green satin muumuu with black velvet trim, a thin black stole wrapped around her arms "like the racetrack" down to her wrists. Soon after, she catered an al fresco luncheon for the owners of the Buena Vista Vineyards. Antonia Bartholomew, wife of Frank Bartholomew, Bureau Chief of United Press International, said that she simply had been appalled when Juanita showed up with vans and pickup trucks loaded with her catering paraphernalia. Sears Raceway was one thing – the beautiful, historical gardens of the Bartholomews entirely another, at least for Antonia, if not for Frank, who was amused. "I never saw anything like it in my life," she said, shuddering with distaste. "We naturally did not ask her back."

Juanita recollected that red-letter day with an altogether different feeling.

"It was this big deal at Buena Vista, and not only did we have plenty of food, but also plenty of ice since it was summer and so damned hot. We had to keep everything covered to protect it from wasps and flies. I'd brought along my big, claw-footed bathtub and filled it full of ice to keep the champagne in. I put the wine in another big tub that had a lid and looked like a coffin. I also had a bunch of little bathtubs that bathtub salesmen used to carry around with them to show farmers, just like the big ones only a lot smaller, and these had lids, too. They made dandy bowls for salads. Since it was a fancy party, I also took my Sheraton along – which I only did at the swankier places. It looked like a pretty, inlaid box, but when you opened it up it was a potty chair. The potty part was real nice for potato salad. I had nice antique urinals for the beans and macaroni."

What did people say when they saw such unusual crockery?

"People had a real great time," Juanita explained, "but I wasn't asked back, so maybe the Bartholomews didn't appreciate having their ritzy guests eating out of urinals and little bathtubs. I don't know why they would've minded though, really. I never used a real toilet. I drew the line."

If she had been a flop at Buena Vista, she was a wild success at Sears Point Raceway and a smash hit at a morticians' convention where she celebrated her own party theme of "after death comes life" by filling her coffin-shaped bathtub full of freshly-hatched chicks. Whenever Juanita was doing the catering, the event was sure to cause talk.

With everything going along so smoothly – and lucratively – it was perhaps inevitable that catastrophe would strike again. One afternoon a repairman came to fix a malfunctioning stove. A part was needed, so he told Juanita he would be back to finish the job the following day. When he returned on the morning of March 26, 1969, it was to find the stove – and the kitchen and dining room surrounding it – all gone. And that morning the rumors budded and blossomed that Juanita, herself, had held the torch.

"Terrible Juanita in Tears"
– *San Francisco Chronicle*

"Hughie was gettin' dressed that morning," Juanita remembered, "and he looked out and saw the fire and came runnin' for me, dressed only in his pajama top. 'Juanita! Juanita! The kitchen's on fire!' he yelled, poundin' on my door. I got up and threw somethin' on and called the Fire Department. Turned out I might as well not have called them at all since all they did was put water on the barn. I told them to water down the stuff in the dining room so we could get it out, but they wouldn't do it and it all just went up in flames. As it turned out, the broken stove had leaked gas all night and the pilot light in my other stove exploded. Once that got goin', all the kerosene lamps I had in the dining room went up like fuckin' fireworks."

The kitchen and the huge dining room were gone. Only the bar, the little hotel and the cabins were left, ringing the huge blackened area like spectators at the scene of a disaster. Juanita was found that morning by employees, barefoot and weeping, in the road. According to Juanita, her insurance agent had neglected to pay her fire insurance premium that month. She was wiped out. Comforted by friends and animals, only several of whom had been singed, she tried to make the best of the catastrophe.

Sears Point Raceway sent men over to help clean up the mess, partly because Juanita was so well-liked and partly because the owners of Sears Point had previously arranged for her to cater a sit-down dinner for three hundred that Saturday night and a tailgate party the next morning. "I was sure glad to have all that to take my mind off the fire," Juanita said, "I had so much to do to get ready that I didn't have time to feel sorry for myself." She rented the cavernous kitchen of Sonoma's Veterans' Memorial Building and delivered the food to be served. The chaos was, as always, a tonic to her.

Three days after the fire her mysterious benefactor, John Stinnet, walked into the bar and pressed a thousand dollars into her hand. "Why do you want to help me?" she asked him, nonetheless tucking away the cash. "Because I want to," he replied. Again she wondered why a man she barely knew would be so interested in her welfare and so eager to help her out. "He didn't even seem to want to take it out in trade," she said, "so I made sure that at least he got a real good dinner."

Her first plan after the fire was to restore what had been destroyed. Sally Stanford complicated matters by publicly announcing that she was going to help her old pal rebuild, and then, according to Juanita, changing her mind. Unfortunately, a lot of people who might have been inclined to lend a hand thought that if Sally was to bankroll the construction, then Juanita wouldn't be needing the contents of anyone else's piggy bank. There were also a few creditors who thought it a good time to collect outstanding bills, perhaps fearing that Juanita, herself, might soon go up in smoke. All of this severely reduced the savings account in Juanita's brassiere.

Gamely, Juanita plowed on ahead, ferrying foodstuffs to the Veterans' Memorial Building and then carting the prime ribs and casseroles back to El Verano, where she had set up a temporary restaurant in the bar and in a small building that had once been a dancehall. This culinary shuttle continued for two months. Business was good, though the service – with reason this time – was much, much worse. People waited at the rickety little tables in the seedy old dancehall for what must have seemed eternity. A handpainted sign out front read, "We may look terrible, but we're here," and "If you think *you* look bad, just wait until you see Juanita!" Clearly, life could not go on like this much longer.

Micki Smircich, Retired Real Estate Agent

I owned a business and sold real estate in those days and, in 1964, I had a place for rent in El Verano. I received a phone call one day from this lady interested in taking a look at the house. She told me her name was Juanita, but the name didn't mean anything to me. We made an appointment for her to come up and see the house. I got there a little early and so I was waiting on the front porch when this big black car drove up. A heavy-set woman wearing jeans and a man's shirt got out and came up the walk and I thought to myself, "Oh, dear." Right away she started telling me all about herself: about her old ferryboat in Sausalito and her drinking and arrest record and everything. Now, my circle of friends had never contained anyone remotely like this woman and I had rarely heard language like hers, and for awhile I thought I was going to drop right through the porch floor! My husband had been a Mason, and I was a past Worthy Matron of Eastern Star and past state officer of Rainbow Girls and past president of the Sisters of Hiram and of the Grange. I mean, we couldn't have been more different. But I showed her the house and she liked it and wanted to rent it and in spite of her language and so on, there was something about her I took a liking to. I ended up taking her for a ride all over the Valley, showing her everything and having a wonderful time. Next thing I heard, she'd bought the old

Verdier's resort nearby and had opened a restaurant.

I decided to retire about the same time Juanita was having trouble with her employees, basically because she hired so many young people who were sometimes not as responsible as they might have been. I started doing a little payroll and bookkeeping work for her and, with one thing and another, after awhile I started hostessing for her on weekend nights. I got so busy that I had to stop all of my extracurricular real estate work, too, and I started working full time for her. I'd do a little bit of everything. When waitresses didn't show up, I'd wait on tables. I'd make salads, seat customers, make change, everything. My husband had died and though I still had a young daughter to raise, my life had become pretty quiet. Suddenly my whole life seemed to center around this woman. I became part of her three ring circus. People would say, "You don't work for *Juanita* do you?" Like they just couldn't believe that I would. But from that first day we met on the steps of that old house, there was just something about her – a *trueness*. It's very hard to find people like that in this world, and when you do, you can't help but want to be around them.

It was very entertaining working for her – wild things went on all the time. Because of her casual attitude about money she kept most of it in her "bank," which was down the front of her muumuu. She'd put it in other places – like the commode – when there *was* any. I had to try to keep up with all of the money she would pay her creditors directly out of her brassiere. She'd give me money to put in her checking account, but sometimes a check of mine would bounce because she'd taken the money out again. Sometimes she'd spend all the money she had on antiques.

Sometimes people complain that she didn't pay her employees, but that wasn't true. Some paid *themselves*. A lot of money never made it as far as the cash register. Also, she hired a lot of young people because she liked them so much, but they were always asking for draws on their paychecks and when it was payday they'd be upset not to get a paycheck because of all the draws they'd taken. I used to spend a lot of time going before the Labor Commission because some kid thought Juanita had cheated him. We always won.

She had an enormous turnover of employees at her place, either because they couldn't take *her* or she couldn't take *them*. One year I had over 300 W-II forms to fill out, and she'd never have more than

25 people working for her at one time. A lot of kids would come in and work for two weeks—some couldn't work longer than two *hours* —and they'd hightail it out of there. People would come in off the street and say, "Can I help?" and she'd say, "Sure, put on an apron!" It was chaos.

We were jammed all the time which made things even more confusing. We gave the waitresses order books, to create some semblance of order, but they'd use half of one, or half of someone else's, and it was impossible to keep things straight. Juanita refused to use anything but the best ingredients and then you'd see some young girl put a tray of English muffins in the oven, forget about them, and then pull them out when they were black. Juanita used only real butter and vegetable salt and the finest meat. She'd serve a whole rib, so much meat that it would be hanging over the sides of the platter. So few people could eat that much that we were spending a fortune on aluminum foil to send people home with all they had left over. Juanita would take the time to wrap it up, herself, in the shape of a swan or a chicken. I couldn't stand to see this, so a waitress and I decided, one afternoon when Juanita was sleeping, to cut the portions in half so we could finally make some money. We thought we'd get away with it, too, but we didn't. Juanita found out and gave us such hell that we never dared do it again!

I have so many memories about all of the good things Juanita did. She'd pick up kids from the side of the road and bring them back to the restaurant to feed. Kids would run away from home to Juanita's all the time, and when she'd run out of room to put them up, she'd rent motel rooms for them.

They loved her at the local thrift shop because she was always buying clothes and household goods for people. For years she received letters from all over from people saying that if it hadn't been for her helping them along the way, they wouldn't be where they were today. One runaway had actually become a minister. So whenever I hear somebody say something negative about Juanita, I really resent it. The outrageous lies are terrible and hard to forgive. You know, when her hotel in Fetter's burned down, she was offered help by a local charity she had helped so much, but she wouldn't take anything. She told them, "Give it to people who really need it." This was after she lost everything she owned.

I started working for Juanita when I was ten years old, just after my mother started working as her bookkeeper. I worked summers and weekends, whenever Mom was there, too. I'd clean the pool and the grounds and cabins, pick up garbage, and then when I was older I "graduated" into the kitchen and could make salads and so on. I peeled thousands of potatoes for her potato salad and bussed what seems now like thousands of tables.

Juanita treated me from the beginning as if I were her daughter and as if she were more like a second mother to me than my employer. I think she was more or less like that with all the kids who worked for her. If she saw some kid doing something she didn't like, she'd say, "Look here, you little brat, stop that!" She didn't care whose kid you really were, you were still *her* kid and she cared if you were up to something you shouldn't have been. Once she found out that I'd been smoking out behind the swimming pool and she sat me down and gave me a lecture and told me that if I went straight home and told my mother, *she* wouldn't tell her. I was scared to death, but I did it. Actually I don't think she loved me more than any of the other kids – but I always felt she did. Maybe everybody else felt the same way, that they were special to her. When there were good, loving moments, you knew without doubt how she felt about you. But then, five minutes later, she could be screaming bloody murder at you. So you had to learn to let it bounce off, knowing it would last only a minute and then be all over.

Of course, in the beginning, a lot of the things she did and said bothered me because I was very sensitive and not very assertive. At first I couldn't understand why people kept coming back, the way she treated them sometimes. But after awhile I learned that a lot of it was just show. Until I understood that, though, I was petrified of her. There were a lot of times I'd leave in tears, vowing to myself that I would never go back, but that was usually because I'd taken something personally that really wasn't meant to be personal. There were a lot of times when I felt "I hate this woman! Why does she do things like this to me?" still knowing inside that she did have a heart of gold and that she really cared for me. She'd yell at my mother too, sometimes, but my mother would just yell right back so she didn't do it to her as often. Most other people would kind of cower or shut up and take it, but my mother wouldn't. After work, we'd go home and talk it over, the good things and the bad things, and usually there were more good things to be happy about than bad things to feel sorry about.

It was often funny and exciting to be around her. One time I was hanging around with a bunch of older teenagers near the restaurant. They were getting a little rowdy, so Juanita came out and yelled at them to go away. Then she saw me. "You get your butt over here right now!" she yelled at me, "You know you're known by the company you keep!" Juanita and I were standing by the old wishing well when the teenagers came back in their car, and as they went past they mooned her through the car windows. I'd never seen another person's bare butt before and at first I didn't know what I was looking at! Juanita was incensed and ran after them, shaking her fist and yelling, and I still didn't understand what it had meant.

These were the Sixties, during the Vietnam War, and there were a lot of hippies around. There were times when I'd be working around the cabins and smell marijuana, although nobody would dare to smoke dope in front of Juanita – she was death on drugs. She hired a lot of these kids, got a lot of kids out of trouble, too, and I guess all of them probably felt what I did about her. I mean, if you stayed long enough, you knew who she was. If you didn't stay that long, you shouldn't have been there in the first place. Kids would be sitting around in the dining room, watching the action, and they'd think how much fun it would be to work for her. They'd ask her for a job and she'd say, "Sure, get off your butt and do something." A lot of them would work one or two hours, listening to her go on and on, and, boy, the next thing you knew, they'd be gone!

She wanted to instill in all of us kids that if something was to be done, it might as well be done right. She could have have hired mature people who would have known already what to do, but she seemed to prefer giving kids a chance to learn. And in spite of her noisy teaching methods, kids would come from all over to work for her in the summer. About half the kids she'd hire were honest, and the other half weren't and they stole from her. I never would've had the urge or the nerve to steal from her myself, but it was easy to do. The temptation was there. She'd send one of us into her room to look for something she wasn't too clear about in the first place, and whatever you'd finally figure out she wanted and took to her would invariably be the wrong thing and she'd start screaming, "That's not the one I wanted, you asshole!" Kids would go in and take things right and left and she'd see them do it – at least that's my opinion – but she'd just let it go. In situations where big things were stolen, she'd let the person know that she knew about it, but that's all she'd do. On the other hand, when customers would walk out on bills, which they did all the time, Juanita would go running after them, chase them down the road, yelling all the way. Most of the time she caught them and got her money from them, too. But she wasn't that way with employees, some of whom would even throw whole prime ribs out the window and then take them home later when they got off work.

She always told us that there was a "right way, a wrong way and Juanita's way," and we had to do it "Juanita's way," or else. If a customer took a scoop out of the potato salad, you had to be right there to replace it, and God help you if you put new salad on top of the old salad, because everything had to be fresh – or else. She'd never tell you about things like this up front, she'd let you learn your lesson the hard way. And she wouldn't just tell you the right way quietly, but she'd grab up the bowl of salad, or whatever, and drag you back into the kitchen, yelling all the way, and you would learn very fast what you'd done wrong, how it was to be done right, and why. And you never, ever forgot. She was this way with everybody. She'd have customers folding napkins or clearing tables, and they'd better do it right, too. Anybody sitting around would usually be told to split muffins, and God help you if you did it with a knife! Forking muffins was a ritual and she was a stickler about it whether or not you worked for her or were a customer she'd pressed into service. She worked hard too, don't forget. Sometimes she didn't take the time to change into a fresh muumuu, and when the one she was wearing would get dirty, she'd just throw a clean one on over it. I remember her wearing five or six muumuus around the restaurant – by the end of the day she'd look like she was wearing her whole wardrobe.

Juanita had a profound impact on my life. Among other things, I learned how to accept people for who they are, not what they are. Not to judge them by the outside, but for their beauty inside. I grew to love her very much.

In 1964, shortly after Juanita had moved to town, I went to work for her in El Verano, doing yardwork. I was fifteen at the time and had been raised as a good Catholic boy in a strict home and had never heard my folks say anything stronger than "darn" or "blame," as in "Put that blamed thing down."

The first three weeks I worked for her I'd hear a lot of commotion coming from the kitchen area, which I learned early to steer clear of. But one day Juanita came out in the yard and said, "Come on in, I'm going to give you a new job," and she put me to work in the kitchen; right smack in the middle of all the commotion. I was a little intimidated, but since I was used to helping my mother in her kitchen, the work wasn't all that new to me. There was just more of it and it had to be done faster. After working for Juanita a little while you could take six dozen raw eggs and have them hardboiled, stuffed and out on the buffet in about ten minutes. Or else. Put it this way: she maybe trained you rough, but she trained you right!

Shortly after I'd been promoted, Easter Sunday rolled around. A traditionally busy day for restaurants, it was always extra busy at Juanita's. Easter morning there were hoards of people just having come from church, dressed in their Easter best, crowded around outside the open kitchen door, which was the entrance to the dining room. Juanita's usual dishwasher was a big guy by the name of Hughie who wore bib overalls and talked in a slow, gruff kind of drawl. I guess he'd had a drinking problem and mainly stayed away from liquor, but the night before he had evidently snagged himself a gallon of wine and had polished it off. He was trying to do dishes, but as he was pretty hammered, he kept dropping whole stacks of plates and platters. Pots and pans were falling all around him on the floor. It was a major catastrophe.

I was working in the kitchen, forking muffins, and starting to get really nervous about the havoc Hughie was creating. People were standing around, taking all this in, when Juanita blows in from the dining room. She saw what Hughie was doing, and grabs up the empty wine bottle and shrieks, "Hughie, you asshole! You're drunk again!"

At this, all of the little old ladies start to look kinda faint and the mommies are clapping their hands over their kids' ears and beginning to look like maybe breakfast isn't such a good idea after all. Hughie stuck his thumbs in the front of his overalls and said, "Well, I might be an asshole, but at least I'm not a lousy cocksucker like you!"

I was so scared by this time that I abandoned the muffins and went to hide in the walk-in cupboard, but not before I saw people trying to tiptoe backwards and out of Juanita's line of fire. She grabbed Hughie and threw him bodily out the kitchen door, which caused even more of a ruckus because we'd been saving tin cans for a local nursery and they were piled neatly in a huge stack outside – they were, that is, until Hughie fell backwards into them. Then, in front of that hushed and fascinated crowd, Juanita put her hands on her hips and shouted, "Did you hear what that nasty shit called me? He called me a lousy cocksucker! I'll have you know I was a pretty good one in my day!"

I had never heard anything like that in my life; neither before nor since, although some other pretty strange things happened afterwards.

One day a couple decided they didn't want to wait any longer for the food they'd ordered and left the restaurant. Right on their heels I saw Juanita running out with a frypan to their car, knocked on their window, and when the guy rolled it down she dumped the eggs and bacon in his lap.

It was well known that Juanita was often a little late paying her bills. I mean, she always paid you, but she didn't always pay you *on time*. It got to be where the driver of one of her purveyors would come in and refuse to deliver her order until she paid the bill in advance. Once I saw this guy drive up with an order of meat. He came on into the restaurant and demanded payment. Juanita took me aside and told me to unload the truck while she kept the driver busy. All sweetness and light, she said to him, "Well, come on in, honey, and have a cup of coffee." Which he did, being none the wiser.

I went and unloaded the truck and put the meat in another room. When Juanita saw me coming back, she said to the guy, "Well, the hell with it. I'm not goin' to pay you any money so you might as well get the hell outta here." And he drove away and didn't discover the meat was gone until his next stop.

It was all quite an education for a country boy!

In the old days, I used to go around to restaurants with my two sons and my husband and offer to sing for one hour in exchange for dinner for all four of us. I never had any refusals, and when I asked Juanita she said, "Oh, honey, sure!" but she was the only one who never asked how many of us there were.

That was the beginning of our sixteen year association. I started singing on a regular basis after that. One thing I learned very soon and that was if you could sing at Juanita's, you could sing *anywhere*. It was always noisy, chaotic – but I sure did learn to project my voice! Everybody came to her restaurants; city councilmen and mayors and movie stars and attorneys and ditch diggers and everybody else you could think of. Eddie Albert came often with his wife, and Tommy Smothers and Jonathan Winters...lots of them. But she treated them just like everyone else, no different.

One night I was tablehopping with my guitar and ran into this man who was drunk and mean and started saying terrible things to me in a loud voice, like, "Why are you singing here? You're lousy!" Somebody told Juanita, I guess, because she came storming out of the kitchen and yelled, "You're a son-of-a-bitch!" and everybody in the restaurant clapped. She returned to the kitchen and immediately came back again and yelled at him, "My lawyer says I can't call people sons-of-bitches, so I'm going to call you an asshole!"

I used to write and sing limericks, as well as ballads, and some of them were what might be considered risqué. I remember I sang a few at one table one night and as I walked away I heard one of the ladies say, "And she looks so respectable!"

The limerick I wrote for Juanita is in a book I wrote called *Bawdy and Soul*. This is how it goes:

Juanita, she has a big bust
And brassieres are never a must.
She relies on her breast
And says with great zest,
"They're the only two suckers I trust."

I went to work for Juanita when I was twenty-one and badly in need of a job to support my kids. I'd just gotten divorced and had never held a real job before, but I got educated real fast and all because Juanita believed that people could do any job if they just set their minds to it. I'd been clearing tables and prepping vegetables and so on until one day when Juanita handed me an order book and made me a waitress, just like that.

After I'd worked for Juanita a little less than a year, a girlfriend and I decided we were pretty tough shit and that we were going to L.A. and show them how it's done. Neither of us had ever been out of Sonoma before, and naive wasn't enough to describe how little we knew, but I left my kids with my Mom and with only a couple of hundred dollars we set off to make our fortunes. It ended up that we couldn't get decent-paying jobs and ran out of money and my friend's parents sent her money to return home and I finally made it back to Sonoma with about four dollars in my pocket. I picked up my kids and was feeling pretty desperate so I went to see Juanita. I told her that I didn't have a place for my kids to live, no money to buy groceries, no money to take our stuff out of storage, and that I didn't know what to do.

Juanita told me she had a place in El Verano where I could move, a little cottage. I was just delighted to have it and told her so. That same day Juanita got chairs and beds and linens and things from her motel and completely furnished the cottage. When I got there with my kids, the beds were all made up and even the refrigerator was full of food. She told me she'd found a babysitter for me so I could start working that same night.

We often filled in where we were needed in the restaurant, and so sometimes I was the hostess. It was an awful job, though, because during the day anybody could answer the phone and take down reservations, and so by the time people were lining up I'd discover that 500 people all had reservations for seven o'clock. It was a madhouse. Impossible. I'd wander around with a clipboard all night trying to figure who should be seated next and dealing with people who felt pretty strongly that they'd waited long enough. Once people were in the dining room they usually didn't want to leave – didn't want to or couldn't – and they'd tie up tables all evening.

Juanita hired me more than once, but she'd fire me pretty regularly, too. I remember once when I'd come in every day for months at five o'clock, one day I got to work and Juanita said, "Why the hell didn't you get here at four o'clock?" and I said, "But I always come to work at five," and so she yelled, "You were late today and you're late every day, and if you can't come to work on time, then you're fired!" So I went home and later on she drove up to my house and yelled out, "Why'n the hell aren't you at work?"

I learned after awhile to hide after she fired me so I could get a day off. We worked seven days a week, and about the only time anybody could get a day off was if you got fired. It got so that when she'd fire me, I'd go pick up the kids at the babysitter and then we'd get packed up and go somewhere for a day or two. When she found out that was what I was doing, she got real mad and when I'd go back to work she'd yell, "Now, Rae, you *know* I didn't mean that, and you *know* you're supposed to come to work!"

June Edelman, Former Taxi Driver

I was divorced and trying to support my two children by driving a taxi, but we were living in a motel and having trouble making both ends meet. The people at the motel told authorities my kids were being neglected and they were taken away from me and put in foster care in a nearby city. My daughter, Lindsay, was then thirteen, and my son, Patrick, was seven.

I didn't have brains enough to fight for them. You have to know the right words to fight with, and I didn't know them. I wasn't offered any kind of legal aid and I was just overwhelmed by things that seemed then to be completely beyond my control.

I had at the time a severe drinking problem, so I went to AA and started working my way back to being sober, and I got two jobs so I would be able to have the money to get my kids back again. Once you get labelled an "unfit mother" by the social services, you have to work your way back up the ladder, rung by rung. Every time I went back to see them, they always had something else I had to do, like be able to rent a three bedroom house. Now, in their foster care home the foster parents had five children of their own and five foster kids and they were not all in separate bedrooms, but it was different for me.

I had pretty much gotten my act together, but still could only manage the money for a one bedroom house when my daughter turned eighteen and came home. When she told me what had gone on while she was in foster care – the emotional hurts inflicted on them and so forth – I almost went out of my mind. I went immediately to the Catholic Social Services about my son but I didn't get anywhere.

I went to Juanita and asked if she could give Lindsay a job and she said, "Of course," and Lindsay went to work right away. The first day she told Juanita, "I wish Mom could get my brother home," and told her about some of the things she had told me about how they'd been treated. Well, Juanita didn't need to hear her talk for more than about two minutes when she got on the phone and called me to tell me that she owned a two bedroom house near her restaurant and that she would have another bedroom built on it right away for my son.

She went ahead and had some of her employees go over that very day and start to work on the house, not only building on an extra room but furnishing the whole thing from top to bottom. The whole operation didn't take more than a month and the next thing I knew, she sent people over to move us out of where we'd been living and over to the new house. I said to her, after seeing how nice it all was, "But Juanita, I don't know if I can afford it," and she said, "How much you payin' now?" and I told her and she said, "Well, that's how much you'll pay here."

Then she said, "Now get on that phone and call those people and tell them you want your kid back where he belongs!" I called them right then but they started saying something about how I first had to have a meeting in front of the referee and on and on and on so Juanita, who'd run entirely out of patience, grabbed that phone and while I can't quote her language exactly, I don't think the Catholic Social Services was ever quite the same! She said, "You will bring that child home where he belongs and I expect to find him on this doorstep one week from today, and that's that!" and she slammed down the phone.

We got a call back right away telling us we could go pick up my son and bring him home, and we did.

I felt just great when my kids were back, and all three of us worked for Juanita for awhile. Patrick was a little wary of me at first, especially since negative things had been said about me in the foster home, and things didn't all go smoothly, but it was wonderful being a family again.

My kids still have problems resulting from the past, but they're doing well now and have real good jobs. We're a close family and I love my children very much. Whenever I hear people run Juanita down I tell them never to talk that way around me. I'll never be able to repay her for all that she's done for us. Never.

Ig Vella, Former County Supervisor, C.E.O. Vella Cheese Company

I had been elected County Supervisor by the time Juanita came to El Verano. The Health Department guys were having trouble with her – she had thrown them out of her kitchen as a matter of fact – so they came to me for help since she was in my constituency. I went over to see her and said, "Come on, Juanita, you can't keep throwing people out of here, because one of these days they're going to come with a big warrant and slap you in the face with it and it won't only be *you* sobbin' and sighin', but all of these hangers-on you have here." "Okay, what do you want me to do?" she said. So I gave her a list of demands from the Health Department and she ended up complying with everything.

People have always wondered how she could get away with having all of those animals in and out of her restaurant and for some of the other stuff she would pull. Well, the answer is that when she had the wherewithal she did a hell of a lot for the indigents and the people who had fallen through the cracks in our welfare system. She had a hell of a lot more patience with them than I had as Chairman of the Welfare Department. What really bothered me was the fact that so many of these people had so little loyalty to her in return; a lack of honor that may have had something to do with where some of them were, as a matter of fact.

I never gave Juanita a hard time, although I had the authority to do so, because she was personally doing so much to help others, and if something happened to her, what would have happened to *them?* She always had half a dozen guys down on their luck chopping wood or something, and she'd stand on her back porch hollering at them, and they'd just shrug their shoulders and get on with it. I sure don't remember any of them not leaving quite a bit fatter than when they came, and she'd give them a few bucks, too. I do have to admit, however, that I was one of the people who kept the Health Department on her kitchen just to make sure nobody would ever get sick, which nobody ever did, to my knowledge.

You know, the English have always had the ability, despite all of their bureaucracy, to put up with and even turn a blind eye to the eccentrics among them, and in a small community where everybody knows everybody else, the constable knows where to find you if you step too far out of line. It was sort of like that in Sonoma in those days. Plus, if you're a judge and you see the same people day in and day out, and then you find somebody like Juanita who will take them off the streets for a month or two and free up a few cells in the county jail, you figure to yourself that you can put up with a lot of blustering because she's saving the county a lot of time and money and maybe reforming a few of these characters who wouldn't have been rehabilitated without her. From the perspective of a judge or other involved official, drunks and derelicts are a nuisance that somebody has to take care of, so we all bent the rules a little bit when we dealt with Juanita. Because the good she did was more important than the difficulties she caused with county bureaucracy. You can fall into the habit of dissecting everything, of trying to figure out the quintessence of legality, and still end up with a big fat zero – or you can be more practical than that and help to see that necessary things get done. That's what we did.

Dr. Dick Danford, Dentist

My family and I have been to most of Juanita's places, most frequently the place she had in El Verano. Our kids loved the place because it was so much fun – you never knew what was going to happen once you got there, except you were sure that there'd be some surprise of one kind or another. You could be sitting in the patio having a drink and all of a sudden a little goat would jump up on your table. Juanita had a little banty rooster that would walk right up your arm and sit on your shoulder. He was a cute little guy and she was real broken-hearted when somebody stole him. She put up a sign saying,

"Will the son-of-a-bitch who stole my cock please return him, no questions asked?"

A couple of my daughters were about to graduate from college and thought it would be fun to get together a bunch of their friends and have a graduation party at Juanita's. We had nineteen guests, including a very respectable professor and his wife. Juanita went all out. She knew I flew planes, so she'd put a big propeller in the middle of the table, and paper cap and gown figures were at each place. Because the college was U.C. Davis, she added a bunch of little plastic farm animals all over the table, too. Dinner was great, as always, and when I later went to pay the bill, I couldn't believe it! She'd charged me $35 for the whole thing.

Since my wife and I and the professor and his wife had finished dinner ahead of the kids, we went out to sit in the patio to drink our coffee. All of a sudden one of my daughters came running out and told us, "Oh, Dad, you just missed something great!"

What had happened was, there was a pretty big crowd that night and this middle-aged couple had spent a lot of time waiting in the bar and by the time they finally got a table they were pretty well sloshed and irritated with everything in general. They no sooner got seated than a waitress came up to the next table with a big platter of English muffins dripping with butter. The middle-aged woman got up and walked over to the waitress and took a couple of the muffins off her tray. Showing remarkable restraint, Juanita, who had seen her do this, called out, "Madam, if you'll just sit down and wait a minute, the waitress will be over at your table."

At that, the woman started berating her to the point that Juanita finally had had enough and hit her point blank with a stuffed egg. The husband then got up and started berating Juanita too, and his parting shot was, "You miserable old broad, why don't you go out and get laid?" She let out a bellow you could've heard for blocks and yelled, "Honey, I'd love to, if I didn't have to stick around here and take care of a bunch of assholes like *you*!"

I've known Juanita since 1965 when she opened her first restaurant in the valley. It was a great place to go in the afternoon to just drop out for awhile. For a businessman, it was perfect. For a businessman to go anywhere else in town at that time was to invite the remark,"Shouldn't you be at work?" Locals used to sneak out in the afternoons to Juanita's because of that. Nobody bothered you. Nobody you didn't want to see would see *you*, nothing you said would be repeated. It was a safe place to be yourself. In a small town there's always somebody who recognizes you, but Juanita was like a bull dog and would keep people from harassing you. If somebody ever bothered someone else, Juanita would look them right in the eye and say "That's off-limits, you son-of-a-bitch!"

At the golf course one day I got the idea of taking the new electric golf cart belonging to this bank manager over to Juanita's for a little libation. A friend of mine decided to come along for the ride although he fell off into a ditch somewhere along the way and I didn't notice he was gone until I got to Juanita's because I was more concerned about going down the road without lights than whether my friend was still in the cart. My friend showed up after awhile and we had a drink and decided maybe somebody might try to steal the golf cart *back*, so we turned it upside down. We were still in the bar when the bank manager showed up. Juanita thought it was all real funny, and we paid the bill for banging lup the cart.

A couple of friends and I decided one day that we needed a little libation, so we drove over to Juanita's and found her standing at the bottom of a telephone pole yelling up at this serviceman at the top. I asked if there was any problem and she told me that the guy was up there to disconnect her electricity because she had neglected to pay her bill and didn't have any money. I asked her how much it was and she told rne a couple hundred dollars, so I gave her the money. She yelled up at the guy,"Okay, you son-of-a-bitch, you can come down now!" I don't know what would've happened if I hadn't come by. I guess she would've just kept the guy up the pole until somebody came along. I want you to know that she repaid me a hundredfold in the years to come. I used to handle the repair of her car from time to time and there was no question of getting paid then, either. I got paid in full for everything I ever did for that lady. She'd tell me if she couldn't pay until later and if she had the money, well that wasn't much of a reach since it was just in her brassiere.

The greatest thing I ever did for Juanita – although she might not have seen it quite the same way – was at the county fair when they were auctioning off the sheep raised by the 4-H kids. You're not supposed to take the lambs, they're supposed to go straight to the slaughterhouse, but I bought a lamb in Juanita's name and took it over to her place and turned it loose in her kitchen. I'd told the Fair Board that I had Juanita's permission to purchase things for her if I wanted to, and that she would be only too happy to pay for it. She did, too. She liked stunts like that, and liked lambs.

Juanita served lots of food and good drinks. The bartender she had for awhile looked a little different because he had two sets of teeth and you'd never know what he was going to say. Juanita never allowed him or anybody else to short pour drinks, either. And if somebody had maybe one too many, she'd come up behind you and slap her two tits around your neck and sort of bang your head back and forth to shake some sense into you. She could control anybody and did it in such a way that you wouldn't feel embarrassed about coming back. Just a great 'ole gal!

Evan S. Connell, Author

I did, indeed, eat a few times at her rotting ferryboat in the mudflat, and once or twice some years later when she had a place in Sonoma. My clearest memory of her was at the Sonoma restaurant. She was lying on a bed near the entrance and simply stared at everybody who came in. It was a bit disconcerting. I had the feeling that she dimly recognized me as somebody who had been there before.

Monsignor John O'Hare, Priest

There weren't many restaurants in Sonoma where you could go and eat in the early 60's, especially if people came up from the city and needed to be entertained. Whenever anybody came, especially someone stuffy, I always took them to Juanita's because it gave me such a kick. Prissy people were afraid of her, but I always found her delightful. It was half the fun of it, to get unsuspecting folks from the big city who were expecting something genteel and ended up in that menagerie. They always looked stunned.

It was most unorthodox. If you wanted a real antiseptic meal, there were other places farther away that you could go to; Frenchified restaurants where they'd say "Monsieur" and all of that business. You'd never get a "Monsieur" out of Juanita – the language was ferocious! The food was always good and abundant. You were always assured of getting a lot, but you weren't always sure what you would get a lot of. And you were never sure what you might see while you were eating it; maybe a cat walking through the potato salad or something. There was always a floorshow and though the hygiene was sometimes a bit obscure, we all got a kick out of being there and often went by for a fizz on Sundays after Mass.

In those days I was Associate Director of Hanna Boys' Center for which Juanita had a kind of devotion. She had a great liking for the nuns and would bring the sisters Thanksgiving dinner complete with after dinner mints in an antique urinal. There was a wishing well at her El Verano place with a big sign saying that any coins thrown in would be given to the Center. I don't remember ever seeing any of the money, but I'm sure her intentions were strictly honorable.

I remember a priest who was involved in child care facilities had flown out to the Center to look over our operation. He was a very stuffy sort and I thought, "Well, I'll take him over to Juanita's," feeling that would fix *him*. When we walked in, he was in a state of shock from start to finish. Juanita was carrying on a battle with one of her dishwashers and was calling him every name in the book – not in the Good Book, either! – and then she waltzed up to us with her rooster, telling this priest that she wanted to show him "*her* cock." It was a great revenge for his having wasted three hours of my afternoon and I'm sure he went back to Chicago telling everyone about the Wild West.

Despite the antics, Juanita was always very hospitable to me and to anyone I ever brought in with me. Maybe I'm not your typical Monsignor, but I always liked her; she was so down-to-earth and with a heart as big as herself. I always felt that the toughness and noise were really a cover-up for a very soft woman. I guess my background in psychiatric social work has led me to see people not as they appear but for what they stand for.

After all, Christ probably spent more time with the publicans than he did with priests. Christ was, I think, much more fond of people who were sincere than of frauds who acted pious and went to church every Sunday. Juanita's religion, whether she knows it or not, I suspect has always been much more oriented in the direction of Christ than a lot of those people who stand up preaching on a Sunday. She's always been a cantankerous woman, but she reached out to those who were down-and-outers and people in need and maybe she beat 'em up a little bit and gave 'em one hell of a time, but she also gave them food and work and a place to stay.

A church is not the only sanctuary in the world; there are many kinds. They're just a means to an end, you know, and people find their path to God in their own way, as disgraceful as that might be for me to admit. Juanita's was always a sanctuary, too, of an odd and wonderful sort.

9

"Step To It, Folks, Juanita Has Returned"

– Independent and Gazette

I n May of 1969, an old friend of Juanita's offered an alternative to what Juanita called "havin' my tits in a wringer." Jack Coffey, a respected local attorney who specialized in criminal law, was part owner of a turn-of-the-century resort hotel in nearby Fetter's Hot Springs. It was a grand old dowager of a building that had seen much better days. Its wide verandahs spoke of rocking chairs and idle summer afternoons with croquet on the lawn and canoe parties on the creek out back. Unfortunately, the verandahs were sagging, the lawn was but a memory and the creek clogged by silt and debris. This was all to Juanita's taste, however, and she had always thought the old hotel beautiful.

Coffey escorted his prospective tenant over to see his white elephant. Though it was indeed white outside, the lobby area had been lacquered black as Egypt, including the mahogany reception desk. "I told Jack I'd take it over right away," Juanita said, "if only to strip off all that awful black paint. I asked him how much it would be and he said a thousand dollars a month, seein' as how it needed a little TLC. I said 'we got a deal' and pulled out a down payment right then and there." Actually the place needed more than TLC, especially since the kitchen had been condemned. "I had to start from scratch with that damned kitchen, same as I always had to. You'd think I'd have learned by then, but I guess learnin' wasn't in the cards."

First Juanita set up her command post—better known as her bedroom—in a room off the lobby and across the hall from the men's bathroom. Her big bed occupied most of the room and an incoming tide of knickknacks and Salvation Army finds filled up the rapidly-disappearing empty spaces. She decorated the men's room with brassieres in the ampler sizes ("They were always gettin' stolen because guys figured they were mine.") The ladies' room was furnished more decorously, its walls hung with lacy petticoats. Woodwork in the lobby was restored and the sagging verandah was once more equipped with rocking chairs.

One day she was out test-driving a rocking chair when a neighbor lady walked hurriedly by, eyes averted. Juanita called out hello. The woman, without raising her eyes, helloed back. This happened several times, with the woman practically breaking into a run, as if in flight from Sodom and Gomorrah. At last, amused and touched by the old woman's evident distress, Juanita hollered, "Now come on up here, honey, and have a cup of tea. My mother is here visiting and I'd like you to meet her." The woman came timidly up the stairs, accepted a cup of tea with trembling hands, and escaped as soon as she could.

"She told us she'd lost her husband and lived all alone," Juanita recalled, "and so the next time she tried to rush past, I asked her to come up on the porch with me again. She just got closer and closer, like a scared animal, and I just kept right on talkin' until she loosened up enough to talk back. Finally she got up the courage to ask me if I really intended to run a house of ill-repute like she'd heard. I laughed and said, 'No, honey, just a restaurant,' and she said, 'But you're Sally Stanford's friend,' and I said I sure was, but that didn't mean we was in the same business! I said, 'I know Melvin Belli, but that don't make me a lawyer!'

"The poor old thing told me she'd been misinformed, then, and had kind of figured the gossip wasn't true when she met my mother. She said she'd been sure that even a madam wouldn't have her own mother visiting in a house of ill-repute."

Juanita told her to drop in anytime, which the widow did. Lured by the prospects both of tea and the satisfaction of her curiosity, she soon was inside the door, then inside the lobby, then in the kitchen where she found "the girls" peeling potatoes and stuffing eggs. She began to bring by her needlework and ended up making blankets for Juanita and every one of the waitresses. Total capitulation came when the widow, who was Italian, mentioned that she made good lasagne. Juanita asked for instructions, and her new friend taught her how to make the dish which became one of the most popular on the salad bar. Encouraged by her lasagne's success, the widow began making mine-strone soup for the restaurant, which also turned out to be a popular addition to the menu. "We sure did keep her busy!" Juanita said. "Which was good for her because she was kinda at loose ends and real lonely. As a matter of fact, she ended up spendin' a lot of time in the Galley and only stopped comin' shortly before she died. I can't ever make lasagne without thinkin' of her."

Ever since Juanita put up a sign in front of the El Verano place informing customers of the move, business had been brisk. Though it was a far cry from the hotel's glory days, still the dining rooms glowed once more with the light of kerosene lamps and the sound of laughter echoed in the hallways and down the wide staircase from the rooms above. On the landing stood a mannequin dressed in Marlene Dietrich's dress from the movie "Summertime." Customers were welcome to wear it to dinner, if they chose. Above the first floor verandah outside, Juanita hung an eclectic assortment of flags, including those of Mexico and Israel and the state of Oklahoma. It looked like election day in Guam. As holidays came and went, the flags were joined by strings of Christmas lights, plastic leprechauns and Fourth of July bunting.

One night several young men stole the flags, but while they rested from their labors in the hotel bar, one of Juanita's employees stole them back. Nobody said a thing. Juanita chuckled, "I guess those kids must've been pretty mad when they found the flags were gone, but they couldn't hardly complain to anyone about it, could they?"

Funhouse mirrors were installed on either side of the front door. The one on the right made a customer slender, while the one on the left must have convinced a few that they had already eaten. Though the mirrors were an afterthought, they gave the entrance to Juanita's just the right funhouse touch. Inside the doors, the Galley had truly become a circus.

Ben Meyer, Cowboy

A bunch of us cowboys went to a horse auction and I decided I needed to have a little mule they had there, name of "Jazzbo." So I bought him and we loaded him up in the truck and took off, stopping to party at all the bars on the way back. We danced and raised hell, just good clean fun.

Well, we went on out to ol' Juanita's and I said, "What the hell, let's bring the mule in, too. Why should he have to stay out in the truck all day while we're havin' fun?" This seemed to make a lot of sense at the time, seein' as how we'd been havin' us a real good time and were a little bit drunk and all, so we took 'im in.

Juanita, she took one look at the mule and told the bartender, "Hey, go get that mule somethin' to eat." He asked her what, and she said, "Go get him some birdseed!"

He poured a pile of seed right in the middle of the floor where everybody was dancin'. That mule just stood there and ate his birdseed while we all went on drinkin' and raisin' hell generally. Then, when the bar closed, I thought to myself, "Now I wonder where in the goddamned hell my mule is at?"

We scoured the place, turned it upside down, and finally decided to go take a look upstairs. There was ol' Juanita lyin' in bed and she had the mule tied up to her bedpost. When I tried to take him, she sat up in bed and shouted, "Hey! Where you goin' with my mule?"

I told her he was *my* mule, but she wouldn't have any of that, so I just untied him and took him downstairs and we all went on our way.

M.F.K. Fisher, Author

The first time I ever saw Juanita was twenty years ago, sitting in the lobby of her hotel, looking like an enormous child. She was only partly-dressed and with her hair freshly washed and hanging down being brushed by two scantily-clad young blond girls who never looked up or spoke to me. They just stood there like slave girls with their eyes downcast, brushing this long, dark, Spanish-looking hair.

I often ate at her place at Fetter's Hot Springs because she was such a colorful character and not because I thought the food was so wonderful. I called it the Ptomaine Palace because of all those animals and everything.

Once I took two very nice, middle-class sort of men there and their chins just dropped. We went into her bedroom, which was just off the lobby, where she was lying in bed like a houri with a girl painting her toenails and another one brushing her hair. She had two tiny tiny marmosets in there that lived in coconut shells and they were climbing around and she had some sort of bird on her arm. "Good evening, gentlemen," she said, very regally, when I introduced them.

Once I went there with Joseph Cotten, who was a stiff and proper sort of man. Juanita met us at the door with a rooster on her shoulder and said, "My cock is bigger than yours, I bet." He died of embarrassment, he was so terribly ill at ease. I think she enjoyed doing that to famous people especially, just to see their reaction to something so outrageous.

I've known both Juanita and Sally Stanford for years, and I've always understood that she was Sally's number two girl in her brothel. Very high up, and that she ran the business side of it when Sally was away. In which case, of course, God help the business! Sally would sometimes leave for days or weeks at a time and Juanita would be in charge of the whole house. Of course she has no sense about money and never will. It isn't an affectation, either. She really doesn't.

The last time I saw her was here at the ranch when David Bouverie was having a Cinco de Mayo celebration with about twenty-five hot air balloons tethered behind his house in a pasture. It was a very nice fiesta. Unfortunately it all ended in tragedy when the captain of one of the things fell out of his little basket and the gentleman riding in it somehow managed to crash land the balloon in a vineyard. I saw him the next day in the market and I said, "Why, you were the hero of the day!" and he muttered something and then fainted dead away. We were in the soup section at the time. Soup cans crashed down around us and on top of him. Terrible noise. The store manager came running back and there the poor guy was, unconscious on the floor and covered with Campbell's Soup cans. That was sad, but it was a very nice fiesta, otherwise.

That day the rest of us were dressed in jeans and tennis shoes, but Juanita arrived all dressed in cloth of silver, like a queen. She swept in with a little gay fellow running along behind carrying her train. She was wearing a turban like a crown with an enormous feather in it. She looked simply enormous and insisted on hugging me. I found myself immediately lost in these great silver robes full of bosoms. She seemed to pick on me because I was so skinny, and every once in awhile she'd turn to me and say, "Darling!" and hug me and I'd disappear.

Meanwhile, the rest of us were rushing around serving people the picnic lunch and going up in balloons, although I wouldn't have done *that* for the *world*, and here she was, all in silver and very grand with this little fairy bustling busily about, rearranging her train for photographs, which she mainly insisted on having taken with me, for some reason. She just kept clinging to me, enveloping me in these enormous embraces of cloth and breasts.

Tommy Smothers, Comedian

The first Galley I went to was at Gate Five in Sausalito with Nick Reynolds and the Kingston Trio and my brother, Dick. We were all working at the Purple Onion and Juanita's was always open for the late night crowd. It was fun, different. When she moved farther north, I kept on going and often took my grandfather with me. He got a kick out of it. I mean, the ambience was something else and the food she served was enormous.

One night I was having dinner at her hotel in Fetter's, the most fun place of them all, and she came up behind me and put her breasts on my shoulders, on either side of my head. It was nice, like a big soft pillow. It was absurd, so far out that she'd do something like that. She did it a lot, too, and I liked it every time.

I felt great at her places, especially when she had goats and monkeys running around. She'd always invite me up to her boudoir, "Come on up, honey," and there she'd be, holding court, like something out of a movie. Bigger than life. She always had a big heart, but nobody messed with her, either – not and get away with it. She'd be yellin' at one of her employees and then turn around and loan him money. I remember her yelling at somebody once and afterwards she turned to me and whispered, "Oh honey, I love 'em, but sometimes I have to take care of 'em a little."

With hindsight, I now think of what a strong, gutsy woman she was to run those restaurants and deal with all of the different people she took in. So many of them were in transition, not quite on solid ground, and she was always the rock, the Rock of Gibraltar for them.

It felt so natural to be at Juanita's. It was refreshing. I didn't feel selected out as special because I was a Smothers Brother. *Everybody* was special to her. She was just as outgoing and dealt just as directly with everyone else. In her place, *she* was the celebrity. All eyes were on her, all the time. She was almost always an incredibly up experience, a fun experience, and a great lady. It was so impressive that she could work that hard and still take the time to give people so much joy. That couldn't have been easy. A big spirit, big spirit. Even bigger than her body was.

Mitch Luksich, Criminologist

I was dating this girl whose parents were customers of Juanita's. They were country people who owned a dairy, but their daughter had moved to the big city and was trying very hard to be sophisticated. The night I met them, her parents took us to the Fetter's Hotel for dinner, just to see our reaction, I think. I was a young guy, only 22 years old, and trying so hard to impress the parents of this girl I thought I was in love with, and all of a sudden these two huge tits flopped onto my shoulders. I remember thinking at the time how lucky it was that I'd been to the bathroom already that evening, because I sure would have gone right then. I knew my face was red and with those huge lungs pressed against my ears I couldn't hear a thing, which might have been just as well since everybody in the restaurant was pointing and laughing. She went away and then shortly afterward came waltzing back in with this rooster on her shoulder and put him on his back on a nearby table. As most country people know, if you do that with a chicken it'll lie there, but it still looked pretty impressive to all the city folk. She held up her hand and stared at the rooster like she was hypnotizing it, and everybody oohed and ahhed, and then she said, "Girls, let this be a lesson to you! If you have a pet cock and you stroke it and treat it right, it'll do anything you want." I mean, this was the sixties but she was still quite a shock. I was so embarrassed I don't remember how my girlfriend reacted – although I think she was mortified – but her parents were just rolling in the aisles. Despite all this – or because of it – by the time we left I was sold on the place and from then on was a loyal customer. As a matter of fact, I always took people there as a kind of trial by fire, like it had been for me, especially if they had some kind of stick up their ass about something. The reactions of the girls I would take there varied between them never wanting to see me again, and getting laid right after dinner in Juanita's parking lot.

Michael Millerick, Public School Administrator

I was nineteen years old and working for the brand new A&W restaurant in Sonoma as a day shift manager. It was one of the old-fashioned kind of A&Ws where customers could drive up and order their hamburgers or whatever outside at boxes that had microphones attached. It was a relay system that went either back into the kitchen on one switch or could broadcast all over the restaurant on another switch.

I was in the kitchen one day supervising the shift that was doing the cooking when this call for an order came in over the outside mike. It was Juanita and she was trying to order five hamburgers, but pretty soon she'd gotten very upset with the kid who was taking her order and when she got upset, *he* got upset and didn't know what to do. I took over the mike from him to try and straighten things out, but she'd gotten so incensed by this time that I couldn't get her order straight, either.

Juanita started yelling and because by this time I was so nervous, I made the mistake of switching on the other mike and broadcasted what she was saying into the restaurant and over the whole grounds, everywhere. So everybody heard her yell, "You can just take those hamburgers and shove them up your ass!" Then she drove away, leaving her five hamburgers on the grill.

I was scared to death that I was going to get fired, what with that going over the loudspeaker and nobody missing a single word, but I didn't. A lot of people in town remember that day – the day Juanita came to the A&W. It's a hard thing, really, to forget.

Walt Wiley, Columnist

Juanita was the kind of story I was always trying to get, rather than some meeting of an official body or an agenda item or some other sleeper. Working for a newspaper like the *Sacramento Bee,* right in the state Capitol, the biggest deal we had to cover was always, of course, state government. But I have to admit those stories were just so soporific! On the other hand, there was Juanita. I'd been working for the *Bee* for about three years when someone told me about her. I went over to Sonoma to find out what kind of story she might make, and at first when I saw all this funky old stuff she had, I started wonderin' just what sort of phony this Juanita was. Lots of places at that time were putting old artifacts on the walls in some kind of spurious attempt to be charming.

When I first laid eyes on her, she was all dressed in this mantilla and comb, gruff and bluff, a giant lady I talked to for about fourteen seconds before I knew that her restaurant reflected in a very genuine way the kind of person she was. It wasn't an attempt to be folksy or charming, like someone else might've tried to do – and failed – this was the real, genuine article. She was so engaging a person, so enlightening, and I can't think of a time after that when I'd do a story about her that another facet of her character wouldn't come out. She was a delight the first time I met her and every time after that.

Through the twenty-five years I've been in the newspaper business, I've written about lots of people, and I take pride on being able to find a story in *anybody.* But right away I knew that Juanita was a natural, one of those stories that, as they say, "writes itself." Interesting, fun, and heartwarming. The kind of story where you could sit down forty-five minutes before deadline and hit it easy with twenty inches of good copy. You almost never run into people like her, a public figure, a celebrity who still always behaved as if she were totally unaware and totally unimpressed by her fame. Other celebrities in the restaurant business today, well, it would be a real song and dance before you'd get to speak with them. Their places are the antithesis of what Juanita's was with everybody yuppying in there and oohing and aahing over a stalk of asparagus and a little slice of rabbit meat.

Juanita was, on the other hand, a gourmand. She served so much food you couldn't hardly waddle out of the place!

I saw her get mad a few times, too. Anybody she thought had it comin', she'd speak her mind and do it in such a way that it seemed just to fit in with everything else. Her snits never lasted anyway. They were kind of like dust-devils that would blow through and then, after the sound and fury were over, everything was okay.

I remember once there was a group of gays there and they were gettin' out of hand; squealing and goosing each other and runnin' around. Now Juanita was always real tolerant of anything that wasn't hurtful to someone else, but this time she had to calm these guys down a little. I don't remember exactly how it went, but the shouting started and there was a long exchange of insults involving the term "cocksucker." One of the gays said something like, "Don't think you're gonna insult *me* by calling me a cocksucker!" and Juanita came right back, real loud, kinda heated, but real funny, about her being one too, as I remember.

Now all of this happened right in front of me. It didn't matter to her at all if I was going to write about her fighting. I guess she was already so public with her behavior that maybe it didn't matter that the press would magnify the number of people who would then know about it, too. She'd do what she'd do in front of the press the same way she'd do it in front of her customers, and if some of it was an act, then she did it real well. I hate talking about her in the past tense, because as long as she's alive she'll be great copy. She doesn't need a restaurant to be a wonderful character.

Larry Linderman, Author

Friends of ours, editors at *Playboy,* came to visit my wife and I in 1972. One of them said something about Sonoma being so "cute," which annoyed me for some reason. I decided right then to take them to Juanita's. You gotta know, the place was full of birds and monkeys and bikers that would come in and hang out, and though it looked like a dangerous joint, it really wasn't. Juanita, herself, was a madwoman who could curse like a sailor and if anybody got out of line she would tell them straight out, "Don't you use that fuckin' language in here!" She'd kick out truckers without batting an eye. A real Tennessee Williams kind of character.

These friends of ours fell in love with the place. They'd never seen anything like it. I hadn't, either, and all of us had lived in *Chicago*! Four or five days later they asked me to write a restaurant review of Juanita's for *Playboy*. I never wrote things like that, but I thought, "What the hell" and did it. Even before it was published, when my wife and I went to Juanita's for dinner, she wouldn't let us pay for a thing. The second time she picked up the tab I told her, "Juanita, if that's the case, then we can't come back here again, and I really want to."

When the review came out, the effect was really extraordinary. Instead of the pickup trucks and motorcycles, there were Jags and BMWs jammed around her place, and she was completely sold out for several months. That was the first time I saw for myself how powerful *Playboy* could be. I'd written celebrity profiles of people like Muhammed Ali, Sylvester Stallone and Burt Reynolds, but I hadn't seen any immediate result before. It was great, all these expensive cars in front of such a dump. As for Juanita, she was pleased – but not really impressed or silly about it. She didn't throw out the birds or the monkeys or change her hat size or quit cussing. I think she knew all along that people like that would enjoy her place if they ever got the nerve to get out of their cars and get down and dirty. Try it out. It was fun to see it happen. Those yuppies sure didn't have any restaurants like it where *they* came from. Maybe there was nothing like Juanita's anywhere else at all. Maybe no other place like it has ever existed.

10

"Animals, Junk, Juanita and a Restaurant"

– Los Angeles Times

I f Juanita had had a menagerie before, at Fetter's it soon became a zoo. The old hotel became a sort of black hole into which all of the unwanted chickens, sheep, goats, peacocks, pigs and mules in the surrounding counties seemed to fall. Juanita found herself unable to refuse to take in any creature, no matter how serious its afflictions or nasty its temper. A poodle arrived blind and so aged that he could barely stagger from where he hunted scraps in the kitchen to where he slept the rest of the day on a loveseat in the lobby. Nice customers would reach down to pet him only to be snapped at and, on six occasions, bitten. Juanita had to post a sign on the wall above the sofa reading, "Do not pet Pierre, he is blind." Either people did not read the warning, or thought it a cruel attempt to rob the poor old poodle of much-needed caresses, for they went on attempting to pet him. "The assholes!" Juanita snorted, "They oughta have known better than to pet a blind dog. But you know, that dog could walk outside and not bump into anything, just like he had a cane. One time he'd gone out and by the time he was on his way back to the lobby, a linen truck had parked in front of the door. Pierre bumped right into it. I told the driver that from then on he was just going to have to park his truck somewhere not on Pierre's route."

Ducks, dropped from car windows and dumped from trunks, invaded the hotel grounds in droves, establishing a beachhead in the front yard fountain. Swimming round and round, quacking and crapping, they soon persuaded Juanita that it was time for a duck-pond, not, of course, because the noise or the mess might upset customers, but because baby ducks might topple over the side of the tall fountain. Minus the ducks, the fountain was afterwards transformed into a giant Easter basket tied with ribbons and filled with plastic flowers.

Once Juanita decided something needed to be built, or added to, or torn down, she wasted no time. Soon a duckpond graced the hotel's backyard and was from the beginning a wild success.

(Juanita was "grubbing around" in the pond one day and lost a sapphire ring that Sally Stanford had given her. It didn't show up until many months later when Juanita found it in a packrat's nest in her closet. "I guess a duck ate it," she explained, "and then crapped it out on the lawn, and a packrat found it and carted it off to my closet." Around Juanita, stranger things happened.)

Chickens and ducks congregated around the duckpond in convivial groups, taking time out from conversation to lay a few eggs in the bushes where they were least likely to be found. Rabbits in cages watched the action as if it were some sort of Aquacade presented daily for their express amusement. This idyll was interrupted one morning when Juanita heard an ungodly racket and raced outside to the duckpond to find her red fox, Rommel, with a Muscovy duck, petrified with fear, in his teeth.

"I knew somethin' was up when I heard the chickens tellin' me something naughty was happenin'," Juanita explained, "and here I find Rommel had escaped and was playing merry hell with my ducks. I yelled at 'im, 'What in the blue blazes are *you* doin'?' and he let the duck go and then just stood there with white feathers all over his mouth, actin' real innocent like a kid in a cookie jar. And then another day he got loose and came up to where I was sittin' on the porch with a baby Cochin chick in his mouth. He dropped it and then ran off and came back with another one, so I took off after him and found he'd got another one. I was so mad I yelled, 'I wish you were dead!' As God is my witness, he ran out in the road at that exact minute and got run over by a truck.

"I felt terrible, but there were a couple of employees near me and they just said, 'Boy, we ain't never gonna make *you* mad!' The word got out that I had this witch power to do away with people and that was when I started talkin' about 'stirrin' my brew' as a kind of teasing thing—only sometimes I wasn't teasin', what with some of the stuff that's been pulled on me. I thought about havin' that fox stuffed but I already had a couple of marmosets in the freezer and didn't have enough room."

The marmosets had come to her via the animal underground,

the purpose of which was to provide homes for animals destined for the tallow works.

"They were just so little, with tiny little hands and clever, sweet little faces. They slept all curled up in coconut shells. They used to sit on top of my closet door and watch me, just like little African men. The problem was that they liked dinner mints too well—mintaholics was what they turned out to be, and all because Everett, one of my bartenders, after he gave them their meal worms he always let them have all the dinner mints they wanted. Joe Foley thought they were comin' down with malnutrition, but they were frisky enough to have babies, all the same.

"I always thought they would be just like man and wife and didn't know you were supposed to divorce 'em when babies are born. First the father ate the babies and then the mother died. You sure wouldn't have thought he'd do a thing like that. He seemed like a real concerned kind of guy, but he died not long after, so maybe he regretted what he'd done, eatin' his family that way and all. I put the two monkeys in the freezer and one of my cooks used to bring them out and tell new employees that he was goin' to put them in the stew. He'd do that with the iguana that was in there, too, and just give everybody fits." (Before this zoological twist on the Donner Party tragedy took place, a customer had walked into Juanita's bedroom, saying, "I have to see this bedroom I've heard so much about!" Just as he said it, a large cockroach ran across Juanita's bed. She yelled, "Catch it! Catch it!" and then told the man that she raised cockroaches to feed her monkeys. "I don't remember the man's name," Juanita said of the incident, "but I'll never forget the look on his face. I think he thought I raised cockroaches right there in my bed! Whooooeee!")

After the marmosets had been mummified, five squirrel monkeys took their places on Juanita's closet door. Not nearly as shy as their predecessors, they played in the hotel lobby and swung by their tails from the big brass chandelier that had been a gift from a local undertaker and hung above the hotel's grand staircase.

With a macaw on the staircase landing and the monkeys chattering in the chandelier overhead, the old Victorian must have had quite a South Pacific atmosphere, especially with Juanita and many of her employees dressed colorfully in Hawaiian muumuus. The macaw had been taught to say "hello," as missionaries had often taught natives of those tropical climes, as well as words no missionary would ever admit to knowing. At the dinner hour one evening, a family of loyal customers arrived, bringing along Grandpa, who was visiting from the East. Right away the children traipsed upstairs, dragging Grandpa.

"Hello! Hello!" they chorused to the bird, delighted when it answered "Hello" back. "Say hello to the bird, Grandpa!" the children entreated, but the old man grumpily refused, saying that he wasn't about to talk to some "stupid bird." After the kids had pestered him long enough, however, he shrugged his shoulders and grudgingly greeted the macaw.

"Fuck off!" the bird replied. Speechless, Grandpa hauled the children downstairs to their parents. "Just what kind of place is this that you're bringing my grandchildren to?" he growled. Though the old man was persuaded to stay for dinner, it is probably safe to assume that a second visit did not occur too soon.

Though Juanita was a stickler for keeping floors clean and tablecloths white as a bride's nightgown, she let her beloved roosters do what came naturally. One of her earliest and most faithful fans was Judge Ernest Zunino. "Juanita had a rooster that she had trained to defecate in ashtrays," he recalled. "That bird would come over, hop up on your table and walk around. If he felt like doing it, he would— and God help you if you said or did anything bad to the bird, because then you had to deal with Juanita, and she was a pretty tough lady!"

A friend who shared her appreciation for birds—although he liked shooting them as much as he did collecting them—was the winemaker, August Sebastiani. He would drive his pickup truck over to the Galley wearing his trademark striped overalls, and demand that Juanita immediately accompany him to see what new pigeon or duck or dove he had added to the collection he kept in rows of cages behind his house. Many people found it difficult to say no to August, and Juanita was no exception.

"We were great friends," Juanita remembered. "Most of the time I even paid my wine bill. But when I didn't, August would tell his family and employees to come in and 'eat the bill,' as he called it. Most of the time at Fetter's we didn't carry Sebastiani wines, though, because the girl who handled the wine list told me that she didn't think too much of them and wouldn't serve them. But August was just always a great guy."

When Sebastiani died, newspapers noted that among those attending his funeral was "the zany restaurateur" Juanita. After the rites, she threw herself a private wake in honor of her lost friend. "I tried to drink all the Green Hungarian in the world," she said, "and I damn near succeeded. I ended up throwing everybody outta this bar nearby on the plaza because it was such an ugly modern place built right next to an old adobe. The cops didn't put me in the tank, though, 'cause I was in mourning."

The day that Beauregard moved in was one of the happiest days in Juanita's life. Expelled from pre-school ("For teachin' the kids to masturbate, can you imagine!") he walked into the hotel lobby as if he owned the joint. Juanita gathered him tenderly into her arms as he sank his teeth into her hand. "That Beauregard!" Juanita said affectionately of the big woolly monkey, "He was the next best thing to bein' human! If he didn't like somethin' you were doin', he'd just bite you, and that was that. You learned fast or you got bit, one or the other."

In the beginning, Beauregard did not return Juanita's affection. He attached himself to Micki Smircich, the bookkeeper, and though Juanita offered him a variety of treats, he would not be seduced. Then Micki was absent for a week and when she returned, Beauregard gave her one long, unforgiving stare and bit her on the arm. From that time on the monkey was Juanita's. When he was ill, she kept him warm inside her muumuu. He slung himself around her neck by day, slept with her by night, and supervised all activities both inside and outside the restaurant. Like Eloise at the Plaza Hotel – only hairier and considerably more naughty – there was very little that went on that Beauregard did not know about. He ran underneath the waitresses' long skirts and, if the spirit moved him, nipped them on the ankles. He snatched cherries from cocktails and, if he were quick enough, the green onions hanging over the edge of the buffet. It didn't matter with the green onions, but Juanita found herself replacing quite a few drinks. Beauregard quickly developed a fondness for maraschino cherries and gin, and could snatch a stem or polish off a martini before a customer knew they were gone. Juanita tried to curb his intemperate ways, but customers would sometimes slip him a little beer when she wasn't looking.

The alternative was to keep the monkey in a cage, but after the tragic deaths of Sally's parrot and her own iguana, Juanita was afraid to keep anything locked up, figuring that a beer now and then was better than a life spent behind bars. She was concerned about his nutrition, however, and so she shared all her meals with him. "Beau couldn't sit in the dining room because of those fool health regulations," she explained, "so we'd eat in the lobby. We had to eat from one plate, 'cause Beau always figured that what I was havin' had to be better than anything he was havin'. One time I couldn't feed him and so Micki was givin' him dinner. But she wasn't feedin' him his pork chops fast enough, so he bit her. She wouldn't have a thing to do with him after that – just couldn't seem to forgive him. Maybe it was the shots."

As hotly as Mr. Blackwell cherishes an aversion to miniskirts, so did Beauregard detest wigs. According to Juanita, he had almost a sixth sense where wigs were concerned. She had hung a swing from the lobby ceiling and as the bewigged would stroll unsuspectingly beneath, Beau would swing down, grab the wig, and run off screeching. "If he knew a woman was wearin' a wig," Juanita said, "he would climb on her lap and pretend to be real sweet, pattin' her on the head. Then all of a sudden, he'd grab her wig off, put it in the crook of his tail, and just tear across the dinin' room with the poor woman runnin' after him, her hair every which way, screamin', 'Give me back my wig!' All the women were so mortified because their hair looked so awful underneath, if they *had* any hair. Some were bald as turnips. I finally had to take that swing down, but then ladies were just on their own if they trusted his intentions. He wasn't a bad monkey – just sorta prejudiced."

When Beauregard and his merry band of squirrel monkeys were up to no good, there was hell to pay somewhere. The squirrel monkeys couldn't open the front door by themselves, but Beauregard could, ushering them all into an unready world outside. Many were the drivers on Highway 12 who witnessed six monkeys swinging hand-over-tail across the road on the telephone wires. A man on his way to a party once saw Beauregard above the highway in the company of three chickens. "He was goosing them along the wire," the man recalled, "obviously having a high old time in every sense."

More than once, Beauregard ran up Sunnyside Street where there lived a woman who – with some justification – feared and hated him. He would cavort in her yard when she was gardening until she took up a broom to shoo him away. More times than not, Beauregard would wrest the broom away from her and she would run into her house and call the police, telling them 'that mean monkey' was terrorizing her again. Bored with the lack of action, Beau would then head on uphill where there lived another woman who loved him and would sit with him out on her porch in her rocking chair. By the time the police had tracked the vicious monkey down, there he would be, looking as innocent as a sleepy child in his grandmother's arms. "Mean?" the woman would say incredulously. "I just don't understand that at all! This is the sweetest monkey in the world, officer! Why, just look at him!"

Then came the day of the Mexican Standoff. Juanita described it like this:

"Beauregard wandered down to the corner market and stood in the doorway, not lettin' anybody in or anybody out. He was just mad at everybody that day, I guess. Everybody inside had to twiddle their thumbs and everybody outside had to just go away. A few people tried to talk him into movin', but he wouldn't and nobody got up the nerve to walk past him, probably because they were afraid he would bite – which he probably would have, he was so upset about things in general. Finally somebody called the Humane Society and they came out and put a noose around Beau's neck and took him away in their truck, although they would've been saved a hell of a lot of trouble if they'd just dropped him off at the hotel. It cost me $3 to get him back, but it cost them a whole lot more to clean up that truck!

"When I got Beau back he was such a mess and just miserable. I gave him a bath and then put Jean Naté all over him, but he still sulked. He sulked all day and wasn't himself at all. The problem was that he was just too smart for his own good. I mean, he could even use a toilet just like a little man!"

A young attorney, his wife and little daughter often came up on weekends. While the child's parents sat out on the verandah to rest and study, she would go to the small room with the four poster bed that Juanita had bought especially for her. There she would play with Beauregard. Though Juanita had spent both money and effort getting the canopy bed for the child, she wasn't in the least upset when the child and the monkey tore the canopy to shreds. Indeed, Juanita would smile indulgently at the sight of the two of them bouncing on the mattress and climbing the posts.

After dinner one evening, a famous English actor was standing in the lobby talking to Juanita when he felt something plop wetly on his head. "I say, is that chickenshit?" he asked anxiously, reaching up tentatively to test the limits of this small, but distasteful, public disaster.

"Nah, honey," Juanita reassured him, "that's not chickenshit. That's monkeyshit."

Another evening, two men light in their loafers were chatting in the lobby when one of them was surprised to feel a sudden, warm shower. Looking up, he saw Beauregard hanging from the staircase bannister. "Did that monkey piss on me?" he asked Juanita incredulously.

"Yes," she replied, "I guess he likes you."

Animals, as far as Juanita was concerned, were not only better-behaved than most of her customers, but were much more deserving of absolute license to misbehave if they chose. People often pushed her off her emotional trolley – animals never did. Enrico Banducci was dining at Fetter's one evening and recalled, "A deer and a turkey and a monkey were running around the dining room and Juanita came tearing through, yellin', 'I've had it! I've had it! I'm gonna open all the doors and let all the animals in, and then I'm gonna kick all you people OUT!'" He never did find out why she was so upset, and later in the evening, she was as affable as ever.

People from all over the county—all over the state—dumped off, delivered and otherwise presented Juanita with so many animals that she had to hire employees just to take care of them. Cages piled up like condominiums in downtown Waikiki. Juanita fenced off part of the verandah next to the dining room for a large pig named Erica, who stood on the other side of the window from the buffet – so near and yet so far. When she was set loose, she would take aim at anyone with food. One customer recalled being pursued from one end of the restaurant to the other until he had given Erica all of his French bread. She still wouldn't let him go, however. Penning him in a corner, she rolled over on her back with her legs in the air, forcing him to scratch her belly before she at last got up and wandered away. "It was like being pignapped," another customer remembered. "If you didn't do exactly what the pig wanted you to do, she wouldn't let you go."

A young boy from the nearby mobile home park came by to plead with Juanita to adopt his two white mice. "I don't like mice," Juanita told him. "But if you don't take them, Mom is gonna flush them down the toilet," he told her, sealing the deal. Up on the upper verandah they went, the two of them becoming four, the four eight, in a geometrical progression that soon required a small village of cages just for the mice. Near them went cages full of pigeons who cooed from morning until night. Chickens too old or infirm to brave the streets were saved from being pecked to death by safe incarceration next to the pigeons.

A man from San Francisco brought Juanita a rooster he had kept as a pet for years. It was blind in one eye, but otherwise lovely. Juanita released it into her chickenyard where a brawl soon erupted that resulted in the loss of the rooster's other eye. Bedraggled, and by now totally blind, the rooster was brought indoors where he took up residence on a parrot stand on the reception desk near the cash register. Bowls of water and seed were placed nearby so that he need do nothing but sleep and eat and let the chips fall where they may. Joe Foley, the practical joker, hid his tape recorder near the rooster and would often play a tape he had made of Juanita snoring. Since the rooster often appeared to be asleep, the sound effect proved quite successful. There were many credulous souls who couldn't wait to tell their friends that Juanita now had a blind rooster that sat snoring on a parrot stand in the lobby.

It is fascinating to imagine what new customers must have thought as they walked up to the hotel's front door, flanked on either side by funhouse mirrors, and then into a lobby in which a blind poodle was asleep on a loveseat and a sightless rooster perched, often snoring, nearby while squirrel monkeys swung gaily from doorbell wires strung from the desk to the door. To find Juanita present, holding another rooster on her shoulder and sharing pork chops with a large monkey, must have provided just that extra touch of surrealism so important in the restaurant business. Celebrities like Kirk Douglas, Joseph Cotten, Tommy Smothers and Don Johnson may have been relieved to find themselves off center stage at Juanita's Galley. It is well-known in the theatrical business that animals and small children upstage mere actors every time.

A flight attendant finally brought trouble to paradise. Juanita recollected this sorry incident in all its sordid detail.

"My squirrel monkeys would sit up on my closet doors, and sometimes they'd watch me sleep and sometimes I'd watch them sleep. Well, one day this stewardess came into my bedroom and tried to get one of the monkeys down so she could hold it and it bit her. It was self-defense, as far as I was concerned, but she didn't see it the same way. We poured gin on her hand, which is the best kind of medical care for monkey bites. She said she was fine and went home to Florida. Once she got there she decided to sue me, maybe because she was too far away for me to snatch her baldheaded. She called the D.A. and complained about my monkeys and chickens and I got called on the carpet so the D.A. could tell me I wasn't supposed to do things like that. I told him the stewardess was just a plain asshole for tryin' to grab a sleepin' monkey and she shoulda known better.

"That broad raised so much hell that I started to raise a little hell, too. I called the guy that owned the airline she worked for and he called *her* on *his* carpet. The story went that she cried and cried and was so sorry for all the trouble she'd caused that he married her. She sent me a present, too, but I sent it back. I heard later that the marriage didn't last too long, but she caused me trouble for years. I had to put all my babies into cages on the porch and in one of the guest rooms upstairs. They had to stay there all the time, except when the coast was clear and we could let 'em all out."

Beauregard was given a large cage in the guest room. To stop customers plying him with drink, Juanita put up a second screen six inches from the first. She couldn't figure out why sometimes he still seemed kind of tipsy until she found someone feeding Beau a beer long distance, through a drinking straw. "He went downstairs headfirst," she remembered with a reminiscent smile, "and hit the ground runnin'."

Even though the circus atmosphere lessened indoors, outdoors it grew ever more outrageous. Peacocks shrieked like terrified women from the oak trees, an old mare nibbled at nonexistent grass in her jerrybuilt corral, skunks and rabbits and foxes hopped and prowled in their shaded cages, while scores of ducks and chickens made certain nothing around the hotel had an opportunity to grow. Enjoying the best of both worlds, Erica the pig could contemplate the dining habits of guests both indoors and out by merely turning her head.

A young waitress came to Juanita in tears one day because her mother was going to turn her pet donkey loose in the hills. Juanita always hated to see anybody cry ("Unless they'd done somethin' *real* stupid") so she told the waitress that if she could get the jenny over to the hotel, she would take care of it from then on. At that point it was perhaps inevitable—as these jokes in life so often are—that a jackass would enter the picture next. He did.

"What happened was, this other young girl told me that she had this jackass and that her boyfriend had sent it to the knackers to be ground up into dogfood," Juanita explained. "Well, I just couldn't stand by and see somethin' like that happen, so we rented a trailer for $55 and went up to the glue factory and paid them another $55 for the sorriest-lookin' jackass you ever saw.

"When we got him home we found out he'd been shot in the flank and had this awful, oozin' sore. The rest of him looked like an old, empty leather handbag. We had this grumpy old vet and he came over and fixed Rattle-Ass up and showed me how to keep the wound clean and give him his shots. I wanted to do it all myself because I wanted it done right. Soon as that jackass was himself again, wouldn't you know that girl's no-good boyfriend showed up again and wanted Rattle-Ass back! Naturally I told him he was fuckin' crazy, that I had the bill of sale and everythin' else and so he said he'd take me to court. I said, 'Fine, go right ahead, asshole.'

"The judge on our case was Judge MacMahon. The asshole boyfriend stood up and said he wanted to use Rattle-Ass in a pack train in the Sierras and my grumpy vet spoke right up at that and said, 'Since when does a stud jackass go in a pack string?' We had him there, boy! I told the judge how I didn't think it was fair for that two-legged jackass to get Rattle-Ass after I'd saved 'im and all. Judge MacMahon just listened to all this. I finished up by sayin' that I guessed we'd done such a good job fixin' that four-legged jackass up that now he was worth a lot more than he was as dogfood or glue, and I looked real hard at the boyfriend when I said it. MacMahon said he'd give the matter some thought and that he'd let us know by letter. We waited and waited and waited. Finally the letter came that I'd been awarded the jackass! Rattle-Ass meanwhile had been shacked up with our jenny and so when her first baby was born, a little male jackass, I named him Judge MacMahon. It was kind of an honor for him and the newspapers all printed stories about it. MacMahon was real pleased, I think.

"You know," Juanita added reflectively, "someone once said about me, 'If you do something real nice for Juanita, chances are she'll name an animal after you,' and he was right. I never have been able to think of a nicer compliment than that."

Just after final adoption papers had been signed for Rattle-Ass, another waitress brought over a mare she couldn't keep anymore. "We had the idea we were gonna mate her to a purebred Morgan horse somebody had," Juanita said, "but Rattle-Ass got to her first. Her baby was born on Father's Day.

"I named him Monsignor O'Farrell after this groovy Monsignor we had in the valley. When he used to bring his Irish relatives by to visit, he always showed them his namesake first. Well, you know he should have been happy because it was the prettiest mule you ever saw, with his mother's lines and his father's good big ears."

After a couple of years, Juanita erected a sign on the property reading, "City Zoo." Few would have argued with her.

▪▪▪▪▪▪▪▪▪▪▪▪▪▪▪▪▪▪▪▪▪▪▪▪▪▪▪▪▪▪▪▪

Diana Willson, Artist

One evening we were having dinner in one of Juanita's private dining rooms, when her monkey walked in. It was a funny-looking monkey with hair all over its face, and it went over to a little sink that was in one corner and began to play with the taps, turning them on and off. After awhile, my husband, Archibald, went over to turn off the water and the monkey bit him. Quite savagely, too. Then he ran over to where Archibald had been sitting, climbed into his chair, and began throwing peas and vegetables around.

I wasn't so fond of the monkey, but there was really quite a lovely pig on the porch, a nice big white pig, and while I thought she was just beautiful, there were a few complaints about her because she was really quite close to the food. I like pigs, though, so that didn't bother me. I liked to paint pigs, actually, and still do. I have always enjoyed painting big things, because it's easier for one thing; pigs and hippos and other large creatures. I loved to paint Juanita, too, because she had all of those ample curves and such lovely skin, which was sort of luminous. You never see paintings of skinny women, you know, because they aren't nearly as pretty as big, fleshly people. There was so much sadness in her eyes, though. Underneath all the toughness and obesity there was always a sweet and vulnerable quality I loved to try and capture. For a period of time I'd always come home from dinner at Juanita's and try and paint her from memory.

It was funny to find out that her mother was so tiny, not much over five feet tall, and with little, skinny arms. I went to visit Juanita once when she was sick in bed, and her mother came in, bringing Juanita a cup of tea. I thought she was a wraith, she was so frail. And there on that big bed next to Juanita on one side was that terrible monkey and on the other side she had these two enormous iguanas. Awful, snakey things, not a bit attractive, really. When I went out to my husband, who was waiting for me, I said, "My God, Juanita's mother is a midget!" At least she looked that way next to Juanita, who had to have weighed three hundred pounds at the time.

After her second place burned down I wanted to cheer her up, so I painted on a bedsheet, like a banner, a picture of Juanita rising from the flames like a huge phoenix. I wrote on it, "We shall rise again!" and we hung it in front of the old burned-out building so all her customers would know this wouldn't be the end of her. Which it wasn't, of course. And though now she doesn't have a restaurant, she's still the same old Juanita. The other day we were in the post office with a very prim and proper friend of ours. Juanita had had her first knee operation and was apparently very proud of it because she lifted up her muumuu to show us the scar. "And I could show you a lot more than *this*, honey!" she said with a wink.

A few years ago I needed a job and since I knew Juanita had a place up at Fetter's Hot Springs, I went to see her. She asked me what I did and when I told her I was a bartender she said right away, "Good, I need a bartender. I fired my last two this morning." She fired them because she thought they were stealing from her, only they weren't. It was the guy who delivered her liquor. I tried later to tell her about him but she only said, "No, no he wouldn't do that." She was that way; sometimes trusted the wrong people.

One real slow night she was asleep way at the end of the bar. There was only one table of four customers who were all drinking expensive drinks, lots of expensive drinks, having a good time, nice and quiet. Then this lady comes in and asks for Juanita and I told her, "She's over there, but she's asleep and I wouldn't wake her up if I were you." But the lady says, "Oh, I know her real well," and goes over and taps Juanita on the shoulder. Juanita woke up and just flipped out. Just flipped out and started yellin' and threw everybody out. I tried to explain to her that the customers were running up a nice long bar tab, but she just kept on yelling, "Get the fuck out! I want everybody out!" and cleared the place. I closed up right after that since there obviously wasn't any reason to stay open.

Actually, I was one of the few people who could wake Juanita up if something was going on. She wouldn't slug me, at any rate, though she might tell me to get lost. I always thought she was drunk all the time because of how bizarre she acted, but I never saw her take a drink. I couldn't figure out how she could get drunk and never come to the bar. I ended up thinking that maybe she was just like that *sober*.

She did other weird things. One time a good friend of mine was having dinner with her boyfriend. Unfortunately she was wearing patchouli perfume, which Juanita hated for some reason. Juanita came out of the kitchen into the dining room and went sniffing around until she located my friend and told her to get the fuck out. Their dinners had just arrived, but they had to go right that second. Another time these guys parked their car in front of the restaurant steps and she asked them to move it and they said, "Fuck you." So she went to the kitchen and got a frying pan and then went outside and walked around the car, smashing out all its windows. She got away with that, just like she got away with having her animals in the restaurant in spite of county regulations.

She had this monkey named Beauregard who used to hang out a lot in the bar because he liked to drink, especially gin. One day a lady comes in, a steady customer, and orders a martini. I see Beauregard get up on the stool next to her and the lady goes, "Oh, what a nice monkey!" and starts to pet him. Then she reaches out to take her drink. The monkey reaches out for it too, however, and he's a little quicker on the draw. So the lady tries to take her martini away from the monkey and he gets mad and bites her hard on the wrist. She let out this ungodly scream and I reached over the bar and slapped Beauregard, knocking him end over end. He landed on all fours and then fluffed out all his fur like a cat, only now he suddenly looked like King Kong, and he leaps off the floor right at my face, pissed as hell and scratching and biting. I don't mind telling you, he scared the shit out of me. I said to Juanita that she'd better lock her fucking monkey up but all she did was get mad at me because I'd slapped him and then she yelled at the "dumb broad" that she shouldn't have ordered gin in the *first* place!

Juanita also wasn't above stiffin' you your paycheck from time to time. Once she owed me money and I was gettin' miffed at her and kept asking her for it. She put me off and put me off until I was real upset. About this time my birthday rolled around, and she found out about it somehow. I was just getting off work when my wife, Donna, came by to pick me up and Juanita said, "Come here, both of you!" and I thought, "Oh, no, not more of her bullshit," when she leads us into this small special room with a table in it all set with flowers and candles and a birthday cake and a bottle of champagne and two prime rib dinners. Then she said, "When you kids have finished eatin', there's a room all ready for you upstairs and the jacuzzi's turned on." We had just a great time.

Another time she owed me about $400, which was a lot more money in those days than it is now. I was late on my rent and needed the money, so I told her she just *had* to pay me and she said, "Sure, you'll get it," like she always did. That night I took in over fourteen hundred dollars and the next day I went to Juanita and said, "You promised me, so hand it over," and she said, "I don't have it." "I know that's bullshit," I told her, "because I took in fourteen hundred dollars last night."

Juanita looks at me a minute and then says, "Well, I don't have it anymore because I spent it all this morning." I said, "What?" and she took me over to the window and pointed out all these pots of flowers all around the hotel outside. "On those," she said. I was so pissed, I said, "Get the fuckin' *flowers* to bartend for you, then!" And I quit.

You know, I'd been stiffed by other people before – the bar business is notorious for people doing that to you – but Juanita was somehow different. I mean, she never discriminated against anybody, including Workman's Comp. or the IRS. One day, when I still worked for her, a sheriff came in and showed me his badge and said, "I'm here to take the receipts tonight." I asked him what for and he told me that he had a lien on her place. He came in behind the bar and counted all the money in the till and then sat there all night, watching me ring up sales. At the end of the shift I said, "Closin' time," and he took all the money out of the cash register and left.

I knew she didn't use my money to go on vacation or invest in the stock market. She was just trying to keep things together, most of the time, and there are lots of us who kind of forgave her because of who she was and things she did – like that birthday dinner. I mean, how can you really get pissed off with someone who does something nice for you like that?

Jack Varney, Paint Shop Owner

I had a paint store in them days and Juanita was always coming in for a kind of pink paint she called "Titty Pink." She musta painted most of the inside of her places pink because I sold a whole lot of it to her over the years, especially when one place burned down and she was fixing up the next. The problem was, she didn't like to pay her bills. You'd be a gentleman for the first coupla months and then when it was clear that she wasn't going to give you a dime without a little encouragement, you'd have to get a little tougher on her.

So on Monday morning I'd go on over to her place, knowing that she would have all the weekend receipts in cash dough. There'd be a bunch of guys there, maybe ten or twelve of us, all with the same idea of waiting for her to come out and pay us what she owed us. It was really the only way to get paid usually. She'd come out brushing her hair and full of greetings like, "What in the hell do you bastards want now?" And a couple of us would remind her, as if she needed reminding! She'd say, "Okay, how much do you need?" and reach down the front of her muumuu and pull up a big roll of dough. She'd pay two or three of us off and that would be it. You'd have to go away and hope that the next Monday would be your turn to get paid.

Finally I got so disgusted with her, I said, "Look, Juanita, if you want any more paint, you're going to have to bring the dough with ya." So after this every once in awhile a couple of hippie-looking guys would come in, some nice and some bums, and I guess she must've put them through some kind of training program. They'd go over and look at the color guide for the right number and then waltz over to the counter and say, "Hey, we want three gallons of number so-and-so to paint a bedroom and a hallway." I'd check it out and sure enough, it would be "Titty Pink." I'd say, "By any chance, is this paint for Juanita?" They'd usually try to slide out of it and I'd say, "Look, for people I don't know, this is strictly a cash business. And if this is for Juanita, you'd better go on back and tell her to fork over the money first and *then* I'll mix the paint for you." I got to where I could almost sense when they walked in the door that another con job was on the way. When they'd tell me what color they wanted, I'd know for sure.

She was just tough as hell on local businessmen, but when groups like the Rotary would meet at her place for a special dinner, people would come out of the woodwork and really pack the place. That's one thing I sure have to say for her – she ran a hell of a restaurant!

Ron Duer, Pharmacist

Juanita's always called me her "banker." She's often come in on a Friday night, short of money, and I've always cashed a check for her to get her through the weekend. She's always paid me back on Monday. Only twice she forgot, but that was when her restaurants had burned down, and a couple of years later she came in and paid me what she owed me. I've always known that if she had it, she'd pay me. I've never worried about that because I know how honest she is. Besides, I've always felt that she's done so much for the community that she has deserved some help, too. Part of living in a community is helping each other, I think, and being a pharmacist in a small town means you have to understand when your customers are a little short of money. A different way of doing business today, maybe, but life's too short on this planet to be an ogre.

Juanita has always come into the pharmacy yelling and joking around, and sometimes people will be a little alarmed until they see how we react to her. Then they relax. That's standard Juanita, and we all love her for being just exactly who she is. For years she always came in on Christmas Eve, right before we were to close for the day, and buy a bunch of holiday things, things I'd have had to just sit on for another year, to give away to kids and friends and customers at her restaurant. I don't know if she ever realized that all of this stuff she was buying would be worth a whole lot less the next day, and that she was helping me out a lot more than I was helping her, but I always appreciated her doing that.

At one point she got worried about people shoplifting from me – why, I don't know – and so one day she brought over a mirror and gave it to me so I could keep an eye on things. It was touching to me that she would be concerned for me like that. I've never put the mirror up, but I still have it. Another time, late one night, I got a call that the front window of the pharmacy had been shattered. My manager and I got there to find Juanita already there, kind of standing guard over the place. How she knew it had happened, I don't know. She then drove home and picked up some boards and woke up a friend of hers and he gave her some nuts and bolts, and back she came with everything and helped us cover the window and secure it so we were able to go home that night instead of spending it watching the pharmacy until morning. I gave her what I thought her efforts had been worth to us and she just handed it back and said rather grandly, "Please put this on my account." Of course she didn't stop to help because she thought she'd be paid for it, and though I know she could've used the money, she didn't take it. I wished, however, that she had.

213

You know, I really hope she's not disappointed with all of the people she's helped over the years, because that would be a very sad thing. I tend to think she never will be disappointed, because she's always been the kind of person who gives without the thought of being given something in return. If she had a whole world, she'd give a world and a half away.

Hal Beck, Former Deputy Probation Officer

I was the assigned Deputy Probation Officer in Sonoma Valley during the early and mid-Seventies. I worked for Judge MacMahon, for whom Juanita had named a jackass, to MacMahon's consternation. The springs area had always been a place where, ever since the Twenties, people from various rackets – mobsters, criminals – went to hide out or retire. It's always been a place where you could be invisible. There were lots of parolees in the area and Juanita accepted people like that without a problem. She would hire our probationers for several reasons. First, they were pretty desperate for a job and, second, she didn't have to pay them very much. Sometimes, she didn't pay them at *all*, knowing that they were unlikely to go through the normal process of filing complaints with the State Labor Commission. She was fairly well known for not paying some of them but, on the other hand, she fed them and clothed them and gave them a place to stay. She really had a good heart to take them in at all, of course, since some were guilty of serious crimes.

One of my jobs was to make sure the probationers under my care were doing what they were supposed to, and so one place I went faithfully every week was to Juanita's to check up on them. We'd sit out on her porch and catch up on who was doing what in the valley. She had a good handle on what my clients were up to and where they'd gone in case they'd taken off. She was always very professional with me, very businesslike. I had the impression she was able to turn on and turn off the theatrics when she wanted to and we got along real well, all things considered.

Sometimes there'd be people at her place who were on the run, but usually these would be the younger, not so bright ones who couldn't figure out where else to go. She did protect "her people" after all, and if somebody had asked her not to say something, she probably wouldn't have said it. I didn't want to go rousting through all her rooms, so I had to trust her to be pretty straightforward with me. I knew she tolerated minor things, but if somebody was doing drugs or stealing a lot of stuff, then she'd let me know. The funniest incident I experienced as a probation officer was when she hired one of my probationers who had a twitch. He didn't do anything else, but this twitch just drove Juanita absolutely up the wall. I think she saw it as a personality flaw. She'd get upset with him and that would make him so nervous he'd start twitching. The twitching would then make Juanita yell, which would make him twitch more, until she was yelling really loudly at him and he was just twitching like crazy. By this time Juanita would be beside herself. One day I went by and asked how he was doing and she laid into me like I'd never been laid into before. She shouted at me that she was prepared to hire my murderers, my rapists, my armed robbers, anyone I pleased, "but I will *never* hire anybody again with a goddamn *twitch!*"

11

"At Juanita's, Three Square Meals Are Anything But Square"

– *New York Times*

At Juanita's, animals gathered "On the Outskirts of Heaven, (In the Valley of the Moon)"– as a sentimental ballad of the Forties described sleepy Sonoma Valley – in noisy numbers no greater and no noisier than local teenagers, who wanted nothing so much as to raise a little hell. As it was the Sixties, any sizable gathering of young people usually included the pervasive odor of marijuana, a cloud that would precipitate a thunderstorm if Juanita caught anyone actually smoking the stuff. If kids wanted to hang around, that was fine. If they wanted to get loaded while they were there, they stood in grave danger of being thrown off the property by the seat of their jeans.

One evening Juanita rounded a corner and ran into a group of teenagers smoking dope. Once she started yelling, however, the lighted joints flew like fireworks into the bushes as the kids scrambled for cover. One joint fell near Juanita's feet and she swooped down on it and ran after the kids, cursing. "I ran on inside after the little bastards," she recalled, "and noticed that after awhile everything had gotten real quiet. All of a sudden I realized that I had this lighted joint in my hand and in those days just to be holdin' one could land you in jail. I threw it out the door onto the patio and then sat myself down out there, ravin' like a maniac. There was this guy sittin' there nearby and he said to me, 'Calm down, Juanita. Don't let it bug you.' And I yelled, 'You don't know! You can't get closed up 'cause you're just a customer!' All of a sudden the guy smiles and says, 'We're not after *you*, Juanita.' I asked him what the hell he meant by that and he opened up his wallet and showed me his badge. He was a vice cop. He had been sittin' there just watchin' everything go down, but he was lookin' for bigger fish to fry than those minnows. He also knew how

I felt about drugs."

Rock bands would play outside the hotel on weekends, the amplified sounds of guitars and drums driving neighbors indoors like cuckoos into their clocks. Like clockwork, too, the police showed up and attempted to diminish the decibel level of the music. Juanita strung her Oriental carpets along clotheslines to help dampen the noise and more than once got up on the platform, took the mike and shouted, "Now, look, all you people out there, I'm talking to you! Why don't you come on down here to see where your kids are, instead of bellyachin' all the time about it to the cops! They're down here listenin' to the music and not out stealin' your radio or lettin' the air outta your tires! Now I'm good and tired of it, so cut it out!" The request fell on deaf ears.

It was true that the police usually had a good idea where many of the local demons could be found on "the outskirts of heaven". They were sitting in the side yard at Fetter's Hot Springs, listening to "Mellow Yellow" and trying to hide a little of it in the palm of one hand.

Drinking was a vice Juanita tolerated to a much greater degree than that of drug use, although she once had to bounce a bottle of beer off the head of a young tippler to teach him to "just say no" a little earlier in the evening. Rather than being pleased by this refreshing approach to the encouragement of temperance, the boy's mother went to the Alcohol Board, which then restricted Juanita from using her hands on a patron. "I didn't use my hands anyway," she said grumpily about this new restriction. "I had no choice but to exercise my stomach muscles more. This worked pretty good, though. It got to the point where I could walk into a crowd of misbehavin' people and send 'em flyin' like tenpins. Most of them chose to move before I got to them, though, 'cause I was like a truck." This turned out to be, Juanita believed, a much better idea than whacking people upside the head with beer bottles because "I couldn't be held responsible if they were in my way and just refused to get out of it."

Though most of Juanita's youthful clientele were reasonably well-behaved, there were occasions when they were not.

"These kids started a fight outside, and me and my employees ran out to help stop it. While we were busy, some of their group ran around back and stole everything we had in the refrigerator and freezer – all the hamburger, prime rib, steaks, everything. When the fight was over and we went back to cook, there wasn't anything left to cook *with*. It was a Sunday, too, and I had to ask the guy who sold me meat to send some down right away so I could open up that night. There were a lotta people who just waited around until dinnertime and I had somethin' to cook for them."

It wasn't only the young who sowed their oats at Juanita's. Adults were sometimes guilty of it, too. According to Juanita, the owner of a well-known bar in San Francisco arranged to have a party for his employees at Fetter's. Everyone arrived in quite a different condition from the one in which they finally left. In between, they decided to throw Juanita's dishes—newly purchased for $4,000 after the El Verano fire—out of the windows. Forks and spoons soon followed. Adding insult to injury, the happy pranksters snatched up balladeer Barbara Tabler's antique mandolin and smashed it, too.

Armed with photographic proof of this monumental food and flatware fight, Juanita went to court to recover some of what she had lost, only to have the judge decide against her. (This, admittedly, does not make much sense, but perhaps the judge did not care to have a jackass named after him.) Juanita gave Barbara money for a new mandolin and cherished less-than-loving memories of the men who did her wrong. She also cherished a shard of a platter, because, as she said, "Sometimes I need a reminder to stay mad. Sometimes that madness kind of runs off and I forget to be pissed off when I see the person again."

Sometimes she preferred to forget "the person," however. One of the down-and-outers she fed for months on the "Eat Now, Pay Never" plan was either an aspiring or a defrocked priest who borrowed her pink truck and returned it the following day painted grey. The advertising for Juanita's, as well as her motto, "Food guaranteed but not the disposition of the cook," had disappeared. "I just blew up!" she said. "I got so damned mad that I got the pink slip and I signed it and threw it at him and told him to get that fuckin' truck outta my sight!" Why? "I didn't want *no* reminders of what that son-of-a-bitch had done!"

Another time, someone borrowed her car to run an errand, got drunk, and forgot to return it until nightfall. Juanita was so upset that she had to work while an employee had driven around happily in a mindless stupor, that she went outside with her rolling pin and smashed all the windows out of the car. While that might seem like cutting off one's nose to spite one's face Juanita, who had done it before, maintained that it made perfect sense. The car, after all, allowed the problem to occur in the first place. So the car got spanked.

Antiques, as well as less valuable objects, continued to disappear on a regular basis. All the television sets Juanita would put in the rooms and cabins walked out with the hotel's guests. Once an entire brass bed was gone by morning. All of this made housekeeping difficult, although the houses, themselves, generally stayed put. One might catch fire now and then, but that sort of calamity can happen to anyone. The life of a hotelkeeper is never easy.

Usually it was Juanita who kept things at the simmer. Most of her customers were so cowed by their hostess that they didn't dare take a second muffin, let alone a piece of hotel furniture. "One woman had just come from Ireland on a visit," Juanita recalled, "and as soon as she arrived we had an earthquake. A day or two later her friends brought her to the Galley for dinner, and I guess her friends musta told her that if somebody made me mad I'd hit 'em on the head with a baseball bat, because all through dinner she just sat there without sayin' a word, watchin' me with these big, frightened eyes. She musta thought all restaurants in America were like mine, poor thing."

On New Year's Eve, 1970, as Juanita took a bubble bath before the fray, Joe Foley surprised her by snapping her photograph lolling, buns upward, in her claw-footed tub. Juanita was so fond of it that she had hundreds of copies made, which she then sold for a dollar each when her bank account was low. These photos proved so popular that Juanita often ran out, and had to promise to send one when she had a new batch. Requests came in from as far away as Japan, England and Australia, always with a dollar, or its equivalent, enclosed. Juanita would tuck the rolled up photo in a paper towel tube and mail it, often for more than a dollar's worth of stamps. "May your blessings be as many as the bubbles," she wrote in her beautiful convent-taught penmanship on every one. It is a curious fact that, though thousands of these photographs were sold or given away over the years, many recipients framed and cherished them as if they were rare and difficult to obtain. Scratched and grainy and in shades of grey, copied on cheap paper, the photographs seem to have been a souvenir not only of

Juanita herself, but also a reminder of a past she enlivened with her own brand of shoot-'em-up hospitality. They are cherished the way one cherishes an old prom corsage or a Valentine as proof of goofy, tender, carefree days.

Juanita collected photographs, too. Her favorites were portraits of people taken in the 19th Century, although she wasn't picky about it. She cherished the photographs of strangers long dead as if they were ancestors of her own. She said once, "I always wonder if I'm related to them somehow. Could be, you know. My grandfather and grandmother came to Oklahoma in a covered wagon. She was a schoolteacher and he was a land surveyor. When I look at my old photographs of people, I always think maybe I woulda known them if we all lived back then. Really, I like them just as much whether they're related to me or not."

Joe Foley, who probably knew Juanita better than anybody else, said, "Juanita likes to dwell in the past. She finds it pleasant. She'll look through old photographs and keepsakes and be a little sad and sentimental – but thoroughly enjoying herself. She once explained to me why she loved three old bent forks she found somewhere. 'See,' she told me, 'little children have grown up eating their mashed potatoes with these. Maybe they had to eat grated carrots or brussels sprouts and that's why the tines are crooked, 'cause the kids were pissed off that they had to eat slop.' She loves pictures that kids maybe looked at all the time they were growing up. This had made them special in her eyes. She'll even buy plaques with the wedding announcements of strangers lacquered on them. Just because she doesn't know Carmen Rodriguez and Enrique Gomez doesn't mean she doesn't care about their wedding. She's just funny that way, always has been."

Louise's husband, Joe, died and Louise came West to live with Juanita. From that time on, Juanita carted both her mother and Hughie around with her wherever she went, as if they were both particularly prized antiques—which, in point of fact, they were. They were both old, and devoted to Juanita, but she probably would have carted them around even if they hadn't been. How Louise adjusted to the livelier life of the Galley is not known. Photos show her swathed in bright muumuus, smiling. When she finally got hold of one of the notorious bathtub photos, she murmured, "Oh, how I remember kissing that bottom! Of course, when I did, it was much *much* smaller." Juanita, who had been on tenterhooks, was relieved.

By the mid-Seventies Juanita had everything she had ever wanted except for Dick and a passel of kids. By dint of much scrounging in antique shops and yard sales, she owned everything she could remember her grandmother having, including the china hair receivers and the Hoosier cabinets. Any level spaces were filled with lamps and knickknacks and porcelain-headed dolls. One whole upstairs room in the hotel was devoted to religious artifacts. Among the adobe Stations of the Cross, rosaries, Menorahs, brass Buddhas, and images of saints and pictures of Jesus, there was an electric cross that glowed with inspiration night and day. In the guest rooms were chests of drawers full of antique clothing and fans and beaded purses which were available to anyone who chose to dine in costume. That many customers felt inclined to wear the costumes right on out the front door was something Juanita refused to fret over. "Oh, they're just kids havin' fun," she would say indulgently. The rooms were supposed to be like guest rooms in Grandma's house, and if the children chose to rob Grandma, that was the old girl's lookout. There were always more yard sales to replenish the drawers, more antique shops to restock the bric-a-brac shelves.

"'Outrageous' Hotel May Soon Belong to Juanita"
– Sacramento Bee

Sometime in the mid 1970's, Juanita decided she wanted to own the Fetter's Hot Springs Hotel and set about trying to acquire a down payment. It wasn't so much that she coveted it for herself. She hoped it would be the bait with which to hook Dick and land him again, for good. It wasn't that she wanted to be married again. She just missed the man who, above them all, knew her, loved her and accepted her for exactly who she was. Through the years since her separation from him, she had always secretly hoped that if she owned a restaurant sufficiently large and successful, she might be able to persuade him to return, with the excuse that she needed someone to keep the books. (She didn't need anyone when Micki Smircich was around, but she wasn't about to tell Dick that.) This long-cherished hope finally died when Dick married a woman who had been his secretary. When Juanita heard about it, she went on a tear and spent much of one week drunk and more than usually disorderly. In the intervening years she had visited Dick from time to time, arranging his furniture and sewing new curtains, but wedding bells signalled the end of their freeform married life, even though the bells did not, in point of law, signal the end of their marriage. None of the three realized this at the time, nor did any have the slightest suspicion that when the first Mrs. Musson moved over for the second, it was not really very far.

Juanita had not taken the veil upon Dick's departure. Men were always too much fun to have around. "My first husband was a Greek and my second was French, and after both of them, I was still a virgin," she complained with a naughty sparkle in her eye. There was more than just a sparkle in her eye the day she was dallying with a chiropractor and someone sent the police to stir things up. Not wishing to have his wife find out about his extracurricular activities, he climbed out the window and hung by his hands from the ledge until the police went away.

Men of all temperaments and occupations shared Juanita's bed. Cowboys and veterinarians, car salesmen and doctors, carpenters and attorneys came and went while the monkeys, foxes and chickens stayed on and on.

Despite Dick's escape from Juanita's castle in the air, she still wanted to be her own landlady and buy the Fetter's Hotel. It became a kind of mission for her, particularly since she had seized upon the idea that the owners planned to raze the rambling old structure and build a shopping center in its place. "I want this to stay country," she told reporters at the time. "I don't want it to end up some damned parking lot."

The down payment was $35,000, a sum vastly greater than any Juanita had thus far been able to accumulate—possibly because her generous bosom was not quite large enough for a savings account of that size. Lack of money had never stopped her from doing what she wanted to do, and it wouldn't stop her now.

On March 11, 1975, Juanita held a much ballyhooed auction of all her possessions. Although it had been only six years since she had lost so much in the El Verano fire, she had not lost her will to haunt yard sales. One of her first possessions to sell was the bishop's bed, minus cats and chickens, costing her a pang to see it go. Unfortunately, she sold little else the two days of the auction, perhaps because most people were interested in bargains and Juanita was interested in making as much money as possible on everything. It was hard enough to part with her treasures; she wasn't about to sell them cheap. The only thing that sold like flapjacks was her bathtub photo. A thousand a day were sold, all of them signed with her name, the date, and her bubblesful of blessings. Profit from the sale was a drop in the bucket, but still she didn't give up hoping someday to add the biggest white elephant yet to her collection. She tried hard to curb her wilder financial excesses. She opened other savings accounts. In addition to her anti-theft techniques of hiding money inside tottering piles of knickknacks and – with an uncharacteristic lack of originality – in her mattress, she hid rolls of bills in an old apothecary chest behind the sofa in the hotel lobby. "Maybe the drawers were just too small or something," she said without a trace of regret, "but I just couldn't save enough money to buy the place."

On the morning of March 23, the bubble burst. Rumors that someone intended to set fire to the Fetter's Hotel had circulated for months. Juanita confided to several people that "somebody's tryin' to burn this place down," and she began to keep a pistol between her breasts in case she was lucky enough to catch the arsonist in the act.

Easter morning came. Hundreds of eggs had been hardboiled and dyed. Easter decorations were strung up among the flags and leprechauns on the verandah. Dozens and dozens of English muffins were just waiting to be forked. Easter Sunday buffet was the busiest day of the year at the Galley. Customers were usually lined up by the time the restaurant opened, with bikers in black leather beside ladies in fluffy dresses. Egg hunts were scheduled to go on most of the day, with children scrambling through the dining room and peering under the furniture in the lobby. Juanita had gotten to bed late the night before, and though her waitress, Chris Hill, wanted to sleep on the sofa in the lobby, Juanita convinced her that the noise from the bar would keep her awake and that she would be much better off upstairs. Early morning found Chris Hill sound asleep in the Cornbread Room, a few guests down the hall, and Juanita snoring in her bedroom off the lobby.

There was a pounding at her door and a shouted "Juanita!

Fire!" She bounded out of bed in her red flannel nightgown and squash blossom turquoise necklace and rushed into the lobby where Pierre was asleep on his loveseat and cats were curled like sofa cushions on the couch. There was no sign of fire and she accused the boy who'd given the alarm of playing a prank on her. She became a believer, though, when she looked up the staircase and saw filmy veils of grey smoke drifting down toward her like slender phantoms.

Shouting "Fire! Fire!" Juanita took the stairs two at a time and got to the landing in time to see Chris totter groggily out into the hall. "Save the animals!" Juanita cried, running to the room where Beauregard and the squirrel monkeys lived as pampered guests. Smoke from the burning roof of the bar had filled the room and the monkeys were already unconscious. The keys to their cages were gone from the hook. Without thinking, Juanita picked up a little bantam rooster from the floor where it had collapsed, overcome. The second floor verandah, where she ran next, was filled with cages of chickens, pigeons and white mice, all of which were hallooing and dashing excitedly about. Chris was not out on the verandah, but Juanita assumed she had already made her escape.

Juanita immediately set to work unlatching the cages. Pigeons circled out and away from the hotel while chickens tittuped unsteadily along the verandah rail as if they were walking a tightrope. Figuring the bantam rooster was dead, Juanita dropped it over the side, shouting for someone below to catch it. The catch was made, but when it was unceremoniously dumped to the ground the little rooster lay for a moment as if lifeless, and then jumped up, shook itself and scooted away. "I guess he had the smoke knocked out of him, is what I figure," Juanita said, "and when we tried to catch him later on, he wouldn't have anything to do with us so the dogs ate 'im."

Fire engines roared into the front yard. Hoses spit and sputtered and then gushed onto the bar roof where the fire had apparently been started. Crowds began to gather. Within a short time, considering the size of the hotel, the whole structure was in flames. One fireman ventured inside only to be hit on the head with what he believed to be a piece of falling ceiling. As it turned out, one of Juanita's employees was throwing her possessions down from the second floor landing and dropped a dulcimer just as the fireman stepped into the line of fire. After he staggered out like Chicken Little with the news of imminent collapse, firemen began urging Juanita to get on the ladder they had placed against the side of the building. At first their entreaties were urgent, but pleasant. As time passed and she showed absolutely no intention of doing what they asked, their shouted directions grew markedly less friendly.

Meanwhile, Juanita was desperate. She dragged the blind rooster from his cage and, leaning over the side of the verandah, yelled to one of her employees to take special care of him. Then she tossed the bird overboard and watched as it fell squawking to earth. A fireman shouted, "Get your ass on the ladder, Juanita, right now or we're gonna move it!" In a frenzy, she threw a cage full of chickens over the side, followed by a cage full of terrified mice. Sobbing, she left the rest to be barbecued. With a one-eyed pigeon under her arm, she climbed up on the verandah ledge and onto the ladder, cursing and crying while a fireman, his head muffled in yards and yards of red flannel nightgown, tried to guide her down.

The firemen must have been in two minds about their wisdom in rescuing Juanita. Alternating pleas with the most bloodcurdling curses, she yelled at the firemen to put more water on the hotel, to save what they could of her possessions scattered out on the verandah, to let her go back inside to salvage her apothecary chest, the loveseat, her pincushion dolls, her Hoosier cabinet. Employees ran distractedly about trying to do her bidding while exasperated firemen shouted at them to get out of the way. Police had to be called in to control them; one cop found two of them trying to drag the funhouse mirrors off the verandah and when he warned them he would put them under arrest if they didn't drop the mirrors then and there, one of them said, "You can arrest us, but Juanita will *kill* us if we don't save these things." They were among the very few items of value that were saved. (One of them later broke when a drunk walked into it and the other fell victim to a billiard ball.)

It was chaos of the most complete kind. One observer described the scene as "comparable to what might have occurred had there been an explosion on Noah's Ark." Lights flashed, sirens wailed, firemen and policemen shouted. Juanita swooped about in her red nightgown with the one-eyed pigeon under one arm and Rommel, the fox, under the other, and with goats, chickens, peacocks and small bands of hysterical ducks quacking in circles. It was a ghastly sort of cross between Dante's "Inferno" and "Old MacDonald's Farm." Erica the pig was the only creature able to profit from the spectacle. Set loose from her pen on the porch, she discovered a large inviting puddle where she settled down happily for the duration.

Through the noise and dust and smoke, Juanita heard a cry that haunted her ever after. Standing at the edge of the crowd of curious onlookers, she heard one of them shouting, "Let the fucker burn! Let the fucker burn!" That, coupled with the way the fire appeared to have started outside on the roof of the bar, convinced her that it had been deliberately set. The fire investigator assigned to the case believed it was Juanita who had torched the place, presumably for the insurance money, basing much of his opinion, according to Juanita, on the fact that her large collection of copper kerosene cans were suspiciously empty. "Naturally they were empty," Juanita snorted, "they were antiques."

As much as Juanita loved "her" Fire Department, she accused them of fighting the fire halfheartedly. "Why didn't they put fans in to blow the smoke away and fight the fire where the flames were?" she asked herself and others repeatedly over the years. "After that idiot got hit on the head with the dulcimer, they just sat outside on their asses spraying water in the windows where there wasn't any fire yet!" A member of the Fire Department is in disagreement, naturally enough, with both the opinion of the fire investigator and Juanita's heated comments on the actions of the Department that day. Firefighters did all they could to save the old building, he said, but it was so old and the fire so hot that it didn't stand a chance. He is in agreement with Juanita, as are many others, that it was most likely a case of arson, although a case would have been impossible to make due to the disruption of evidence at the scene.

Unlike the El Verano fire, involving the loss of mere property, the Fetter's Hot Springs Hotel fire was a real tragedy, causing as it did the death of one of Juanita's closest friends. Chris Hill had not left the upper floor as Juanita had believed, but had turned the wrong way down a side hallway where she was overcome by smoke. Her remains were discovered at the end of the next day and Juanita was inconsolable. "It's all my fault!" she cried, putting her face into her hands. "I told her to sleep upstairs!"

It is more for this reason than for any other that few who know

Juanita well find it even slightly plausible that she could have set the blaze. Not only did she lose a loved friend, but Beauregard perished in the flames, as well as the multitude of beloved creatures that she had been unable to rescue from their cages in the old wooden structure. Gone was everything Juanita had accumulated over twenty years. The little money she recovered was saved because a courageous firefighter lay bellyfirst in the ashes, hunting for the money she told him she had put for safekeeping in the tank of an upstairs toilet, while another volunteer poured water over his back. Neils Chew at last arose triumphant with a roll of wet bills in one hand and a sackful of loose change in the other. "There weren't thousands of dollars," he explained, "but she sure was glad to get them."

After the fire, Juanita did not have one pair of shoes or a mantilla comb to her name. The silver lamé and velvet muumuus were but a memory, as were the electric cross, the apothecary chest, and her enormous collection of pincushion dolls. Gone were the Hoosier cabinets, the antique shoes, the Spanish dolls; gone were the loveseats, the pool table, the honkytonk piano. Gone were the photos of somebody else's relatives. Gone was the brass chandelier. Everything she loved was gone.

Keith Schwarz, Firefighter

I was a volunteer firefighter the first time I met Juanita, a rookie with the Valley of the Moon Fire Department. One evening we were called for a roof fire at her place in El Verano, and we quickly discovered that the fire was caused from sparks going up her fireplace chimney and setting fire to the leaves on the roof. I went inside and checked around and then I took the garden hose and put out the fire which was still blazing away in the fireplace; eliminating the sparks but also eliminating the only source of light they had in the bar at the time since the power was off. Well, Juanita came out and grabbed a hold and tore into me, yelling that not only had I put out their only light but that I'd used *her* water to do it! I'd never met the lady, and of course in training we'd always been taught to be very polite to the public even if someone gave you a lot of guff, so I tried to be as polite as I could be and at the same time get the hell away from her. I was a mess when I finally escaped.

I learned after that if you stood up to Juanita, she respected you. She might give you a bad time but if you gave it right back to her, you had no problems. I found out pretty fast that though she was kind of a rough character, she was also a great old girl underneath. I mean, no matter what she's always said about us, she *loves* the Fire Department. We have annual dinners at Christmastime for the kids and when she had a restaurant she never failed to send over ham and turkeys and so forth. One year we failed to mention the date of the dinner party, she only heard about it later, and we got our frames climbed unmercifully because we hadn't let her know. She just gave us hell.

Now, she might yell at us, and did, but she sure as hell wouldn't tolerate *other* people yelling at us. She might say bad things about us, but *you* better not say bad things about us because we were *her* Fire Department. We used to work twenty-four hour a day shifts, and sometimes a couple of us would decide we wanted something different for dinner and call Juanita and order a steak sandwich. She'd have them personally delivered on foot by one of her employees, served on a big tray on china and with silverware, and all for two dollars each. Someone would be sent later in the day to pick the plates back up. That's how she treated us – when there wasn't a fire. When there was, she wasn't quite as gracious.

We got a call late one night and responded over to her place at Fetter's and found a feed shed burning pretty bad. It was surrounded by cages of rabbits and other little animals and Juanita was out there real upset about how her animals were getting too hot next to the shed. She asked us for a pair of our gloves so she could move the cages and wasn't any too pleased that we couldn't loan her a pair since our guys all needed them to fight the fire. She followed one guy, yammering at him, until just to get rid of her he backed all the way into the burning doorway.

Lo and behold, the following week, in comes one of the fire supply companies with a gross of gloves for us. She'd ordered twelve dozen pair of gloves, paid for them and had them delivered to us, although we had only about 35 men in our department at that time and didn't exactly need one hundred and forty-four pair of gloves!

We took out enough to supply our department and ordered the rest returned and Juanita reimbursed. We also took out an extra pair for her. We painted an old helmet red –signifying a captain's rank – and we went over to her place and presented it to her with the pair of gloves in it. That helmet hung on the wall behind the check-in counter from that day on until the place burned down. She wouldn't let anybody mess with it, either – it was hers from the Fire Department.

Now, the Fetter's fire was a sad one, sadder than the one in El Verano because one of her waitresses died in the fire and also a wonderful landmark was destroyed. The call came in early one Sunday morning. We had crews there all day and all night long, fighting that one. It was an extremely hot fire, there was just no stopping it. At no time did we make the decision to let it burn down, as she has alleged. We were pumping all the water that the fire district could supply to us. It was just a very old building that was burning faster than our guys could put water on it.

She kept a lot of chickens and pigeons and things on the second floor verandah and that was where she was when we arrived, trying to release them from their cages. We yelled at her to get on the ladder but she wouldn't; she wouldn't leave those birds. One of the guys finally yelled at her, "You either get your ass on the ladder right now or jump, because we're moving it!" We had other people to get out of the building and weren't about to wait around for her to set all her pigeons and chickens free. She was angry at us, of course, for not coming up and helping her rescue her birds, but we weren't going to lose a firefighter for a bunch of pigeons, even though that might sound cold to some people and certainly did to *her*.

Finally she did get on the ladder in her big, flowing muumuu and come down. She was very upset and swore at us constantly as she was climbing down the ladder and during the rest of the day. Nothing we did was right, we were a bunch of assholes, the whole bit. Some of her employees who'd been living in the hotel hassled us about the way we were doing things until it got to the point we had to call in law enforcement to put a lid on them. After it was all over, Juanita went back to being the woman we knew and some of us loved.

When everything, including Juanita, had cooled down, some of us went back there and searched through the rubble. One of the guys who knew where her bedroom had been went to check if anything of hers had survived the fire. He found a huge roll of bills that she had apparently kept in the toilet tank. Other than being wet, the money was in good shape and Juanita was glad to have it since she'd lost everything else.

The rumor was, of course, that she had burned her places down herself. The investigation on the Fetter's fire was, at best, a futile attempt because of the fact that the waitress was lost, and that took priority over conducting an arson investigation since we first had to locate the body and that took until late the following day and with the aid of heavy equipment, which destroys evidence. The state investigator was working the fire and he told me that he was sure in his mind she was responsible for it and he was going to prove she did it if it killed him. I am a fire investigator myself, now, and so I can say that is not a good attitude to take into a fire investigation, although I've also thought it not impossible she might have set it. The investigator died not long after and nothing was proved one way or another; the exact cause of the fire is still unknown to this day.

There's a guy in San Francisco that could have been responsible for the fire, since we know he's responsible for I don't know how many other places torched for the insurance money, but we can't prove it. A lot of people were positive in their minds that Juanita set the fires and some people will never be convinced otherwise, although there are people who will swear she also burned down places in Sausalito, Texas, Port Costa and any other place on the globe where she's been, and some where she never was. People like to talk, about someone like Juanita in particular.

Alice Yarish, Journalist

I covered Juanita for the *San Francisco Examiner* when she was in Sausalito. Everybody I worked with in the newspaper business – myself included – thought she was a fascinating character. I've always loved wild and crazy people, and Juanita was never boring. For awhile she had a pet white turkey that wore a rhinestone necklace and a little red rooster that would sit on her shoulder all the time and when people would come up and say, "Oh, how cute! What's his name?" she'd say, "Chickenshit Smith," sweet as pie.

I remember the first time I saw her away from her restaurant, and that was when I was covering the county jail one Sunday. Two cops came walking in with Juanita between them. She had a bloody rag around her head and blood was streaming down her face and her blue jeans and white shirt had blood all over them too. "Hi, Alice!" she called out, "How're ya doin?" Jaunty as ever. She used to drink and fight and carry on in those days, and I guess she told me she'd gotten in a fight in her restaurant over something. I don't remember if she'd won. I doubt if *she* remembered.

Later on, in Sonoma, she was in all kinds of financial trouble so the next time I went up there to lunch, I put a hundred dollars in an envelope and gave it to her. She said thank you, balled it up in her hand, and I didn't hear another word, which I thought was funny since she's a very responsive person. A couple of weeks later I sent her a check for fifty bucks and when I next went to see her she said, "Thank God for that check you sent me! They were about to turn off my electricity." Again I thought it was odd that she didn't say anything about the hundred bucks I'd given to her previously, so I asked her if she remembered the blue envelope I'd given her last time we were together and she said yes. I asked, "Did you open it?" She said no, she hadn't, she'd forgotten. Maybe it was lost, she said, or maybe somewhere in her bed. I told her then what was in it and she said, "Oh, my God!" She called the next day to tell me that she'd gone through all of her desk drawers and finally found the envelope all crumpled up in the bottom of one of them.

She was in Fetter's Hot Springs when I talked the *Examiner* into doing another story about her. A photographer and I went up there and took a lot of photos of the hotel. About a week later the place burned down and Juanita called to ask me if I could bring her the photos we'd taken so she could show them to her insurance company. I told her I'd mail them, but she said, "No, I want you to bring them up yourself." I told her I was awfully busy but she talked me into it and up I went with the glossies. The place was so heartbreaking, and such a mess! I gave her the photographs and as I was leaving, she slipped this amethyst ring on my finger. I appreciated the kindness of the gesture but I figured it was just cheap dimestore jewelry. However, the more I looked at the ring the better I liked it and at a party the next night one of the other guests was a jeweler, so I asked him about it. I said, "Is this for real?" and he said, "Of course it's real. It's a beautiful ring."

Of course, considering the dire financial straits she was in, I figured she didn't know the value of the ring, so the next morning I called her and said, "Hey, Juanita, you made a big mistake. That ring you gave me isn't costume jewelry. It's real and it's worth a lot of money." She said, "I know it is. I knew that when I gave it to you." And I said, "But why did you give me something so valuable?" She answered, "Well, you probably don't know this, Alice, but in the old days when I was drinkin' and in trouble all the time, gettin' in fights and gettin' arrested, you were the only reporter who wrote about me as if I were a whiz-bang human being. You helped me quit drinkin' and go straight because of your regard for me. I've always been real grateful to you and I wanted to give you one of the few valuable things I have left."

12

"Juanita's Hotel-Zoo Comes To End In Charred Ruins"

– San Francisco Examiner

"Juanita Not Down Or Out, And Planning To Rebuild"

– Independent Journal

Whatever was not ashes, was dust. Juanita, her mother and twelve employees lived in the old cabins surrounding the ruins of the Fetter's Hotel without water or electricity for two months. Dressed in a hastily-sewn muumuu, wearing cast-off shoes on burnt feet, she wandered sadly in the ashes. Cooking on an antique woodstove that had survived the blazing verandah of the hotel, she prepared pots of stew in the middle of the dirt parking lot to keep "her people" fed. After water was hooked up, life was easier, but memories of the tragic fire kept the atmosphere of the improvised camp-out anything but cheerful.

"People will tell you that we were given our meals, but we weren't," Juanita explained. "I kind of take an offense to receiving charity." This, from the woman whose many acts of charity, as much as her swashbuckling demeanor, had made her a legend.

"Everything had to be bulldozed right away and carted off to the dump, and this was even though there were lots of burned-out places around in the valley that had sat there since the first trump!" Juanita said, disgusted. "In my case, it had to be done right away. I'd lost my voice from shock so somebody gave me a police whistle so I could stop the guy on the bulldozer if I found somethin' I wanted to save." One can almost hear the incessant tootle and the indignant flap flap of her sandals as she went in hot pursuit of a charred piece of cherished china, a twisted bit of metal.

"I'd whistle at the guy and he'd stop and I'd root around for awhile and load up stuff in my apron. Once I whistled at him but he was pissed off and wouldn't stop. Served him right; he ran into a water pipe and tore a hole through his radiator." She said this with all the complacency of virtue, as if the hand of Providence had skewered the bulldozer before her eyes, giving the driver exactly what he deserved for daring to ignore even one toot of that frantic refrain.

"He had to quit for two days, and during that time we picked up four gallon jars of pincushion dolls and melted silver! I found the little fire engine I'd tied to an old leather horse collar, too, even though the Fire Marshall pooh-poohed the very idea of finding anything. Ha!"

This happy triumph was shortlived. Soon the whole area was as flat and black as the top of Juanita's salvaged stove. People still scrounged around in hopes of finding treasure, but there was very little left to find. Rumors flourished that Juanita had now burned a second restaurant, a rumor fueled by the fact that the grease cans she was saving to be picked up had been found empty. Eyewitnesses to the fire declared that, yes, indeed, they had smelled burning grease. The spotlight focused ever brighter upon the fat and forlorn figure of Juanita as she stood, hair greying and unkempt, stirring her pots, surrounded by a bewildered assemblage of chickens, pigs and jobless employees. The accusations that she had "struck again" were painful and infuriating, but there was nothing Juanita could do about them. She had long ago made her peace with the fact that if she were to cultivate an aura of notoriety, she would have to accept unavoidable backlash. She thought sadly of the last Thanksgiving Dinner, when she had served six hundred people and the *San Francisco Examiner* had given the event excellent press by publishing a photograph on the front page of the paper's food section of her favorite turkey stepping majestically out of the cold oven. Wonderful times seemed far in the past, and her dreams lay in ruins around her. Many of her beloved animals had to be given to adoptive homes when it became clear that she could never rise again from those particular ashes, and she was deprived even of that undemanding devotion.

In the spring of 1975, and for the following ten years, Juanita took her show on the road. Like the Ringling Brothers, she took her cast from town to town, staying in a place anytime from two months to two years, taking along her mother, Hughie, her ongoing – if terribly diminished – animal acts, and a repertory company of employees who either slunk offstage after a few minutes or remained with rare devotion for the duration of what must have seemed the world's oddest and unluckiest vaudeville show.

Glen Ellen, several miles away, was her first stop. A charming country hamlet, it had been loved by Jack London, who had lived for years at the Beauty Ranch in the hills above town. Juanita took over the lease of a restaurant in a grist mill that had been built in 1835 as a sawmill by General Mariano Vallejo, who had been sent from Mexico to the Sonoma Valley to protect the northern flank of the Mexican Empire. It was a structure sufficiently old and wooden to please Juanita, and therefore sufficiently old and wooden to make a few other valley residents nervous. Attached to the side was a reproduction of the original water wheel, again in running order.

Most of Juanita's surviving pets were loaded into vans and pickup trucks and transported to their new home. Survivors of the fire who had been in hiding straggled tardily into Glen Ellen with the weary disenchantment of luckless goldminers. One such straggler was Dominick the peacock, who gave Juanita's Grist Mill a wide berth and went to live with Russ Kingman, owner of the Jack London Bookstore across the street. Russ, the world's leading authority on London and his works, gave houseroom not only to the peacock, but to Erica the pig. A man of unusual tolerance, he allowed them the kind of freedom they had known under Juanita's wing. A few chickens made the journey, although most of those that had gone back to the wild had long since become dinner for valley dogs. With mixed emotions, Russ watched Juanita settle in.

The beautifully-restored old building had one major flaw. With her bedroom upstairs, Juanita was forced to make too many trips a day for knees that had been abused ever since the days she knelt to scrub convent floors. She could not bear not being on hand to wrap her enormous breasts around the necks of the unsuspecting, or to let kitchen activities go unsupervised. Yet she needed her naps in order to function from dawn until near-dawn. Dragging her three hundred pounds up and down stairs as many as twenty times a day frequently landed Juanita in bed, where, in her frustration, she hired and fired employees with restless abandon. She would rather have been whacked with her own skillet than to have anyone see what pain she was in; and so, as though to emphasize her undiminished capacity, Juanita threw herself into the constant brouhahas with undiminished zeal. One evening she overheard a ruckus in the dining room and hurled herself downstairs from her bed of rest in time to see one young man menacing another with a knife and a broken pool cue. Without a word, a savvy onlooker handed her an unbroken cue. She began to wallop the attacker about the head and shoulders. "That hurts, Juanita!" he cried, trying to shield himself from the blows raining down upon him. "How does it feel to have a fuckin' pool cue up your butt, you moron!" she yelled. Both were taken to jail, although Juanita was soon released to go home and the young man released to go to the hospital for treatment of his lacerations.

Business prospered. Tour buses were frequently lined up outside the restaurant like suckling piglets on a hog. Yet Juanita still found it difficult to keep up with the constant—and often hotly contested—demands from creditors, landlords and governmental hired hands. She generally paid her bills, but did so later rather than sooner. Her philosophy when dealing with entities such as Ma Bell or the electric company was to wait until she received an urgent notice of pending disconnection before jumping in her car and hurtling to the nearest office to pay what she owed. On occasion she did not make it. Twice she had to keep a serviceman treed until a messenger could be sent to pay the bill while she stood at the bottom of the pole like a mastiff until the serviceman could be permitted to climb down.

Before long, Juanita's landlord insisted that the rent be paid on a daily basis, delivered each morning before the doors of the Grist Mill could be opened for business. It was all just so … unsportsmanlike. That, "those damned stairs," and the fact that her remaining animals were not allowed inside but were forced to mope out of doors, kept Juanita from driving her tent stakes in too deeply. Within a year she was approached with an offer to take over running a restaurant in Port Costa, a tiny railroad town on the San Francisco Bay, some fifty miles from Glen Ellen. She accepted the offer, folded her tent and, after a spirited debate over who owned what, left the Sonoma Valley with a sense of resignation and her usual high hopes.

No doubt local business people watched Juanita leave with mixed feelings. Though she could be generous to a fault, it was rarely with people to whom she owed money, although she mostly managed to pay her bills, or had every intention of doing so "real soon." A small convoy of pickup trucks loaded up Juanita, Louise, Hughie, Rattle-Ass, Monsignor O'Farrell, the blind rooster and the one-eyed pigeon. Erica the pig had gone to live on a farm, the horse and jenny had been adopted along with most of the goats and chickens, and Dominick the peacock had recently died in a freak automobile accident. Juanita had had a year in which to begin a new collection of antiques and knick-knacks and she had not let one acquisitive opportunity pass her by. Treasures filled two trucks and every available human lap. It was "Port Costa or Bust."

It would be hard to find a more charming old town than Port Costa, reportedly the setting for Jack London's cautionary novel, *John Barleycorn*. Its glory days as a busy shipping port were long past. Fires had destroyed the town's wooden docks and no one had been sufficiently roused to rebuild them. The short main street with its Victorian saloons and hostelries had been purchased by Bill Rich, an entrepreneur interested in preserving whatever had managed to with-stand the years of desertion and neglect. On one side of the tree-lined street, the Burlington Hotel conjured up memories of the time when a hundred trains a day came puffing into town. On the other was the old grain warehouse, whose cavernous insides resembled nothing so much as the dark dwelling of gypsies who had amused themselves by nailing their possessions to the ceiling and walls. Chandeliers, bird-cages and farm implements hung like stalactites from the ceiling. A spiral staircase, a theatre box office, and assorted hatracks rose like sta-lagmites from the floor. Interesting or artistic clutter filled the corners. The place was already a restaurant, and so as far as Juanita was concerned, all the Warehouse needed was a little more of everything to make it just perfect.

Right away, she had the beautiful carved bar moved further back into the shadows, and a couch installed in the entrance where she could greet customers and take her naps. Velvet valances were hung from the rafters. Buffets, antique stoves and old refrigerators sprouted like mushrooms in the gloom, providing level spaces to hold a variety of electric and kerosene lamps. Mirrors were hung on the walls, although it was too dark for them to reflect anything in their murky surfaces but shadowy forms and distant small pools of lamplight. Over the salad bar, she erected a red satin tent that glowed from within like a Bedouin version of a red light district. The whole effect combined the Casbah and a Salvation Army collection center.

Juanita had just finished putting rugs down everywhere when there was an autumnal flood. According to her, it "raised all the rugs three inches from the floor. We were a foot and a half under water in the restaurant and the crap from the sewer system started coming up, too, so we had to close down until everything could dry up. Right away I saw a problem and so I had a guy cut a groove in the floor so water could go down a drain." What Bill Rich thought of this improvement was not mentioned, but she did add, somewhat irrelevantly, that when Bill eventually decided to pour a new concrete floor, he left all of the furniture where it was, instantly making everything a permanent fixture, "even the tables, honey." If this was really what happened—and it is hard to imagine that it did—it must have instantly solved the problem of pilfering of the café's furnishings.

It was to be expected that the pool of available employees in such a backwater would include some characters. One waitress wore earrings made out of goat droppings, prompting Juanita to comment, "I really didn't think that was right in a dinin' room, but she sorta liked the bottle and maybe that persuaded her." Another waitress, lashed into a frenzy by a lethal combination of booze and bullying, took a knife to Juanita and when that didn't do the trick, smacked her with a frying pan.

The Warehouse Café had been a popular watering hole for years, but with the addition of Juanita, business boomed almost as if the good old days of Port Costa had returned. The antique shops upstairs and those along the main street benefited from the increase in foot traffic. Juanita, disappointed that there was no bedroom connected to the Warehouse dining room, found the next best thing and set up her bed in the lobby of the Burlington Hotel across the way. There was plenty of room, she explained, "and I could just say hi to everybody who wanted to rent a room for the night and tell 'em how they had to eat dinner across the street." She felt that the rooms of the Burlington lacked that lived-in look so she put old clothes in the closets and old shoes under the beds and scattered knickknacks on top of the antique dressers. None these homey touches cost much – of course neither did the rooms – which was fortunate since they regularly disappeared with departing guests.

"I recognized some of the clothes when people came in for dinner," Juanita admitted, "and I was real happy they felt like dressin' up. Pretty often, though, they just kept wearin' the clothes right on outta town." This was okay, too, she added, since they wouldn't have stolen the clothes if they hadn't needed them.

A very needy guest indeed disappeared one morning with all of his room's knickknacks, as well as a dresser drawer to cart them away in. "Shoulda used a pillowcase, the asshole," Juanita commented. "It was a nice birdseye maple dresser, too, and I had to make the place where the drawer was gone into a shelf," where she put a doily and more knickknacks.

Did Juanita ever get fed up with the larcenous nature of some of her customers? "Nah. I never got bitter about people stealin' from me. When I found myself gettin' a little bit cynical, I'd go see Sally. I always told myself that no matter what happened to me, I never wanted to end up as cynical as she did. If you're cynical, it doesn't matter how much stuff you own 'cause you can't really enjoy it. I'd just as rather not have anything at all than end up like that."

According to Juanita, Bill Rich repeatedly suggested that the hotel should stay locked to keep the merely curious from trespassing and making off with of the furnishings, but she always rejected the idea. "I wanted it kept open so anybody who wanted to could go in and look around. If they stole somethin', that's just the way it was."

Her tolerant philosophy did not extend to breaches of good sense and decorum in the Warehouse Café, however. Many customers were told, in no uncertain terms, that their behavior was unacceptable to their hostess. At lunch one day a young woman and her boyfriend were helping themselves from the salad bar when the girl dropped a serving spoon. Alert to impending mischief, Juanita watched as she replaced the spoon in a bowl of salad. With a roar, Juanita thundered up behind her and slapped her soundly on the posterior. "Now I have to throw out this whole bowl of beans because you did that! If you worked for me, you'd be fired!" Mortified, the young woman dragged her highly-amused boyfriend out the door. Another time, Juanita stood witness as a man hacked clumsily at a large baked ham. "Just stop that, you asshole!" Juanita bellowed, "you're just makin' a mess of the whole fuckin' thing!"

Juanita regularly reprimanded customers who filled their plates so that the foods overlapped. "Why are you sloppin' everything together like that?" she would say, chin thrust out and hands on hips. "You won't be able to tell a damn thing apart! I might as well just slop it all into a bowl in the first place, you moron!" She would also tell people to leave if they dared to mention other restaurants as their favorites ("Then get your ass right on outta here!") or if they made unkind remarks about the help ("Out!") or if they decided to get a little too rough. A one-time member of an infamous motorcycle gang recalled that he was in the Warehouse Café one night with a few fellow members when Juanita decided it was time to crack some heads. Of what dreadful lapse they were guilty he never knew, but he made the observation that he doubted they would ever do it again, "at least not anywhere near Juanita."

Her many kindnesses were greater in number, although considerably less spectacular, being largely unmentioned, and determinedly unpublicized, by herself. Lee Rae Mullins remembered a man, obviously down on his luck, who came into the café late one afternoon and stood for a long moment studying the price list posted on the wall. Unaware that he was being observed, he pulled out his trouser pockets and counted his money. Shoulders drooping, he was just about to leave when Juanita shouted across the room, "Hey, where the fuck do you think *you're* goin"? Understandably startled, he stood rooted to the spot. "Come on over here," she called in a softer voice, "come on over here, honey, and have somethin' to eat." He walked shyly toward her and after she told him to sit down, she ordered Lee Rae to help her fill two large platters full of food. They plunked these down in front of the man who, looking embarrassed, murmured, "But I can't pay you for all of this food." "I don't want your money, honey," Juanita replied, putting a warm hand on his shoulder. "Now you just eat all you want and don't think another thing about it."

A lesser woman might have patronized such a man, or given him a token serving of the cheaper dishes, or watched cautiously as he nervously served himself. Not Juanita. Ordered to sit down and eat, he might have been reminded of his mother, or his drill sergeant, and be reassured that he was not accepting charity but obeying a more powerful authority. No one stood around to watch him as he ate and his thanks were accepted with friendly indifference when he left. "Things like that happened all the time," Lee Rae said. "She just could never stand to see a person or an animal go hungry. That's always been her way."

Of course, Juanita herself would have insisted that it was no big deal. And perhaps it wasn't, except to a man who did not have to trade his dignity for a full stomach.

Coming to the aid of the underdog was always Juanita's avocation. "This one day," she remembered, "a guy was walkin' down the street with his little dog on a leash. A biker started makin' fun of him and somebody came runnin' into the restaurant to get me. I ran on out and saw what was goin' on, so I grabbed that biker by his hair and held on. He started yellin' that he was gonna sue me for pullin' his hair, but I said, 'Hey, buddy, I just got ahold of it. You're doin' all the pullin'. About this time Bill Rich came runnin' out with a gun and I let go and the biker took off. When I went up to Bill, he just had two barrels of a gun and that was all, no trigger or nothing else connected to them. I said, 'Bill, how in the hell did you figure you were gonna protect me with that?' and he said, 'Well, the guy left, didn't he?' I sure couldn't argue with that!"

As if customers, employees and other troublemakers were not enough, Juanita's animals were as mischievous as ever. Rattle-Ass, who was camping for the summer on a nearby ranch, went AWOL on a regular basis. People would catch him and, knowing to whom he belonged, call Juanita. "I tell you, that Rattle-Ass walked me all over those hills," Juanita recalled. "I knew every damned rock. Once I tried to bring him back in a Camaro –with me ridin' in the trunk and leadin' him – but he wouldn't cooperate and so I had to walk him all the way to town. Once I brought him right on into the Warehouse to sing Happy Birthday to a guy ." Never much of a hiking enthusiast, Juanita regretfully agreed to retire Rattle-Ass to a large ranch where the fences were sturdy and the resident jenny agreeably wayward.

On a sadder note, Monsignor O'Farrell disappeared. As Juanita recalled, "There hadn't been any horse rustlin' in the county for over ten years, and nobody ever had rustled a mule. This was the first time, and he was gone for good."

Romance blossomed at the Warehouse Café when the blind rooster and the one-eyed pigeon fell in love. "They used to walk up and down the main street," Juanita remembered, "and the pigeon would never fly when he was with the rooster, just always walk right alongside him so as not to hurt his feelings. They were real pals, except when we caught them doin' it a couple of times. They were gay, I guess. Some people from Minneapolis spent all of one evening watchin' that pigeon bring twigs to the rooster, who was buildin' a nest in a big watering can. He was just inside there, cluckin' away like a hen.

"You know what? That very night somebody stole that pigeon. That's the God's truth. The nest got done, anyway, but it sure took the wind outta that rooster's sails. He just wandered around after that, lookin' for him."

Perhaps it was heartbreak that soured the rooster's good nature. He became so nasty after his love departed that he began nipping at everyone who tried to comfort him in his sorrow. "Sombitch" he was soon re-christened, and "Sombitch" he remained until his grief was spent and he no longer bit the hands that fed him.

Though Juanita loved Port Costa and added so many artistic touches to the decor of the Warehouse Café, she was nonetheless restless. When a couple of businessmen expressed interest in bankrolling a Galley in Las Vegas, she gave the idea some thought and even accompanied them on a fact-finding mission to the town where anything goes but money. Swept from pillow to post in a limousine, wined and dined to a faretheewell, even given a tour of Liberace's museum by the glittering songbird himself, Juanita still hated the town. "I mean, could you see a buncha high rollers eatin' enchiladas at my place?" Juanita demanded. "And what would I have done with Sombitch and Rattle-Ass and my mother and Hughie? So I just said, 'Thanks but no thanks,' and went back home."

A "skinny bald guy" sidled up to her one day with another business proposition—one much closer to home—and she leaped at it. There were no hard feelings when she left Bill Rich and the Warehouse Café, although it is reasonable to wonder whether customers felt they were getting their money's worth without the bawdy floorshow. A grandmotherly sort had knitted Juanita a pair of woolen "breasts" and these she thoughtfully left with Bill's sister, Sue, to wear if she ever felt so inclined; they must have seemed a puny substitute for the originals.

Vallejo was the next stop on Juanita's culinary odyssey. The "skinny bald guy" owned a large Spanish-style hotel/restaurant that might have seen better days, had it not been in Vallejo where the good old days could never have been many. Vallejo was the kind of large town that decided long ago to take a few half-hearted steps toward "progress," and gave itself a center of town that was shabby, grimy and an architectural mongrel. Most of the few nice Victorian buildings were boarded up and derelict. Though there were some charming old houses, they were obviously struggling against weather and neglect to remain standing. "At that time," Juanita explained, "Vallejo was doin' a lot of tearing down of old buildings and puttin' in parking lots. There wasn't much in the way of business downtown— there wasn't much of a downtown, period—but they were sure puttin' in a lot of parking lots, anyway, maybe in case somebody might wanta go there someday."

Juanita rented a house for her mother and got Hughie settled in, then rolled up her sleeves. The Casa de Vallejo restaurant was lovely and even had a mural on one wall depicting Spanish priests bringing Catholicism and conquistadores to the new continent. Everything in the kitchen had to be brought up to code, however, including a new hot water heater. When opening day finally dawned, Juanita discovered she would not be allowed to open after all. Inspectors had discovered that the hot water heater had been installed incorrectly. "I wondered why in the hell it was takin' so long to get hot water," Juanita said. "Then we figured out that pipes carried the water all over the whole damn hotel before it would get to the kitchen, lukewarm." That night she gave away everything she had prepared, since it was already cooked and she wasn't about to see it go to waste. Of course she also suggested that her new customers might like to contribute "donations," just so, as she said, "everything will be on the up and up." Most everybody did.

Sorry that she couldn't have her animals in the restaurant, Juanita started keeping a small iguana on her shoulder, attached by a leash to a pin on her sleeve. Sombitch lived in her house, although their hospitality did not stop him from nipping Juanita or her mother whenever they fed him. Faithful customers found where she had gone and kept on coming, although nobody—except perhaps the locals— seem to have thought too highly of the Galley's new location. There was, as Gertrude Stein wrote once of Oakland, "no there, there."

Eight months later, the building was sold out from under Juanita to investors who planned to turn the Casa de Vallejo into a senior residence. She was told, nicely, to pack and scram. She moved to an old Victorian, also badly in need of renovation. Once the necessary caulking and plumbing and spackling had been done, she discovered that a nearby church was raising hell about her selling wine and beer. She had as much chance of getting through the eye of a needle, they seemed to be predicting, as she did of getting a permit. By now she had also discovered that so few tables could be crammed into the dining room that many of her customers were forced either to wait impossible lengths of time to sit down (all the while remaining quite unintentionally sober) or to be served on the back steps. Having her customers gnaw their prime ribs while contemplating the garbage cans was not even Juanita's idea of gracious dining.

The stakes were pulled up once more and Juanita, vowing never again to stray, returned to Port Costa and the Warehouse Café. This time she stayed three years, from 1979 to the spring of 1982. In February of that year, her old friend and sparring partner, Sally Stanford, died of heart failure. The colorful madam-turned-mayor, who was once quoted as saying, "I should have run for President of the United States. At least there's some dough in it," left the ring without ever once hanging up her gloves.

"When Sally Stanford died," Sue Rich recalled, "Juanita said she didn't have the right sort of muumuu to wear to the funeral. Somebody made her one out of a damask tablecloth, and she wore a beautiful black mantilla and her tortoiseshell comb. Then she said she didn't have a car that would get that far, so I loaned her my red convertible. Off she went with the top down, her mantilla blowin' in the wind. On the way she was caught speedin' but the cop recognized her and when she told him where she was goin', he told her to go right along and have a nice time, even though she didn't even have a driver's license since it was burnt up in the last fire she'd had and she hadn't bothered to get another one."

Shortly after Sally's passing, Juanita decided it was again time to pack her shoeboxes and go. Cabin fever, and an accumulation of old arguments, once more illuminated the yellow brick road to an Oz always just beyond reach.

Emily Pickens, Vice-President/Bank Manager

My husband and two children and I had just moved from the suburbs to a small farm with a stable and a chicken coop in Glen Ellen. Shortly after we arrived, I took the girls, who were five and seven years old, down to the feed store to see about getting each one of them a chicken. They were really excited to see all the baby chicks in the coops and kept saying, "Mommy, come look!"

All of a sudden a very large woman in a floor-length muumuu came out of nowhere and put her arm around me. "Are you looking for chickens?" she asked. I said yes and she said, "Well, don't buy them here. I have plenty you can have for free." She turned to the girls then and said, "Would you girls like to have chickens?" Oh yes, they said, yes they would! "And I bet you'd like to have goats, too, wouldn't you? And a pig? I bet you'd like to have a *horse*, too, wouldn't you?"

Here she's talking to two children who have suddenly gone to heaven. I mean, the idea of two baby chicks was as far as I had planned to go and they'd been completely satisfied with that. Suddenly they were getting much bigger ideas – thanks to this strange woman who told us her name was Juanita. She gave us her address and told us to come over right away and bring a couple of cardboard boxes.

My husband and I talked about whether we should go at all, but we decided I'd really sort of promised and of course the girls were not *about* to let the subject die. So we went, telling each other that we'd get the girls one chick each and since we already had a coop, how bad could it be? We didn't even know where Fetter's Hot Springs was, but a couple of days later we piled into our Volkswagon and drove on over.

When we got to her place we couldn't believe our eyes – it had burned to the ground! It must have just happened because the ruins were still smoking. Juanita was there and right away she told us to start sifting through the ashes because, she told us, there was a great deal of money in there and if we could find it we could keep it. We told her that we really didn't want to start searching through ashes—I mean, little plumes of smoke were still erupting from them—but we would be very grateful to be given two chickens.

She told us then that we could have the chickens just as soon as we could catch them since they were all wild. I mean, I'd sort of pictured them in coops like they'd been at the feed store, not running around in the bushes! She had these two "characters" there—I don't know how else to politely describe them—one of whom was wearing a long overcoat down to his ankles and buttoned up to his neck, and it was a hot day. Juanita started yelling directions accompanied by every four-letter word imaginable. After several hours of these guys stumbling around after these chickens they finally managed to catch a couple and put them in one box. Then Juanita said, "I just absolutely love these kids, so I'm going to give you my prize – Sir Cock!" This turned out to be the rooster she used to carry on her shoulder in her restaurant. We looked all over and he finally turned out to be in her bedroom in this rundown motel nearby. There was chickenshit *everywhere*, even all over the bed, and Juanita said "It's okay if you want to go jump on the bed, kids!" but they sat rather gingerly on the side of it. Sir Cock was standing on the dresser and she went over and grabbed him and then put him in the other cardboard box.

Then she took the girls over to see her goats, Charlie and Ferris. These were two full-grown, neutered male goats who, as it turned out, had learned the trick of running up behind people and knocking them over backwards. She gave them to the girls. Then she said, "Come on, kids, now I want to show you my horse, Star." The horse was just darling and very quiet and somehow we agreed to take the horse, too, although we managed to put our feet down about taking the mule and the jackass, insisting that we didn't have the room, however delightful we knew they would be as pets. Fortunately we couldn't take the pig because, thank God, we weren't allowed to have pigs where we lived.

We told Juanita that we didn't know anything at all about taking care of animals since we'd lived in the suburbs all our lives, but she said, "Oh, they'll eat anything!" Which, of course, turned out not to be true at all. We told her that we didn't have anything but the Volkswagon to transport animals in but she just waved away that objection and said, "Oh, don't worry about that. Where do you live?" I think she actually wanted to check out what kind of home the animals were going to, although I think we'd already "passed" as a typical American kind of family.

The next Sunday morning she arrived in a step-van. Not a horse trailer, not a cattle truck, but a step-van. I don't know how she had ever managed to get the horse into it, but she backed up to the side of the barn and unloaded the goats and Star. The girls were beside themselves. Then Juanita came into the kitchen, told me she was going to cook breakfast, and moved me gently out of the room. She made the most wonderful pancakes.

One of the goats turned out to be really old and had to be put down after awhile because his arthritis was so bad. Stephanie rode Star for years, everywhere she went she went on that horse. The chickens were nice and laid green and blue eggs and had lots of chicks, thanks to Sir Cock who bred them morning noon and night. The girls were always saying, "Mommy, why is the rooster jumping on our chickens all the time?" He was also the most amazing escape artist. He could crawl under or fly over anything and then he'd always head for our neighbor's back porch where he'd sit and crow at four o'clock in the morning and attack all the neighborhood dogs, including ours.

At other times, Sir Cock would sit by our back door, which tended to be a little messy and frequently dangerous if you didn't look where you stepped. He would try to get on our shoulders and we'd have to keep batting him down all the time. He also liked to get on the table and investigate whatever you might be eating. He'd insist on pecking at it or stepping in it or climbing on top of it. Obviously he'd had a lot of freedom and was used to walking wherever he pleased.

Russ Kingman, Author/Bookstore Owner

Juanita moved across the street into the Grist Mill Restaurant with a big pig named Erica. She put the pig up on the hill behind my bookstore and had a fence built around her to keep Erica in, but because she'd get lonely she'd break out and come on down to see me. She fell in love with me and after awhile there was this path beaten from her pen to my door. We'd push her back on up the hill and fix the fence, but she'd just lean against it and since she weighed five hundred pounds, the fence would fall right on over again and down she'd come. Finally we all gave up and let her do what she wanted and she took up residence in a little grove of redwood trees nearby. One of the first things she did with her freedom was eat up all of our patio furniture cushions, so we told Juanita and she said, "How much did it set you back?" and we told her about thirty dollars. Two days later she came into the store with this glass pig full of about forty dollars worth of quarters.

Boy, I liked that pig, but she sure gave me a terrible time. I'd go out and wash the car, forgetting about Erica, and she'd come up and rub against me and all that weight just absolutely crushed me against the car, which I think has a lot to do with the state of my knees today. All she wanted was to be petted, and every morning I'd go out and say, "Good morning, Erica," and she'd say, "Oink, oink," and then flop over on her back with her legs in the air so I'd scratch her belly, but she pretty much killed me sometimes.

One day somebody spray-painted a sign on the side of Juanita's restaurant that said, "Juanita is Erica's retarded sister." Oh, Juanita just laughed and laughed. Thought it was real funny!

One morning a peacock appeared on our roof, and it turned out to be Juanita's peacock that had finally managed to locate where she'd gone after her Fetter's place burned down. He decided to stay with us and right away became a member of the family. His name was Dominick and he used to fan his tailfeathers when I told him to. One day he imagined he was following a peahen or something and was walking alongside our driveway when this woman driver got mesmerized by him. You know how a lot of people will drive where they look? Well, she drove right on over Dominick and broke his neck. Juanita saw it happen and she came running over just when I picked him up. Blood was pouring out of his neck, but he tried to fan for me. Juanita just stood there and blubbered, tears running down her cheeks. I put him inside this 20,000 gallon wine barrel by the store while I attended to something else, and when I got back to where I'd left him, he was gone. A few minutes later a waitress came over and said, "Juanita had me take the peacock over to a taxidermist to have him mounted." She paid for it, too, and gave him to me, and I put him up over the bookstore door where he's been ever since. Nobody else would have thought of doing something like that – only Juanita.

You know, Juanita is really two people: the nicest person you ever met in your life and the worst person you ever met. Depends on how she feels and whether she's been drinking. I'll give you some examples. I had some Hollywood people up here visiting, actors and screenwriters, and we walked over to have dinner at Juanita's. We were sitting there and Tommy Smothers came in and sat down and we all started talking back and forth. One of the guys I was with went over and whispered something to Juanita, who was about half lit, and she went over to him and pulled one breast out of her muumuu and flopped it on his shoulder and then pulled out the other and decorated his other shoulder, too. Tommy was a great friend of hers and had dinner there really often.

My wife and I would go over quite a bit and since we didn't like to eat too much, we'd just have the salad bar, which was plenty. Well, we'd be about halfway through when the waitress would come over with plates full of prime rib, cooked just the way we liked it. We'd always say we hadn't ordered it, and the waitress would always say, "Oh, I know that, but Juanita wants you to have it." Then sometimes a waitress would come across the street at lunchtime with a platter covered by a towel, and she'd say, "Juanita wants you to have something to eat," and under the towel would be this huge slab of prime rib.

On the other hand, just to show you how difficult and strange she could be: one of her waitresses got drunk late one night and didn't quite make the turn at the bridge and ran smack into a tree. A couple of days later, my wife and a friend and I were walking by there and I said, "Juanita's waitress got drunk and didn't make the turn." All of a sudden Juanita pops up from where she'd been sitting out of sight behind some bushes and starts calling me every name a sailor ever heard – and some others I think she invented on the spot for the occasion. I listened for awhile and then I stepped up to her and grabbed the front of her muumuu and kind of twisted it tight and said, "Now look. You act like a man and talk like a man, and if you call me one more name, I'm going to knock you down on your fat rear end just as if you *were* a man! Now call me one more name, that's all I want!" Well, she was all apologetic and there's never been a harsh word between us since. I have to say, all in all, that she's really one of the nicest people I've ever met and has a heart bigger than she is. No put on about it either. She's just honestly good.

My ex-husband and I operated the Grist Mill restaurant in nearby Glen Ellen, but as we had decided to divorce we were selling the lease. My ex-husband got the cash part of the deal and I got the note, so I went to work for Juanita in a kind of managerial position, mainly to keep an eye on things. We moved out one day and she moved in the next, and in one day the clientele changed completely. Isn't that strange? The very first day everybody was different. I kind of figured that my clientele wouldn't be the kind that Juanita attracted, but then the atmosphere of the place was so utterly transformed. That first day Juanita had decided to put on a "Turkish Thanksgiving," whatever that was, and I guess that pretty well signalled the changing of the guard.

I discovered right away what a great showwoman Juanita was. She knew that a restaurant is a personality business and she milked that to the nth degree. Groups of people would come in and usually she'd go up behind the shyest or cutest male at the table and plunk her breasts on his shoulders. Now that's pure showmanship! You'd hear the people at the table all talking about which ten people they were next going to bring to Juanita's, and if that doesn't prove what a good businesswoman she was, I don't know what would! Every time she'd do something outrageous you'd always see people elbowing each other delightedly and saying, "See? That's why I brought you here!" They just loved it. She'd be on stage all day. I'd usually close up at night and so I'd see her after a long day and she'd be in agony with her knees, but none of her customers would have known the pain she was in.

I started training bartenders and almost as fast as I could train them, Juanita'd fire them. It was a revolving door; bartenders in, bartenders out. One night, soon after she had taken' over, she was telling this biker to get out when he flipped her over on her back and really hurt her. She had to take to her bed for awhile where she spent her time being aggravated and firing bartenders.

With all the showmanship, Juanita was no fake. She was as honest as it's possible to be and a shrewd restaurateur. She controlled the inventory and knew where every penny was going. Many employees had been with her for years and were excellent, professional people. Juanita didn't pay great wages, but the tips were so good, especially if she yelled at you in front of a customer. She never had trouble finding help.

Most people quickly learned that underneath all the shouting, Juanita was loving and giving to a fault. I had started a lunch program for patients at the nearby mental hospital. Someone had come in asking if they could bring some of their developmentally disabled over for lunch so they could experience what it was like to eat in a restaurant. I thought it was a good idea and it worked out so well that it became a weekly thing, and Juanita continued the tradition all the time she was in Glen Ellen. They were always made welcome, just as everybody always was at Juanita's.

At the very beginning of the exodus of the "boat people" from Vietnam, Juanita was one of the first to volunteer to take the refugees in and give them work. Nine refugees came up to work for her and from the start it was hysterical. A translator was supposed to accompany them, but there was some kind of snafu. I knew a little bit of Lao, as it happened, which they sort of understood, and I'd try to interpret for them in the frequent crises. Juanita really tried to do her best, but these people just drove her crazy. It was "show and tell" time with them every day, and they'd watch patiently and then go ahead and do things their own way. Juanita had a definite way of doing things, a consistent way of having things done which is a necessity in a high-volume restaurant like hers. She'd yell and scream at them out of pure frustration, but they wouldn't have the slightest idea what she was yelling about. They were Buddhists and there isn't much yelling in the Buddhist culture, so Juanita was probably something of a shock to them. However, since Buddhists feel that life is purgatory and you're supposed to do good works and then go on to nirvana afterwards, they seemed to shrug things off. I think her yelling soon became kind of funny to them, once they'd caught on that her bark was much worse than her bite. Besides, she was paying them and feeding them and clothing them and I think they knew how good her heart was, in spite of all the noise that went along with it.

In 1979, Juanita came to manage the Warehouse Cafe, which my brother Bill still owns. The Warehouse was always kind of wild looking, with revolving doors at the entrance and a big spiral staircase in the middle that reached all the way up to the high old ceiling. One time this guy came down it naked as a jaybird and streaked the place!

Right away she made changes. She moved the bar from the front to the back and put a long couch in the entrance hallway where she took her naps. She'd lay down there and snore in front of everybody. When somebody would come by and start laughing, she'd sit up and yell, "Why you son-of-a-bitch, what's wrong with *you?*" It was hilarious, sometimes.

In the beginning I just couldn't stand her shouting at me the way she did, because my feelings got hurt real easy. I mean, you could never put a spoon in the salad bar the way she wanted it – she'd come over, yelling, and pick up the spoon and then put it back exactly the way you had put it in the first place. People would be waiting around for Sunday brunch and she'd start up with, "Goddamn it, there isn't one fuckin' person around here who can do one fuckin' thing *right!*" At that I'd start to cry and she'd turn on me with, "What the hell are *you* crying about?" I'd tell her, "If you don't know then just go ahead and do everything yourself!" and I'd walk out and go on home. Later on, when I got to know her better, we talked about it and made a pact that she'd warn me when she was about to go on a tirade in the dining room. "Sue," she'd say, "I'm gonna get on your butt now and cause a little disturbance, so get ready, honey." When I was forewarned, it was okay. She could be ferocious, but not as ferocious as people thought she was because some of it was an act. Of course, some of it *wasn't* either! I remember once there was a line of people waiting outside for brunch and when we opened the door and the crowd started coming in, all of a sudden a lampshade burst into flames. One of the customers said, real loud, "Well, I guess Juanita's at it again, trying to burn *this* old place down now." Juanita overheard him and started shouting, "I'm gonna *kill* the son-of-a-bitch that said that!" But she couldn't figure out who it was and nobody volunteered the information. She didn't mince words at all. I've heard her with local people who would say to her that it was the first time they'd come to the Warehouse, that they usually went to eat in other places. Boy, she'd just fire up at that and yell, "Well, what the hell are you doing here *now*? Why don't you just get your asses *back* to those other places if you like 'em so well?!"

People would come from miles around to hear her and to see the wild things she would do. There were those people who would get real offended and say they weren't ever coming back – but there were a hundred times more people who would come back time and again because they loved to see Juanita in action. She'd go out and get on the tour busses when they'd arrive. Sometimes they'd be full of senior citizens so old they would have to be helped down, but she would have them all laughing in no time at all! People would come from overseas to visit the United States, and one of the big attractions they weren't going to miss was Juanita. I've personally talked to people when I was on tours overseas and they'd know who Juanita was!

Of course, her food was as famous as her tongue. It was wonderful and she served these enormous portions of food – food my brother had to pay for. It wasn't coming out of *her* pocket. But then she always had served huge amounts of food and had never been too concerned that a lot of it got wasted. She just never has had any sense of money whatsoever. My brother just kept buying all this food and she'd cook far too much for the number of people, and then give away the scraps to all the animals around in Port Costa. Of course, on the other side of it, she also brought in quite a few customers, too.

Russ Riera, Restaurant Reviewer/Radio Personality

I first became acquainted with Juanita's Galley when I started writing restaurant reviews in 1971. I wrote about her until 1979, so I knew what most of her places were like. My first book was called *The Good Time Manual*, and the idea was just to read about colorful places and have a good time. The thing about Juanita was that you didn't have to try to write colorfully because colorful copy was always supplied to you by the woman, herself. There was a ton of material around since she was so wonderful to write about. I venture to say that no restaurant person was ever written about more than she was.

She always seemed wonderfully eccentric, like a madam out of the movies, an outrageous woman who was ready to do anything and say anything to anybody. People would make pilgrimages to her places, which were each one like a movie set. Added to this, her staff was always this hodgepodge of people, a lot of free spirits who were drifting around during the more hangloose seventies. It was like those forties' movies where a bunch of people say, "Oh come on, let's all get together and put on a *play*. To heck with the money and the business, let's just have fun!" Like an Our Gang comedy. Customers really pulled for her, too. It didn't matter if you had to get your own water or help in the kitchen or put up with lousy service, it was like you were part of the show.

She transcended the mere running of a restaurant. I mean, nobody could start out with the idea of running a restaurant that way. The right alchemy has to happen. The times have to be right, the place has to be right, the character has to be genuine. People can tell if a character is the genuine article and they gravitate toward that person. For instance, if the hostess came out in a muumuu and swaggered cursing among the tables, and the place was a little on the scruffy side and in a weird location, what would happen is that the place would go broke. Even if the person running the restaurant was as generous with food as Juanita was, still those things alone would have *killed* another restaurant.

Of course, there was less pressure on a restaurant then. You could afford to make more mistakes. Today you can't afford to do that and, maybe as a result, there aren't as many warm, family-type places now. Health codes and high rents have fazed them out. I mean, no way would Juanita be allowed to run a business in the Bay Area today the way she could in the good old days.

In my twenty years of restaurant reviewing, Juanita is by far the most unusual restaurant personality I've ever known. Stands above everyone else. Through the years since she went out of business, I've looked for other characters like her because they make such good copy and are so much fun to know, but there just isn't anybody at all. Maybe there never *will* be.

Juanita's: Vallejo
Prime rib, 2½ lbs. an order/The hostess, a legend in progress

Juanita has the body of Mother Goose, the personality of Mae West, and the voice of an Army drill sergeant. This combination has made her eligible for a unique occupation—the job of being a character. And she's good at it. This lady is what restaurant legends are made of.

Juanita had a definite reason for opening a restaurant. "I love catering to men," she told us, "and the only way I can do it legally is feed 'em." And Juanita does it right. She serves a 2½ pound cut of prime rib for dinner. "And honey, that ain't all," Juanita always reminds us. Dinner also includes a buffet—a giant spread of stuffed eggs, olives, ten different salads, three kinds of fruit, hot muffins, and country ham. With Juanita around, the plenty never ceases.

When Juanita isn't looking after the buffet, she can usually be found walking around the dining room in a volcanic-red Hawaiian muumuu. She shifts among the tables, always talking, constantly laughing, and occasionally firing off a smoking hot salvo of four-letter words. But this never shocks anyone. Or fools them, either. Everyone knows that Juanita is about as tough as cotton candy. Yes, Juanita is special. And that's why everybody likes her. A whole lot.

The locations of Juanita's restaurants have always been as unusual as the woman herself. She's served dinners on a dry-docked Sausalito ferryboat, an El Verano chicken farm, and when she ran the Fetters Hotel, she even served dinners *in her bedroom*. When Juanita said, "Come and get it," you had to think twice.

Juanita's latest restaurant is located in a Spanish Colonial-style hotel that was built in 1928. The dining room has an interesting time-mellowed appearance, and it's been made even more interesting with the addition of Juanita's amazing collection of antiques. And it looks like Juanita's here to stay. She recently told us, "Honey, this shack and me are permanent partners." And when Juanita said that, her voice was so loud, the ashtrays started to dance.

*Review from **Two Hundred Good Restaurants**, by Russell S. Riera and Chris Smith.*

Working at Juanita's was like working with the Addams' Family, there were so many strange characters. One time in Port Costa, a waitress named Josephine got into a fight with Juanita, who was drunk, in the kitchen. Neither of them were exactly pussycats, and they were yelling and calling names at each other. I think Josephine really wanted to provoke Juanita into hitting her so she could take her to court, but Juanita just stood there like a stone wall. So Josephine picked up a small frying pan and started hitting her on the head and shoulders with it while Juanita just continued to stand there as if she couldn't feel a thing.

Really upset by now, Josephine then grabbed up a steak knife and started stabbing at her with that, too. I don't know if it was because Juanita was drunk, but she just stood there, motionless, while the other woman kept hitting her on the head with the pan she held in one hand while she was stabbing at her with the knife she had in the other. I guess Juanita finally got tired of this and she reached over and grabbed hold of Josephine's hair – only it turned out to be a wig and Juanita pulled it right off. This was probably the worse thing she could have done since the woman had all her hair tied up in this tiny little pigtail on top of her head. But that was the end of the fight. Juanita won, just like that. Josephine turned around and left without another word.

With the seagoing Wattles on board the Charles Van Damme, 1960.

Stomping grapes in El Verano, 1966.

The day after the fire, 1969.

El Verano, 1966.

Fetter's Hot Springs Hotel (Courtesy Press Democrat).

*Monsignor O'Farrell on Father's Day.
(Judge MacMahon and Rattle-Ass on
other side of fence.)*

*Combination advertisement and public
service announcement, Fetter's Hot
Springs, 1972.*

Juanita snuggling Jeff Kan Lee, newspaper photographer, in her famous bishop's bed. (Photo by Tim Tesconi)

A favorite form of communication.

Louise and Juanita, with dogs and unknown child, 1972.

Erica

Beauregard in his cups.

Sorting through the ashes.

In the ruins.

Discussing firefighting strategy with a Fire Marshall.

Another opening, another show. Juanita's at the Grist Mill, 1976.

Juanita and her blind rooster.

Having a chat with authorities before leaving the Grist Mill, 1976 (Courtesy Press Democrat)

Wildlife at the Warehouse.

Catering for a bibulous throng, 1976.

In her lobby apartment in the Burlington Hotel.

Juanita with "Cuz," one of Port Costa's colorful pioneers, 1976.

Juanita's at the Warehouse, Port Costa, California, 1976.

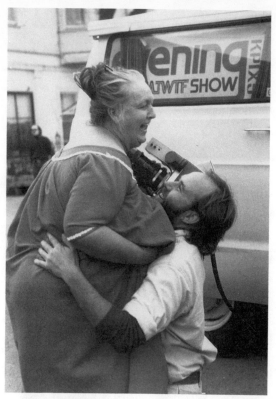

Giving the "ear muff treatment" to a KPIX cameraman, Port Costa.

Juanita's in the Casa de Vallejo, 1977.

Opening day, next door to the ill-fated Victorian Juanita's, Vallejo, 1977.

Celebrating her 57th birthday during her Warehouse reprise, 1980.

L: Playing the conga drums in the Apache Room, Fairfield, CA, 1982.
R: Casting bread upon the waiters.

Contemplating her next move
(Courtesy Press Democrat. Photo by Jeff Kan Lee)

Publicity photo for animal welfare fundraiser, Sonoma, 1989
(Photo by Joanie Morgan)

Taking the waters of the Agua Caliente Pool, 1989.
(Photo by Mary Carroll)

13

"Juanita's Port of No Return"

— San Francisco Chronicle

"Where did Juanita Go?"

— Sausalito News

I n probably her strangest move of all, Juanita next hung her banner outside a bowling alley in nearby suburban Fairfield in what had heretofore been called the Apache Room, for reasons probably too dim for scrutiny. She tried to add her own personality to a decor dominated by orange vinyl booths and hotly-colored posters of Indian warriors. The artistic effect of doilies, kerosene lamps and antique chamber pots in among the warpaint and tomahawks must have been nothing short of visionary. The entrance had two sets of glass doors with a dreary sort of garden atrium in between. Into this Eden Juanita released Sombitch and a hen. The hen laid eggs right away and sat on them contentedly while patrons passed in and out. The resulting chicks were a source of joy to children, who much preferred petting them to eating dinner. The chickens were, however, much less than a source of delight to the county's Health Department, which took a dim view of a restaurant with a chicken coop as an entrance.

Ron Scheufler, the Environmental Health Specialist given the dicey job of inspecting the premises, told Juanita that she had to close down until the chickens were moved. "What's the matter, honey," she cooed, "don't you like my cock?" He was amused, but not *that* amused, and Juanita was forced to take the chickens back to the house she and her mother were renting. Louise did not complain since she found the hours long without the agreeable company her daughter unfailingly provided.

Maybe it was revenge, or it could simply have been mischief, but Juanita from then on teased Ron Scheufler something terrible. "She always made some kind of mention when I was there that she wasn't wearing any underwear," he said unhappily. "When she had finally complied with all of the regulations and I told her she could open the place for business, she grabbed me and tried to plant a big kiss on me. We got in a sort of struggle."

It came to Juanita's attention that a meat packing plant was up for sale and that the property included 28 acres. Immediately, she set her heart on having it. The building was big enough, even bigger than the Warehouse Café, so she would be able to feed more people than ever before. Almost more exciting was the fact that most of the land was a bird sanctuary where, she was sure, nobody would have the right to exclude chickens. "If birds were okay, chickens had to be okay, too," she explained. Nobody was going to tell Juanita that a robin had more rights than a rooster. She visualized it all as the kind of place where hundreds of people could come and eat and hundreds of chickens roam free. "It would have been ideal for everybody," as she put it.

How close she might have come to realizing her dream we will never know. It dried up and blew away on the afternoon she learned that the venerable plant was to be razed and a shopping center built in its place. "I just couldn't believe it," she said. "Here they could've kept that nice old building and gotten to see a little wildlife, and instead all they did was build more crap."

By now it was 1984, and her world was beginning to look as bleak as Orwell's. Louise was unwell and the chickens, while endearing, made disorderly roommates. The atmosphere of the bowling alley was charmless while the Apache Room, to be blunt, was beyond redemption. Juanita herself was beginning to fear that the tide had turned against her forever. For the first time in her life she wondered if she was ever going to manage to rise again. Her savings had dwindled to almost nothing with so much of her profit having been plowed into ramshackle or ill-equipped buildings. Many of her customers had lost track of where she had gone and those who managed to smoke her out at the Apache Room found it as much like the old Galley as the Galley had been like the Fairmont's Venetian Room. Business, not to put too fine a point on it, was lousy.

Hope was stirred anew by the discovery of a restaurant available for lease a few miles north in the town of Winters. The town had a pleasantly rural air; the building should have had a revolving door for the restaurateurs who one after another had tried and failed there. Though there seemed to be a curse on the place, Juanita was undeterred. After all, hers was not just any restaurant, and she was not your average restaurateur. Loading up Louise and Hughie and the ragtag family of chickens, she headed north.

Right off the bat, she came to grief with the Health Department. They would not let her chickens inside. They would not permit her to screen off a part of the dining room as a bedroom for her mother. ("So convenient, too!") Neither her charm nor her fury got her anywhere. "Seemed like I was losin' my touch," she confessed. But she was still determined to make a go of it and plunged in with her customary zeal, dragging in employees off the sidewalk and drafting perfect strangers into an army of dishwashers who came and went so regularly that many nights she had to do the dishes herself. After hours spent schmoozing in the dining room with customers— with her feet and her knees in competition to be first to give out— facing a sink full of greasy platters was not a pleasant prospect.

A one-time employee remembered going to Winters for dinner and finding Juanita with thirty steaks on the grill and no one in the kitchen but herself. "She had grease burns all over her arms and all the way up to her neck from splattering grease," the former employee said. "She didn't complain none and I guess she was just tryin' to ignore it and keep on cookin', puttin' Bag Balm all over herself. I got roped into forkin' muffins, and it was just like home."

Disgruntled ex-employees complicated the situation by informing the Health Department that Juanita was letting her chickens inside, after all, and that she was washing her dirty underwear in the dishwasher. Especially aggravating was Juanita's policy of charging careless employees for the crockery they dropped. Juanita saw it as a method for slapping slippery fingers; they saw it as an unethical attempt to prune their paychecks.

On New Year's Eve, 1984, Juanita's was booked for the entire City Hall staff. Juanita was up by daybreak, baking hams and boiling potatoes, but as the hours passed and not one employee showed up, she became a little concerned. Forging on alone through mountains of macaroni, forking muffins and stuffing eggs in a frenzy, she finally received word that all her employees had gotten so drunk in happy anticipation of the evening ahead that none of them were conscious enough to come. As Juanita told it:

"Everybody from the City Hall got there, all dressed up and lookin' forward to a good time. There I was, all alone, hair all over the place, a dirty muumuu on and no shoes. Also I was pretty wild by that time and not about to take lip off nobody. When they saw what was what, everybody started helpin' out at the salad bar and bussin' the tables and resettin' them. One guy ran the cash register. A woman came up to me and said, 'Juanita, you do the cooking and I'll get the orders out,' and she did. The City Clerk, bless her heart, went home to change her dress and came back to wash dishes for me. Boy, I tell you, they were great! I always did feel that my restaurants were partly owned by the people who ate in them, and the Galley sure belonged to those people that night!"

Not all the people in the vicinity were as tolerant.

"I'd been in Winters about six months, and though I'd paid my electric bill, I hadn't paid all my deposit yet. I was supposed to pay it monthly, but I forgot, maybe. The girl down at the office shut the juice off Friday, so I had to close for the whole weekend. I just sat there watchin' the food rot. The service guy who came on Monday, I made him help me throw out all the stinkin', rottin' stuff and he was cussin' like crazy. My mother was sick, just outta the hospital. Hughie had broken his hip and I was tryin' to take care of him, too. So I went out and bought a doll that looked just like that broad and I was goin' to stick pins in her, but I never did. I just put its arms on backward and left it at that."

That double whammy was enough. Even Juanita was not prepared to wait around for a third calamity. Bag and baggage, she moved on to Allendale, a wide spot in the road a few miles south. Only Juanita, however, would have chosen as a solution to her troubles a building so derelict that the surrounding chicken coops were in better shape.

"They were nice knotty pine," Juanita explained, "and so I fixed a couple of them up and made cement stairs for them, and mother and I lived in one and Hughie in the other. Mother liked being there because she could sit right in her living room and feed the chickens and ducks that would come right up to her door. It gave her somethin' to think about while I was workin'.

"It was all a real challenge, I tell you! I made a fence outta an old wine cask and put in geraniums and got everything lookin' real homey. Where I was goin' to put the restaurant was a building that used to be a roadhouse and the old Allendale Store for years. But it was in such awful shape that the Health Department wouldn't let me open up until I took buckets of money and dropped them into the place. It needed a foundation and a 10,000 gallon holding tank for water. Also I found out that its zoning had changed and I couldn't open a restaurant there even if I did do all that work. Since I didn't know what to do next, and mother was havin' such a nice time, we just stayed on about six months. I hung up my Juanita's Galley sign on the side wall, anyway, so at least we always had some company drop in.

"You know," Juanita added, cheering up somewhat, "because of me, my good customers got to see a lot of the country. Just followin' me around, they got to see pretty much of the countryside of Marin County, and then to Sonoma County and Contra Costa to Yolo County, and then Solano County last of all. They got quite a cook's tour, if you wanta look at it that way. Whoooeee!"

It was not, however, a happy time. First of all, Sombitch was "just run to death" by his thankless male offspring, who then stood around the corpse as if it were a sort of buffet and ate its innards. Ron Scheufler, the Health Inspector who had gone several rounds with Juanita in Fairfield, and a few more in Allendale at the twilight of her career in the restaurant business, said, "Some of the life was going out of her, like things were running down. It was sad to see her spirit getting broken in the fight and the spunkiness kind of draining away from her. That happens sometimes to people, but it was especially sad to see it happen to someone like her. I'd never met anyone in my life like her, professionally or any other way, and I felt bad that things weren't working out for her."

When a friend came by one day to ask Juanita to help him settle a property dispute in her old stomping grounds of El Verano, she seized upon the excuse to go. "Maybe I never should've left Sonoma in the first place," she admitted matter-of-factly. "It sure felt good to be goin' home."

Edward Baciocco, Owner, California Meat Company

I used to sell meat to Sally Stanford when she had her bordello at Taylor and Broadway. She had a dining room where the girls and the customers could eat together. Then I started selling meat to Juanita, too. People used to say that Juanita worked for Sally, and other people thought she was a madam, like Sally, but she was a very different kind of person altogether, though the two of them were friends.

Juanita had the best damn food, and in such huge portions! I know, because I sold her meat during all those years she was in business, and she was a good customer – if you count the times she actually paid for the meat! I think she still owes me about twenty-five thousand dollars. She could've gotten rich, too. If you ask me, I think she's got some hidden away somewhere. Otherwise, where did it all go?

One time I got mad at her and told her I wasn't gonna sell her any more meat. Then, after awhile, I got an employee to call her up and tell her I had some good beef but that she was going to have to pay cash on the barrelhead. I had learned somethin', see. So for awhile she'd come into town on the bus and buy – with cash! – two prime ribs weighing maybe twenty-five pounds each. She'd put them under her arms and go catch the bus back home. Once I asked her, "How you gonna get 'em home?" and she said, "I'll get 'em home, don't worry." She'd catch the bus and then sleep all the way home, she told me, with her head resting on the ribs.

When she was in Winters and PG&E cut off her electricity, I bailed her out with a thousand dollars and I don't think she's ever paid that back, either. However, I do have to say that she sold me some property she had and I turned around and sold 'em for more than I paid for 'em, so I guess that was something. I know that some of the money she owed me she gave to different charitable organizations, but she never gave me any credit for it! She's done lots of things for lots of people, but when it came to payin' bills, she wasn't too good at it.

I met Juanita in the late Seventies at a place she wanted to open just west of Winters, a restaurant that had a history of owners coming in and going broke. I'd spoken with other people in the County Health Department and had gotten a general idea about the way she ran her restaurants. They told me the places were real unconventional-looking, but the main problem was that she liked to have animals in them.

I went out with the city building inspector who was also the Baptist minister in town. I'd worked around a long time and had seen just about everything – and heard it, too –so that nothing was really shocking to me. That wasn't true for the inspector, however, who was immediately put off by Juanita's mouth. About every other word had four letters and every time she opened her mouth I could see the building inspector getting increasingly unhappy. I think the corrections he therefore required of her were probably substantially increased the more familiar he became with her vocabulary! The next time I went back by myself. She was pretty upset with me that I hadn't warned her that the inspector was a Baptist minister and that if she had known, she told me, she would've watched her mouth. She said she'd felt like kicking herself when she found out who he was.

We had to practically invent a new restaurant code, since existing regulations didn't seem to apply to Juanita or her situation – as far as *she* was concerned, anyway. One of our requirements was that you couldn't live in a restaurant. We had quite an argument about that, since she'd already walled off part of the place as a bedroom for her sick mother who was living there.

On one of my first visits she said to me, just out of the blue, "Don't you ever believe that lie that my monkey used to piss on the grill! Don't you ever believe that because the monkey wasn't tall enough." I told her I hadn't heard that one before, as a matter of fact.

We early developed a kind of line over which neither of us would cross, and that helped our relationship. I told her in the beginning that if I ever caught her doing anything wrong, I'd close her down. On New Year's Eve I did manage to catch her in a violation and we had a fight in the parking lot, sitting there and screaming at each other. I told her that I'd see her locked up in the county jail if I ever caught her again doing whatever it was I'd caught her doing. It almost came to blows at one point, but then it kind of simmered down and we came to an agreement.

We were always somewhat concerned about the possibility of fire, too, since she seemed to have some bad luck that way. It was implied that since the fires were of unknown origin, she might have been responsible; and it was also implied that if things started going downhill then a closer eye better be kept on the buildings she was in, just in case.

We spent a lot of time at Juanita's due to all of the complaints the Health Department received. We got complaints about her from disgruntled employees about not being paid or being charged for the breakage of things they hadn't broken. They'd also say pretty regularly that she had animals in her restaurant and that she was washing her underwear in the dishwasher, which we caught her doing once, as a matter of fact. The last time I was there a sheriff was handling the till. Juanita was being pretty resigned to it, like she sort of knew the way the wind was blowing.

14

"The Inimitable Juanita"

– Press Democrat

The little row of tourist cabins left from the heyday of the Fetter's Hot Springs resort were, inevitably, in need of work when Juanita moved in. The owner, a man who owned a public mineral pool several hundred yards away, had planned to bulldoze them, but he made the mistake of leaving them standing long enough for Juanita to become their champion. The little house at the end of the row was perfect; it was rundown enough to have character, but not so ramshackle that the roof leaked. Juanita immediately busied herself planting gardens and cleaning up the mess previous tenants had left behind. Busy, she kept herself from looking back. She would not let regret set foot inside her door.

Louise had been ailing for years with a series of strokes that finally necessitated her being placed in a convalescent facility. Juanita visited her daily, a vision of the tropics in her bright muumuus, full of quips and insults and smiles. When Louise finally died, Juanita could not help but feel it was a blessing since her mother had been so sick for so long. But she missed her, this loyal companion.

In the cabin next door, Juanita still had Hughie to fuss over, and her faithful friend, Joe Foley, lived nearby, but it was her husband, Dick, she worried most about. His second wife had died, mercifully unaware that their union, however blessed in the eyes of God, certainly had never been in the eyes of the law. Toots had also checked out by this time, so there was no one left to nurse ill-feelings if Juanita spent some time with Dick again. North to Washington she went.

Dick had smoked himself into the abyss of emphysema by then and had to be on a respirator. Juanita cooked for him and held his hand, ("And not just his *hand*, honey!") and they talked about old times. One day Dick remarked, "Life with you was sure never dull, anyway." Stung, Juanita replied, "Well, it was great with you." He

283

smiled and patted her arm. "Oh, it was great with you, all right. Just never dull." Juanita took his words home with her, treasures no one could ever steal.

Dick died two days after Easter, 1987. "I think he did that on purpose, dyin' after Easter, " Juanita decided, "because he knew how much Easter meant to me and he didn't want to leave me with a sad memory on that day."

Oscar Hudspeth had died some years earlier, but in 1988 Juanita received a letter from the woman who had become his second wife. It came as a belated answer to a question Juanita had asked her some years before, never expecting an answer. The question had to do with whether or not Oscar was her real father. For years she had suspected he was not. For some reason, her intuition had caused her to look closely at John Stinnet, who was big and hardworking and capable, and who had always seemed to appear just when she most needed help. He had known her mother when he and Louise were teenagers, but Louise would never speak of him. The one time Juanita – whose name in Spanish is the feminine diminutive of "John" – mentioned him, Louise became so agitated that Juanita never spoke of him again. John Stinnet had died in 1977, but his death only added to the mystery, for a week before his death he called Juanita to say that he was on his way to tell her something "very important." A heart attack suffered enroute silenced him forever. Had he wanted to tell her he was her father, Juanita wondered; out of deference to her mother's feelings had he kept silent through the years until, at last, he decided to tell her the truth?

These were late days to ferret out the answer to such a mystery, but the belated letter from Oscar Hudspeth's widow shed more light upon the matter. It read, in part, "...you wanted to know if you and Oscar were a blood relation. No, Juanita, you and he are no kin. He adopted you but I would like you to know that no father could have loved a child more than he loved you. He loved you so much he went to a lawyer and tried to get you but they told him no court would give you to him because you were adopted. Because he wasn't allowed to see you, he thought it was best for you and he to break all ties and go away. But Juanita, don't ever think you wasn't loved by Oscar. What I have told you is what he told me. Oscar was a truthful man."

It was, of course, too late for the whole truth. Juanita would never know who her real father was. "I guess if it was Stinnet, he must've loved me because he tried to make things easier when the going was rough," she said. "That's what a real father does. So I decided I might as well believe he was my father, because that's what I'd *like* to believe."

Orphaned and widowed, without money or a job, it might have looked like the fat lady was finally going to sing. She did not. The row of little cabins might not be Easy Street, but then Juanita never expected to live on Easy Street and would probably just complicate matters if she ever were to find herself without botherations of one kind or another. What is life, after all, without a passel of stray animals to cluck over and a bunch of people to push around?

Joe Foley died in 1989, leaving Juanita his big orange cat, Wally, as her share of his modest estate. "Wally only had one tooth," she explained, "but it was a real big tooth. He kissed me all the time, but maybe he was just tryin' to gum me to death. I was teachin' him to say 'Mommy' when he got sick and died."

Hughie had long since been retired from active duty so that he could read the *TV Guide* and care for his two ancient dogs, Fanny and Skippy. Juanita had given up trying to get Hughie to eat right since he had always given his dogs whatever Juanita had fixed for his meals and was not about to change. "Maybe he's just makin' sure that what happened that summer on that ranch, when all those animals he was takin' care of almost starved to death, never happens again," Juanita explained, "See, Hughie is a real devout Catholic, but he believes his dogs have souls too. Every Sunday morning he sits in bed and he helps the dogs get up on the bed, too. He rings his bell and says his rosary beads, and those dogs sit real quiet, like they're prayin' too.

"I know he prays for me a lotta time because I can hear him all the way outside, just prayin' as hard as he can for God to save my soul and not give me a cold. He says he thinks my soul may be all right, but if I don't start wearin' a coat, I'm gonna get a cold, anyway."

In the neighborhood were many recent immigrants from Mexico. Juanita fussed over the children until she noticed they had begun avoiding her. The realization was a dagger straight to her heart. Through the grapevine she heard that a mother had said harsh things about her, warning her children to stay away from Juanita because she was a kidnapper. Caught unaware, Juanita at first could not figure out how such a story could have gotten started. Then she remembered Mai.

"This Cambodian family moved into the old motel near here," Juanita explained, "and they had this little adopted girl. She was forced to sleep on an old couch in front of their room – an awful place for a kid because of all the drunks hangin' around. I was real afraid somethin' bad would happen to her and I said so. Her foster parents asked if she could sleep on the couch in my house and I said okay, fine. A few days later I got home and there was her foster father on top of her. I didn't want to scare the kid – she was only six – so I just told him he had to get out right that second, and I guess I had that sorta meanin' in my voice that made him go quick. Mai was so dirty that I right away took her into the shower and when I was washin' her hair I found that her head was all covered with knots and there were bruises on her legs and arms."

A faraway look came into Juanita's eyes at this, as if she were remembering another girl who had suffered the same abuse so many years before. Her voice hardened. "I decided right then and there that that child wasn't ever goin' back to those people. She didn't want to, anyway, that bastard had been abusing her since she was three. I told her where to run to when the police came. When they knocked on my door a coupla days later, Mai took off out the back way in her bare feet and never stopped runnin' until she reached my friend's house. The cops asked if I had her and I said yes. They told me I had to give her up and I said, 'Well, now, you ain't gonna get her.' When they threatened me with jail, I said, 'Shit, I been in jail before, take me on in.' They put me in the back of the patrol car and when we were about halfway there, one of the cops said, 'Look, Juanita, we don't want you to go to jail for this,' and I said, 'I guess you're just gonna have to, though, because I ain't *never* gonna tell you where that poor little kid is.'

"So what happened was, they gave up. They told me that they'd send a social worker out on the case right away and so I said, 'Fine, you do whatever you do, but that child will never go back to that foster home. Not ever.' We drove on over to where Mai was and she ran out and wrapped herself around my legs, cryin', 'No, Mommy, no!' The cops said she could stay with me just until the social worker came. So I said again to the cops, just in case they didn't understand me, 'Look, I promised this kid that she wouldn't ever have to go back to those people, and as far as I am concerned she never will. I will do anything to see that she doesn't. And that includes anything.'"

It doesn't take much imagination to picture the blood in Juanita's eye. She had brawled, after all, for much lesser stakes. Juanita took Mai home and thought for hours about what it would be like to finally raise a child as her own. When she went to court as a witness, the judge asked her if she wanted to adopt Mai herself. Juanita replied, "I'm sixty-two years old and I've never had a child of my own. To tell you the truth," she added softly, "I don't think I'm the kind of person who should raise this kid. Maybe once I could've – but not now." Mai was adopted by a local family with several children. On the long drive home, Juanita wept for what would never be. When she explained the story to the Mexican woman who had spoken ill of her, and had given an edited version to the neighbor children, she was no longer an object of distrust.

Now mothers ask her to babysit their children. She supplies her charges with kittens and thrift shop knickknacks, and likes to take them out to restaurants where she lavishes praise and criticism on the waitresses. On an almost daily basis, she finds on her doorstep stray animals to care for until, and if, they can be adopted. People come knocking at her door needing bail money, clothing, a place to sleep for the night and, most important of all, someone who will listen and not judge because she has heard it all before. She gives them her attention and maybe a little hell, and puts something in their stomachs and in their pockets before they leave.

The Agua Caliente pool, which is practically in Juanita's front yard, is now her turf. She urges the ill, the old, the aching and the cantankerous into its healing mineral waters. After everyone has gone home for the day, and there is no one left to encourage, cuddle or harass, Juanita dogpaddles slowly back and forth, dressed in a muumuu that floats to the surface around her like Ophelia's long hair. Though she doesn't need to work as hard as she has always done, she insists on scrubbing the pool of mineral deposits and hosing down the bathrooms. As always, she doesn't trust anyone else to clean things the way they ought to be cleaned. She is a demon with a pumice stone and will not rest her worn-out knees until everything has been done "Juanita's way."

John Herbst, Waiter/Writer

One day Juanita and I were over at old Joe Foley's place, cleanin' it up after he died. I live in a cabin real near Juanita and so I help her out from time to time, and she needed someone to help move his stuff out of the house so I said I'd give her a hand. So anyway, I looked down and here's this wastebasket sittin' there and I said, "I could really use that," and Juanita said, "Okay, fine." I brought it home and then forgot, really, where I'd gotten it. It was just there, you know, being a wastebasket.

About this time I bought a big blue plastic ball at the drugstore for 99 cents, not because I needed it but because they look like they're worth 99 cents and they're fun to fool around with. So, I was sittin' at my typewriter kind of playing with the ball and I threw it in the wastebasket. Well, it struck me then that if I cut off the top half of the basket and nailed it above my front door I could shoot baskets every once in awhile, and still have the bottom half for trash. I thought it was kind of an ingenious idea and I proceeded to nail the top half of the basket up and it worked pretty well.

A few days later Juanita asked me if I would pick up a *TV Guide* and a *National Enquirer* at the store. I said I would and she said she'd bring me the money later. So there I was, shooting away, when Juanita came out of her house with the money and saw what I was doin'. Well, she went into a *tirade*. She yelled, "I hope to *God* you're not goin' to tell me that's Joe Foley's wastebasket!!" and I knew then that I'd fucked up and thought to myself, "Oh, shit, man!"

Then she yelled, "You self-centered, egotistical asshole! Everything's fine as long as it's for John Herbst!" Then she launched herself into the longest tirade you ever heard. Finally I said, "Juanita! You're getting upset over a wicker wastebasket!" but she was still really beside herself with rage so I thought I'd calm her down and said, "But I still have the bottom of it for a garbage can!" That did it. She stormed off and got in her car and went to the store for the *National Enquirer*.

I went back inside my house and wrote it all down in my novel before I could forget how crazy that woman can be. I mean, she went on and on and *on* about how selfish I was, fuckin' with other people's property – you'd have thought I was a fuckin' *terrorist*!

I took the basket down because I didn't want her to have a heart attack about it. And, besides, it didn't really work all that well, anyway.

You know, a guy that lives around here really thinks, his explanation of why she is the way she is, is because she has syphilis and that it's affected her brain. He told her that to her face, too, which she didn't appreciate all that much. Personally, I don't think there's a psychiatrist alive who could figure out Juanita. The science hasn't evolved that much.

Helen Clary, Animal Welfare Activist

Naturally you could tell how Juanita felt about animals because she had so many at her restaurants and obviously loved them very much. I think she missed having them when she came back to the Valley after leaving the restaurant business because she became a volunteer with our Pet Population Control Fund, knowing we were desperate for foster homes. You see, our organization tries to make it possible for people on a limited income to have their pets spayed or neutered, but we also try to find homes for the unwanted animals people are always dropping off on our doorsteps. Juanita is just wonderful about this. When it's more than I can handle, I call her and she always says, "Sure, I'll take care of them."

Let me tell you about a recent month this past spring. A girl who was moving called me about a mother cat she had that had just given birth to five kittens. Juanita said she'd take care of them, so we hauled over this big, three-storied cage to her front yard and put the cat and her kittens in it. There were also two pregnant feral cats living in a nearby field and somehow Juanita caught them and put them in one of the cages together, where they soon had *their* kittens. She was taking care of all these cats when a Russian gentleman contacted me that he had to move to a senior citizen's home where he wouldn't be allowed to bring his cat and dog with him. Juanita took them both into her house, this old cat and a cocker spaniel named Chippie, and though at first it was on a temporary basis, she soon decided that she simply wouldn't hear of them ever being separated after spending their lives together, so she adopted them both.

About this same time a friend of mine called to tell me that someone had dropped a mother dog and her nine puppies on a neighbor's doorstep and they didn't know what to do with them. We had no place to put them, and I hated to ask Juanita, since she was already pretty burdened down and had no money to speak of, but as we had nowhere else to put them, we picked up the dogs and took them over to Juanita's house. She fenced off her kitchen for the puppies and they stayed there until they could be weaned and found homes through a local pet shop. All of this was an awful expense, what with parvo and puppy shots and spaying the cats and everything, and Juanita fed all of them out of her own money. One day Juanita fell and hurt her leg pretty badly, but she just kept on caring for all of these animals both outside and inside her house, which was really too small for all of them. To make sure no one went hungry, Juanita had bowls of food on the mantle and under the table and on the windowsill and she'd put their litter in a big laundry basket in the middle of the living room floor. Then, one day, this boy drops in to say that he represented the owner of the mother dog and that he had found somebody who would give her a good home. Well, Juanita was highly suspicious of this and wasn't *about* to let the dog go to just anybody, which she told this boy in no uncertain terms. He didn't know what to make of all this and ended up leaving pretty upset. So there Juanita was with the dog, maybe forever.

As if things weren't crowded enough, one day she went to have lunch at her favorite Mexican restaurant near her house and, lo and behold, back she comes with a mother cat and its kitten. The kitten was wild and unsocialized, but Juanita was determined to tame it, which she did, and then found it a home with a little Mexican boy down the street who really wanted a pet. The mother cat stayed with Juanita.

A rabbit then showed up, a nice rabbit, and Juanita coaxed it somehow into the bottom floor of the "kitty condominium" and let the cats have the upper two floors. They all got along just fine and after awhile a home was found for the rabbit.

A woman in her 80's called me about her Himalayan cat that she couldn't keep anymore, although she hated to have to give him up. Juanita said she'd take care of him until we could find him a home, which we knew would take awhile since he'd been declawed and couldn't defend itself in the outdoors. Juanita took him into her house, with the dogs and her own cats, and named him "Big Boy." During her nightly "animal updates" to me, she'd say things like, "Well, Big Boy and I are having pork chops for dinner tonight." She ended up getting real attached to him and decided to keep him. But by this time she had so many cats and dogs going and coming in her house that she thought Big Boy would be safer for awhile living in a little cottage near her own, so she rented it for him and put a nice big pillow in the window for him to lie on and watch the action in the street. He was happy as could be.

A young man called me one day to say that he was getting married to a girl who was allergic to cats and he had to get rid of the two he had. Right away we found them homes but, unfortunately, the people that adopted one of them happened to live only three doors away from the young man and so the cat kept going on back to its first home. The bride called me in hysterics, so I told Juanita the problem and she said, "Well, bring it on over," and I did. She's kind of a skittish cat and maybe not too adoptable, but she seems to love Juanita and gets along all right in the house, so Juanita will probably end up keeping *her*, too. Then Big Boy got evicted soon afterwards, and so she took him back into her house, where they all seem to get along fine.

With all of this, Juanita helps us out in other ways, too. We make most of our money by selling rummage at the community center, and Juanita often comes down and sells things for us. Lots of times people will come in and look at her curiously for a minute and then say, "Are you Juanita?' and she'll say yes and then try to sell them something. She buys *herself* a lot of stuff, too; in fact, she's one of our best customers. She furnishes her house with some of the things she buys and then she gives the rest away to other people. In the Fall she's going to cook a big Mexican dinner as a fundraiser for us and, considering it's Juanita doing the cooking, we should do really well. Everybody knows who she is, after all, and what a great cook she is. You know, every Thanksgiving and Christmas she puts on big dinners for all the poor people in her neighborhood and any friends who want to come over. She makes lots and lots of food, like in the old days, and not only feeds everybody all they can eat, she sends them away with leftovers. She doesn't forget the animals, either; they all share in the food, too. Even if she doesn't have enough herself, she puts the needs of others way ahead of her own. Of all people, *she* doesn't have a real kitchen, just an old microwave and a couple of electric woks, and if anybody deserves to have a kitchen, it's her. But the money it would take to have a nice stove and everything she just gives away and does without.

You know, very very few people have the instinct to adopt the less adoptable animals; the ones nobody else would want. Juanita will adopt anything, the lonelier and homelier the better, really, as far as she is concerned. Because she can't stand the thought of any animal – or any person, either – going hungry or being without a home.

When asked how she feels about her life from the vantage point of her sixty-six years, Juanita said, "I am really grateful for the life I've had. When I look back on it, I find myself sayin', 'Thank you, God, for not lettin' me fall off the straight and narrow'– 'cause there were some pretty wild days in my youth, I hafta admit! I mean, I'm glad I had 'em, but I wouldn't want to repeat any of 'em, either. I always regretted not having kids, but how things have ended up, I've had more kids by owning my restaurants than I ever would've been able to have myself. They've given me a lot of joy, too. Now when they're all grown up and they bring their children to meet me, they introduce me as the lady Mama used to work for, and they sound real proud and happy about it, too.

"You know, full moons have always driven me a little nuts. Up until the last one, if I knew there was gonna be a full moon that night, I always stayed in bed all day and wouldn't even look outside in case I saw it. That's how bad it was, honey. But this last full moon, I stood out in the cold clear air and just looked and looked at it. I drank it all in and I said my prayers. Then I came on in and went to bed and slept like a child."

Phineas T. Barnum, called the greatest showman who ever lived, once wrote, "Men, women and children, who cannot live on gravity alone, need something to satisfy their gayer, lighter moods and hours, and he who ministers to this want is in a business established by the Author of our nature. If he worthily fulfills his mission and amuses without corrupting, he need never feel that he has lived in vain." If Barnum had known Juanita he might in her honor have changed "he" to "she."

An acquaintance from the old Sausalito days remembers seeing Juanita in 1988, after her return to the Valley. "As the years went by and I hadn't heard about Juanita for awhile, I thought that maybe she'd turned into a nice, grey-haired grandma. Then one day I was at the county fair and there she was, a finalist in the grape-stomping contest. She was crushing grapes in a barrel with her bare feet, her skirts up around her bosom, roaring with laughter and obviously having a hell of a time. It was such a sight, and so reassuring, to know that she was still around, still being the marvelous, colorful character she'd always been!"

It would be a mistake to feel sorry for Juanita in the twilight of her life. Pity instead all of the poor souls who have never seen this woman who has always preferred to be disliked or go to jail than to be someone she was not. Juanita has always seemed larger than life because she has always chosen to live her life so fully and openly. While most of the rest of us are afraid to rock the boat, Juanita has always believed that the trip is not worth taking unless the sea is rough, the wind is wild, and the sun is shining brightly on the farthest shore.

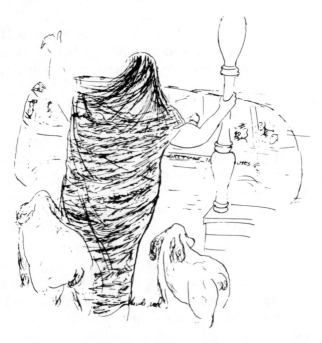

About the Author

Sally Hayton-Keeva was born in Mount Vernon, Washington, and grew up in Corona del Mar, California, where there was lots of sun but very few chickens. After several careers, she settled down to write books because she read books all the time and thought, "What the hell?" Also she could go barefooted. She is married to Joseph Keeva – a man of wit and tolerance – and has one son, Blake, who is a reincarnation of Huck Finn. She has lived with her husband on a ranch in Sonoma for five years, during which time she has collected a variety of eccentric animals and met a lot of eccentric people.

Photo by Richard Ingalls